Elements of
Metalworking Theory

by GEOFFREY W. ROWE
M.A., Ph.D., D.Sc., C.Eng., F.I.Mech.E., F.Inst.P., F.R.S.A.
Professor of Mechanical Engineering,
University of Birmingham

EDWARD ARNOLD

©G. W. ROWE 1979

First published 1979
by Edward Arnold (Publishers) Ltd.,
41 Bedford Square,
London WC1 3DQ

British Library Cataloguing in Publication Data

Rowe, Geoffrey Whaley
  Elements of metalworking theory.
  1. Shop mathematics   2. Metal-work-
  Mathematics
  I. Title
  684'.09'0151   TJ1165

ISBN: 0 7131 3400 3

Text set in 10/12 pt IBM Press Roman, printed by photolithography,
and bound in Great Britain at The Pitman Press, Bath

Preface

Metalworking in its various forms plays a key role in industrial production and development, but it has very ancient origins and still relies in many instances upon the skill of operators with long years of experience. A sound knowledge of the underlying theory can substantially reduce the time necessary to understand and effectively to control a particular type of process. Theory can also contribute to optimisation of tools and schedules, leading to more efficient use of both energy and material resources. In some instances it can indicate changes of method leading to less noise or fumes, thereby improving the industrial environment.

Some metalworking analyses look formidable, but surprisingly little advanced mathematics is strictly necessary for most of the theory. In fact no mathematics beyond sixth-form calculus is used in this book, which is designed for use by students in technical colleges and universities as a course text book. It is based on a larger volume, *Principles of Industrial Metalworking Processes*, and provides all the basic theory necessary to an understanding of metalworking processes. Stress analysis, slip-line fields and upper-bound techniques are described in detail, showing their advantages and limitations.

Numerous examples are given, with complete solutions, so that the book can be used as a self-tuition manual as well as a formal teaching text. A completely new chapter has been provided, giving full descriptions of illustrative experiments on rolling, forging, drawing, extrusion and cutting, with outline suggestions for many more. Most of these can be undertaken either with full-scale instrumented equipment, or with simple machines developed around readily-available electric motors and hydraulic-press units. The experiments include measurements of forces, choice of tools and pass visualisation techniques. Students are strongly recommended to perform as many as possible of these, to establish a feeling for the reality associated with the analytical solutions.

The half-tone illustrations have been selected from many provided by industrial organisations. I am grateful to all who kindly collaborated in this way. I also thank my wife and family for their patience during the production of this manuscript.

G.W.R.
1978

Acknowledgements

We wish to thank all those who kindly provided photographs of modern equipment, and we are grateful to the following for permission to reproduce illustrations:

Rasselstein A. G. (Neuwied),	Plate I
Birmetals Ltd (Birmingham),	Plate IIa and
	Plate Vb
Formtecnic Machine Tools Ltd (Alcester)	Plate IIb
Paul Granby & Co Ltd (London) and	
Maschinenfabrik Hasenclever GmbH (Düsseldorf)	Plate III
ASEA Ltd (London)	Plate IV
Fielding & Platt Ltd (Gloucester)	Plate Va
W. E. Norton (Machine Tools) Ltd (Sheffield)	Plate VIa
Hi-Draw Machinery Ltd (Romsey)	Plate VIb

We also thank Dr J. A. Schey and McGraw-Hill Book Co. for permission to produce Figure 1.2.

Contents

List of Symbols and Abbreviations

(Symbols used for more than one purpose are marked *)

Dimensions

h height or thickness
l length
L length
A area
*V volume
b platen or tool breadth
w strip width
D diameter
R radius
r radius
h_0 initial height in compression
D_b, h_b entry diameter or thickness in rolling or drawing
D_a, h_a exit diameter or thickness in rolling or drawing ($h_b > h_a$)
l_0 initial length
l_1 drawn length
A_0 initial area
A_1 final area

Tensile properties of materials

d_u diameter at M.T.S.
L_p limit of proportionality
L_e elastic limit
E Young's modulus (typically 200 kN/mm² (30 x 10⁶ lb/in²) for mild steel, 120 kN/mm² (18 x 10⁶ lb/in²) for copper
G rigidity modulus, or shear modulus
v Poisson's ratio
m strain-hardening exponent
n strain-rate exponent
*s nominal stress
ϵ_u strain at M.T.S.
e linear strain
e_t tensile strain (positive)
e_c compressive strain (negative)
el% percentage elongation of gauge length
U.T.S. or M.T.S. ultimate or maximum tensile stress
Y.S. yield-point stress, equal to Y'
R.A.% percentage reduction in area to fracture

Metalworking properties of materials

σ true stress (Note that $\sigma \neq s$)
*$\bar{\sigma}$ mean stess
*$\bar{\sigma}$ generalised stress

ϵ natural or logarithmic strain $\left(\int \frac{dl}{l}\right)$. $\epsilon_t = \ln(1 + e_t)$

$$\epsilon_c = \ln\left(\frac{1}{1 - e_c}\right)$$

$*\epsilon$ generalised strain
$*\bar{\epsilon}$ mean strain
$\dot{\epsilon}$ strain rate
γ shear strain ($\gamma/2$ is commonly used)
$\dot{\gamma}$ shear-strain rate
$*B$ constant in yield-stress equation

k yield stress in pure shear $k = \dfrac{S}{2} = \dfrac{Y}{\sqrt{3}}$

$\bar{Y}$ yield stress in uniaxial tension
$\bar{S}$ yield stress in plane-strain. $S = 1\cdot55\,Y$
$*H$ Brinell Hardness Number (B.H.N.), expressed in kg/mm^2
r fractional reduction of area in an operation
$R\%$ percentage reduction of area in an operation
$*c$ specific heat
ρ density

Metalworking analysis

log, ln   logarithms to base 10 and base e respectively
P indentation or extrusion pressure kN/mm^2
$*P$ working force or load, usually kN
$*F$ force, e.g. in drawing, usually kN

$\bar{Y}$ mean yield stress, assumed constant. $\bar{Y} = \dfrac{1}{\epsilon_2 - \epsilon_1} \displaystyle\int_{\epsilon_1}^{\epsilon_2} \sigma\,d\epsilon$

$\bar{S}$ mean yield stress in plane-strain
$*t$ time
$*W$ work
$\dot{E}_b, \dot{E}_d, \dot{E}_f, E_T$ boundary, deformation, frictional and total energy dissipation rates.
F_s shearing force
t_1 depth of cut (undeformed chip thickness)
t_2 chip thickness
T temperature
V_s shear-plane velocity
$*\alpha$ cutting-tool rake angle
Δb width of a zone boundary
χ roll load factor
$*\phi$ shear-plane angle
σ_i flow stress in zone i

Stress analysis

σ_x, σ_y direct stresses on planes normal to X- and Y-axes respectively
τ_{xy} shear stress on a plane normal to the X-axis, in direction OY
$\sigma_\theta, \tau_\theta$ direct and shear stresses on a plane inclined at an angle θ to an axis of reference e.g. OY
$\sigma_1, \sigma_2, \sigma_3$ principal stresses; major, intermediate, and minor
θ inclination of an arbitrary plane to an axis of reference also inclination of the tangent to a slip-line
$\theta*$ inclination of a principal plane to an axis of reference
$\theta**$ inclination of a plane of maximum shear to an axis of reference

$\epsilon_x, \epsilon_y, \epsilon_z$ logarithmic strains
$\epsilon_1, \epsilon_2, \epsilon_3$ principal strains
μ coefficient of friction
*2α included angle of tool or die
B a constant or variable equal to $\mu \cot \alpha$
l, m, n direction cosines
r_m maximum reduction of area

Slip-line field theory

*p hydrostatic pressure in a plastic metal
k yield stress in pure shear
α-line, β-line } mutually perpendicular slip-lines, defined by the algebraically greatest principal stress lying in the first quadrant
*α, β distances along slip-lines
ϕ inclination of a slip-line
u, v velocities along α and β slip-lines respectively
*V velocity of an element of metal following a streamline
*s distance along a slip-line, or along a line in an upper-bound solution
t_x drawing stress derived from slip-line field (t_x includes friction)
t_H drawing stress for work-hardening metal
q die stress (q' includes friction)

$f\left(\dfrac{c}{d}\right)$
and
*$\phi\left(\dfrac{c}{d}\right)$ } the redundant work factors of geometrical parameters

*ϕ anticlockwise rotation of a slip-line
*R extrusion ratio

Rolling theory

*R, R' undeformed and deformed roll radius
L length of projected arc of contact, $L = \sqrt{R\Delta h}$
Δh draft, or decrease in strip thickness
*c an elastic constant, in the Hitchcock equation
*s springback
g roll gap

*H a function in Bland and Ford solution, $H = 2\sqrt{\dfrac{R'}{h_a}}\, \tan^{-1} \sqrt{\dfrac{R'}{h_a}} \cdot \alpha$

w width
P roll load (kN)
T roll torque (Nm)
t_b, t_a back- and front-tensions
k_b, k_s deflection constants of the rolls, due to bending and to shear
α general angular position, measured from the exit
α_N the angular position of the neutral point
α_b* angle of bite, equal to $\tan^{-1}\mu$
p_r radial roll pressure
*p component of roll pressure normal to the strip
p^+, p^- roll pressures on exit and entry sides of the neutral point, respectively
λ lever arm
$\bar{\lambda}$ lever arm for deformed rolls
Q a factor in Sims' equation

Friction theory

A_x area of intimate asperity contact

A_0 apparent area of contact

*$\bar{s}$ mean shear strength of junctions, related to k

p mean yield stress of junctions, related to hardness, and so to k

*F friction force

*W load in a friction experiment

s_i shear strength at an interface

Metal cutting

α rake angle

ϕ shear plane angle

X a ratio defining the rake-face contact length

β the ratio of shear stress to shear yield stress

W work done by shear

t_1 undeformed chip thickness (depth of cut or feed)

t_2 chip thickness

Useful Approximate Conversions from f.p.s. to SI Units

(It is seldom useful in metalworking theory to attempt to obtain accuracy better than 1%.)

Length

1 in = 25·4 mm $\simeq$ 25 mm; 10 mm $\simeq$ 0·4 in

$\frac{1}{8}$ in $\simeq$ 3·2 mm

$\frac{1}{16}$ in $\simeq$ 1·6 mm

10^{-3} in (= 1 thou) $\simeq$ 0·025 mm; 10 μm $\simeq$ 0·4 thou

1 ft = 305 mm $\simeq$ 0·3 m

Area

1 sq in = 645 mm^2

Mass

1 lb = 0·454 kg; 1 kg $\simeq$ 2·2 lb

1 ton (= 1·016 tonnes) $\simeq$ 1 tonne = 1000 kg

Force

1 lbf $\simeq$ 4·45 N

1 tonf (= 9 964 N) = 10000 N

Stress or Pressure

1000 lb/in^2 (i.e. 1000 lbf/in^2) = 6.89 N/mm^2 $\simeq$ 7 N/mm^2

1 ton/in^2 (i.e. 1 tonf/in^2) = 15·44 x 10^6 N/m^2 $\simeq$ 15·4 N/mm^2

Speed

100 ft/min = 0·51 m/s $\simeq$ 0·5 m/s

10 rev/min = 1·05 rad/s $\simeq$ 1 rad/s

Young's Modulus (for rough estimates)

Steels $E \simeq 30$ x 10^6 lbf/in^2; $E \simeq 200$ kN/mm^2

Copper $E \simeq 18$ x 10^6 lbf/in^2; $E \simeq 100$ kN/mm^2

Aluminium $E \simeq 12$ x 10^6 lbf/in^2; $E \simeq 70$ kN/mm^2

Introduction

Metalworking has very ancient origins, but it still makes a large contribution to the prosperity of industrially-developed nations. The main objective of mechanical working processes is to produce metals and alloys, and also polymers, in the wide variety of shapes and sizes required by industry and commerce. In addition, the strength and toughness of alloys is greatly improved by hot-working, which homogenises the material and refines the crystals. Cold-working further increases the tensile strength and hardness, and at the same time gives good surface finish and close dimensional tolerances, but it may require very large forces.

The art of *forging* was well known in the Orient and in Egypt more than 3000 years ago, and force limitations were overcome by using the impact of a hammer rather than a steady pressure, as is still often done today with power hammers. *Rolling* is inherently a continuous process, and the earliest mills, built of bamboo, were suitable only for producing papyrus. Many centuries passed before mills of sufficient strength for the rolling of metals could be constructed. *Wire-drawing* is naturally concerned with small sizes, and soft wires can be drawn manually through a die, as was practised in the Middle Ages and still is in jewellery manufacture today. When larger and stronger equipment is available, a force limitation is experienced in the tensile strength of the drawn wire or tube itself. *Extrusion* is a relative newcomer among these processes, dating from the nineteenth century. The pressures required are very high and equipment of great strength is necessary.

As larger sizes of product in harder alloys are demanded, or heat-resistant materials have to be worked at very high temperatures, the forces assume increasing importance. Metalworking theory has consequently been predominantly concerned with optimising plant and drafting-schedules to reduce forces that might otherwise cause fracture of the equipment or, in tensile processes, of the stock material itself. Modern society is, however, increasingly recognising that power consumption and material utilisation are important features, of more than economic significance. Reliability and the avoidance of breakdown or the production of faulty material are clearly very relevant. Theoretical analysis of metalworking processes can contribute to the making of rational decisions in this context also.

Although the basic theory is still restricted to rather simple shapes and conditions, it is possible to predict flow patterns, final shape and internal distortion in many instances, giving indications of likely fracture or defect locations. It is necessary to make simplifying assumptions relating to both the theory and the practical operation, and there is at present very little relationship between such analysis and the detailed properties of the workpiece material, which may be subjected to steep gradients of strain, strain rate and temperature. Very recently, more realistic but less rigorous mathematical analyses have been made possible by computer tech-

1

niques, some of which can include local variations in metal properties. These make considerable demands on computer time and capacity, and have not yet been extensively developed.

The limitations, as well as the potential of metalworking theory, should be clearly understood by all those concerned with the practical processes. Realistic contributions to improvements in the operations, products, material utilisation and energy consumption can then be expected.

1

Determination of Material Properties

In the design of bridges or aircraft, great care is taken to ensure that the forces applied will not cause any permanent change of shape. The components all deform elastically, recovering their original dimensions completely when the force is removed. The primary purpose of metalworking, in contrast, is to impart major permanent, or plastic, change of shape, for example by rolling a 30 mm thick billet into 0·8 mm strip.

The transition from elastic to plastic deformation can be demonstrated very simply by holding one end of an annealed 0·5 mm copper wire in a vice and stretching it with a pair of pliers. A light pull has no visible effect, but a stronger pull produces permanent elongation, and incidentally makes the wire stiff and straight. The elastic part of the deformation in fact extends the wire less than 0·1% and disappears when the load is released. It has little or no significance in most metalworking and is usually ignored, by assuming that the metal changes from completely rigid to fully plastic.

More precisely, the onset of plastic deformation is defined by a certain yield stress (force divided by cross-sectional area), which is of very great importance in theory and in practice. Real materials, however, increase in strength by strain-hardening as plastic deformation proceeds, which means that the yield stress increases with strain (change in length or cross-sectional area divided by original length or cross-sectional area). It is therefore convenient to represent the mechanical properties of a metal by a yield-stress—strain curve, usually referred to simply as a stress—strain curve or a flow-stress curve.

1.1 Flow-stress curves

Conventional tensile testing is well known and is fully described in many books, but it is of limited value in metalworking because a tensile instability, leading to fracture, occurs at a moderate strain. Moreover, the *nominal stress* (force P divided by original cross-section A_0) and the *nominal strain* (extension $L - L_0$ divided by original length L_0) have no physical meaning. In metalworking, with large plastic strains, it is desirable to use *true stress* σ, defined as the force P divided by the area A on which it is acting, and the *true strain* ϵ, defined incrementally. Thus

$$\sigma = \frac{P}{A}; \quad d\epsilon = \frac{dL}{L} = -\frac{dA}{A} \tag{1.1}$$

The latter identity arises because plastic deformation is a shearing process involving no change in volume. This has been verified up to very high strains and is always assumed in the theory.

3

$$dV = A\,dL + L\,dA = 0; \quad \frac{dL}{L} = -\frac{dA}{A} \tag{1.2}$$

Hence
$$\epsilon = \int_{A_0}^{A} -\frac{dA}{A} = -\ln\frac{A}{A_0} = \ln\frac{A_0}{A} \tag{1.3}$$

The flow-stress curve for most metals in the annealed condition can be represented fairly accurately by a power law

$$\sigma = \sigma_0 \epsilon^m \tag{1.4}$$

This is convenient for analytical work, but even simpler calculations can be made, for strain-hardened metal, by assuming that the yield stress increases linearly with strain over any restricted range considered:

$$\sigma = Y + B\epsilon \tag{1.5}$$

1.2 A simple method for determining a flow-stress curve from a tensile test

In a tensile test the load P reaches a maximum at the tensile instability, usually recorded as the Ultimate or Maximum Tensile Stress, P_u/A_0. This point is defined analytically from the condition for a stationary value

$$\frac{dP}{d\epsilon} = 0; \quad \sigma\frac{dA}{d\epsilon} + A\frac{d\sigma}{d\epsilon} = 0, \tag{1.6}$$

since $P = A\sigma$

But $d\epsilon = -\dfrac{dA}{A}$, so the equation 1.6 becomes

$$-A\sigma + \frac{A\,d\sigma}{d\epsilon} = 0; \quad \frac{d\sigma}{d\epsilon} = \sigma \tag{1.7}$$

Substituting for σ from equation 1.4, in terms of the strain at the maximum load point, ϵ_u

$$m\sigma_0\epsilon_u^{m-1} = \sigma_0\epsilon_u^m; \quad m = \epsilon_u \tag{1.8}$$

Thus m, the *strain-hardening exponent*, can be found from the cross-sectional area at this load, for a cylindrical specimen:

$$A_u = \frac{\pi}{4}d_u^2;$$

$$m = \epsilon_u = \ln\frac{A_0}{A_u} = (d_0/d_u)^2 \tag{1.9}$$

It remains to find σ_0, using equation 1.4 and the measured P_u:

$$\sigma_u = \frac{P_u}{A_u} = \sigma_0\epsilon_u^m \tag{1.10}$$

This is conveniently done by plotting a straight line with slope $m = \epsilon_u$ through the point σ_u, ϵ_u on a ln σ versus ln ϵ graph, representing the logarithmic form of equation 1.4,

$$\ln \sigma = \ln \sigma_0 + m \ln \epsilon \tag{1.11}$$

Experimental comparisons have shown that this power law can often be extrapolated up to at least $\epsilon = 1{\cdot}0$, which represents a reduction in area of 63%, amply sufficient for wire-drawing and single-pass operations other than extrusion.

1.3 Plane-strain compression

The flow-stress curve can be determined with better accuracy and over a greater range by a compression test executed under plane-strain conditions. This implies that the strain is strictly confined to two dimensions only, with no change in the third. If a wide strip is compressed across its thickness, this condition is closely approached. The plane-strain test was first developed to relate to rolling of wide strip, in which the reduction in thickness is exactly matched by the increase in length, but it is now extensively used for flow-stress determination in general. A strip of thickness h is compressed between platens of breadth b, which overlap the strip as shown in Figure 1.1.

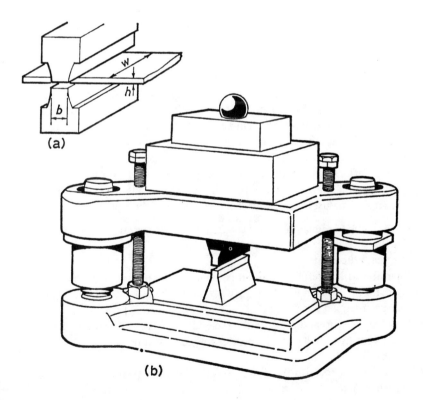

Figure 1.1 The plane-strain indentation test. (*a*) Schematic arrangement showing dimensions (*b*) Outline drawing of an actual sub-press

The width w of the strip should be at least 5 times and preferably 10 times the platen breadth, to ensure that lateral spread is negligible. The ratio h/b is chosen to lie between $\frac{1}{4}$ and $\frac{1}{2}$. If the thickness is too great, then the indentation pressure will exceed the simple yield stress, as explained in Chapter 5, §5.6. In the limit, when the thickness h is infinite, the process becomes one of indentation by a single punch, for which the indentation pressure is 2·57 times the yield stress. If, however, h does not exceed $\frac{1}{2}b$, the maximum error arising from this geometrical constraint will not be greater than about 2%. If h is very small, this error will be even less, but low h/b ratios imply a relatively large platen breadth b, which will increase the frictional contribution. Even when the dimensions are correctly chosen, it is necessary to ensure that the friction is as low as possible. For this purpose, the surfaces are well lubricated. Light rubbing with a soft pencil to form a graphite coating, together with a thin film of machine oil, is found to be best for copper, but a molybdenum disulphide grease is most effective for steels. After each thickness reduction of a few per cent, the specimen is removed and relubricated.

This test has proved useful and reproducible, and can be recommended as a standard procedure. It should, however, be emphasised that the yield stress measured is S, the yield stress in plane strain; not Y, the yield stress in uniaxial tension, as measured in the tensile test. These are related, and it will be shown in Chapter 2, §2.3.4 that

$$S = \frac{2}{\sqrt{3}}Y = 1\cdot155Y = 2k \tag{2.18}$$

A disadvantage of the test is that it takes appreciably longer than a tensile test, but this is counterbalanced to some extent by machining time, since the specimens do not need to have a special shape. The time involved in the actual test depends on the frequency with which the specimens are relubricated, and this can be reduced appreciably if a slightly lower accuracy is tolerable. Further time may often be saved in practice by making the first indentation large, so that the stress–strain curve starts effectively at say 20% reduction of area. Calculations based on annealed or lightly-worked metal are likely to be inaccurate because the yield stress changes rapidly. It may be useful to tabulate the sequence of the test:

1. Choose a platen breadth b between 2 and 4 times the strip thickness h.
2. Cut the strip to a width w at least 5 times b.
3. Lubricate the strip.
4. Align the strip carefully so that it is square to the platens.
5. Estimate the load required to make say 2% or 5% reduction in h. Apply and measure the load accurately.
6. Remove the strip and measure the indentation accurately with a micrometer fitted with tips small enough to enter the narrow indentation.
7. Relubricate.
8. Replace the strip, with the dies in exactly the same position, and repeat the sequence 5–8.

The platens must be accurately ground square and parallel, and mounted rigidly in the sub-press. A standard die-set provided with running ballrace sleeves performs excellently if the load is centrally applied via a lubricated ball-seating. This may easily be made with a 25 mm ball, pressed into two hard copper blocks by a load appreciably greater than the largest to be used in the test. Even when these precautions are taken, it will be found that after heavy cumulative reductions in cross-sectional area, the indentation loses its well-defined shape. This occurs because the platens cannot be ground parallel with infinite precision, and the low friction encourages any tendency to sideways slip. It is also impossible to replace them exactly correctly each time. As soon as this error is detected, it is advisable to start a fresh indentation with a single heavy reduction, ignoring the first reading afterwards and then proceeding as before.

Although the lubrication is effective in this test, the friction can never be reduced to zero, so it is desirable to make allowance for the finite coefficient of friction. This can easily be done by using two pairs of platens, one of width $b_1 = 2h_0$ and the other $b_2 = h_0$. The wider platens will introduce a larger contribution from friction and the respective pressures for some fixed height h_n corresponding to a large reduction ϵ_n, say 1·0, are given by equation 3.34

$$\frac{p_1}{2k_n} = 1 + \tfrac{1}{2}\mu \frac{b_1}{h_n}; \quad \frac{p_2}{2k_n} = 1 + \tfrac{1}{2}\mu \frac{b_2}{h_n}$$

Since the true yield stress $2k_n$ is the same for both, μ can be eliminated, or more conveniently μ can be determined from one test and assumed to be the same in similar tests:

$$2k_n = \frac{p_1 b_2 - p_2 b_1}{b_2 - b_1}; \quad \mu = \frac{2h_n(p_1 - p_2)}{p_1 b_2 - p_2 b_1} \tag{1.12}$$

1.4 Ring compression

A simple test, originally devised for friction measurement, can be made with a series of ring-shaped specimens. The results are less precise, but can be obtained over a wide range of temperatures and mean strain rates.

A ring of fixed geometric proportions, usually $D_o = 20$ mm, $D_i = 10$ mm and $h = 3\cdot3$ mm, or suitably scaled, is compressed between flat platens to thicknesses predetermined by appropriate stops to give height reductions between 10% and 70%. With good lubrication the ring expands uniformly, but if the friction is high the outer regions will be constrained, so the metal will also flow radially inwards, closing the central hole. By suitable calibration, the relative change in internal diameter can be directly related to the coefficient of friction. Male and de Pierre have shown that if the load is simultaneously measured, it is possible to evaluate the yield stress from a formula related to that for the forging stress of a disc, using a computer or a calibration chart as shown in Figure 1.2.

1.5 Torsion tests

Compression tests are reliable up to strains of about 80%, but the very large strains that may occur in hot-working processes such as extrusion or tube manufacture can more conveniently be produced in torsion.

A thin-walled tube subjected to torsion experiences pure shear and yields at the

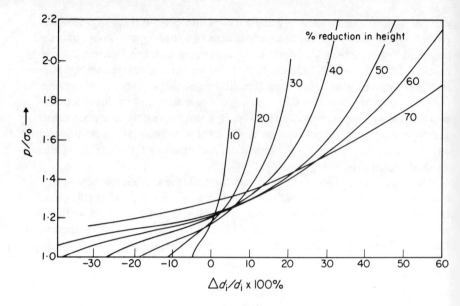

Figure 1.2 A calibration chart for a ring test adapted for flow-stress measurement

shear yield stress k. In solid bar the stress varies radially, but integration of the torque on an annular element gives the overall torque T:

$$T = \int_0^{r_0} (\tau 2\pi r\, dr)r \quad \text{and} \quad \frac{\tau}{r} = \frac{\tau_0}{r_0} \text{ for elastic stress}$$

$$T = \frac{\tau_0}{r_0} \int_0^{r_0} 2\pi r^3\, dr,$$

usually written $T = J\dfrac{\tau_0}{r_0}$

or $\tau_0 = \dfrac{r_0 T}{J}$ (1.13)

The *shear strain* γ is defined as the circumferential rotation $r\theta$ of a point at unit distance from the end of the cylinder:

$$\gamma = r\theta/L; \quad \gamma_0 = r_0 \frac{\theta}{L}$$ (1.14)

Thus a shear-stress—shear-strain curve can be obtained for elastic deformation.

More commonly, the torsion test is used to determine ductility, for example in high-carbon steel wires, or to assess hot-workability.

1.6 High strain-rate tests

Forging, rolling and extrusion may involve strain rates up to and even beyond

$1000\,\text{s}^{-1}$. Simple billet compression can be used, with appropriate allowance for friction, but the strain and temperature distributions are ill-defined. Ring compression suffers from the same deficiency, but automatically includes friction.

More elaborate procedures have been proposed, using a cam plastometer for plane-strain compression, or a Hopkinson bar for torsion.

It is more convenient to use machining as a high strain-rate property test, but the results are less direct and the interpretation is semi-empirical.

The end of a tube is cut with a tool set squarely across the lathe so that the cutting is effectively in plane strain, or, as it is usually described, orthogonal cutting. It is assumed that the chip or swarf is formed continuously by simple shearing along a single plane inclined at an angle ϕ to the direction of cutting. Then if the chip thickness is t_2 and the depth of cut is t_1, the length L of the shear plane is given geometrically by Figure 7.7:

$$L = \frac{t_1}{\sin\phi} \quad \text{or} \quad L = \frac{t_2}{\cos(\phi - \alpha)} \tag{1.15}$$

if the rake angle of the tool is α, the angle of inclination of the tool face to the normal at the workpiece surface. Thus if t_1 is set by the lathe gears, and t_2 is measured, as an average value, ϕ can be determined:

$$\tan\phi = \frac{t_1 \cos\alpha}{t_2 - t_1 \sin\alpha} \tag{1.16}$$

From consideration of the geometry, the shear strain γ can be found:

$$\gamma = \tfrac{1}{2}\,\frac{\cos\alpha}{\sin\phi \cos(\phi - \alpha)} \tag{1.17}$$

Similarly the stress acting along the shear plane is found from the resolved force component F_s and the area. If the width of the tube face is w,

$$\tau = \frac{F_s}{Lw} \tag{1.18}$$

These can thus be recorded and plotted for a given maximum strain rate $\dot{\gamma}$, which is assumed to follow the empirical equation

$$\dot{\gamma} = C\frac{V_s}{L} \tag{1.19}$$

where V_s is the resolved component of velocity along the shear plane. C is related to the spread of the shear zone about the assumed plane in a real material, and is taken to be a constant for a given metal.

This test can easily be undertaken with a wide range of materials at various cutting speeds.

1.7 Approximate yield-stress curves from hardness tests

Hardness testing does not directly provide a stress–strain curve, and it is mainly used for quality control. However, it is possible to obtain an approximate stress–strain curve, for rough calculation of cold-working loads, quickly and simply by hardness testing. The principle depends on the semi-empirical relationship between the Brinell hardness number H and the yield stress Y

$$H = cY \qquad (1.20)$$

If both H and Y are expressed in kgf/mm^2 the constant c is roughly 3. Though the Brinell hardness number is in fact in kgf units, Y is usually required in tons/in^2 or N/mm^2. This involves the conversion 1 ton/in^2 = 1·57 kgf/mm^2, giving

$$Y \text{ tons/in}^2 = (\text{B.H.N.})/4·7; \quad Y \text{ N/mm}^2 = \text{B.H.N.}/0·3 \qquad (1.21)$$

A flat-sided off-cut of any size or shape can be compressed by known amounts, for example in a simple forging press with limit stops, without needing a knowledge of the deformation load. The yield stress after each deformation is then found by a hardness test. It is not reliable for small strains, because the hardness test itself involves some 8–10% strain, and the greater rate of work-hardening for this condition also impairs the accuracy, but the larger strains are usually of more interest. This method provides an easy assessment of yield stress, without using expensive load-measuring machines, which is often of sufficient accuracy for preliminary calculations.

2

Yield Under Combined Stresses

The tests just described can be used to determine when a metal will yield under the action of a simple tensile, compressive or shear stress. All metalworking involves stress systems that are more complex than this, but it is possible to analyse the stresses and to relate them to a criterion of yielding which will specify whether plastic flow will occur.

A representation introduced by Mohr is very useful for this purpose, especially in the two-dimensional states of plane stress and plane strain. The latter is particularly valuable in slip-line field theory.

2.1 Mohr's circle for plane stress

We consider first the direct stress σ acting normal to the plane $ACC'A'$ and the shear stress τ acting parallel to it, as in Figure 2.1a. The other direct stresses are defined

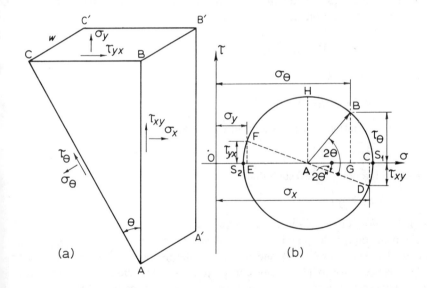

Figure 2.1 (a) The stress system acting on an elementary right-angled prism, in two-dimensional stress (b) The Mohr circle corresponding to the stress system

as acting on the planes whose normals are in the direction specified; thus σ_x acts on ABB'A', whose normal is in the direction x, and σ_y acts on BCC'B'. The shear stress τ_x also acts on the plane normal to the x direction, but it requires a second suffix to show its direction, τ_{xy}. In this example of plane stress, all stresses act in the plane ABC, so $\tau_{xz} = 0$.

If ACC'A' is an arbitrary plane inclined at an angle θ to ABB'A', resolution of forces perpendicular to AC gives:

$$\sigma_\theta \, AC.AA' = (\sigma_x AB.AA') \cos\theta + (\sigma_y \, BC.BB') \sin\theta + (\tau_{xy} \, AB.AA') \sin\theta$$

$$+ (\tau_{yx} \, BC.BB') \cos\theta$$

$$\sigma_\theta = \sigma_x \cos^2\theta + \sigma_y \sin^2\theta + (\tau_{xy} + \tau_{yx}) \sin\theta \cos\theta \qquad (2.1)$$

In fact τ_{xy} and τ_{yx} are complementary shear stresses which must be equal, to avoid rotation of the block.

Resolution of forces parallel to AC gives:

$$\tau_\theta \, AC.AA' = (\sigma_x \, AB.AA') \sin\theta - (\sigma_y \, BC.BB') \cos\theta - (\tau_{xy} \, AB.AA') \cos\theta$$

$$+ (\tau_{yx} \, BC.BB') \sin\theta$$

$$\tau_\theta = (\sigma_x - \sigma_y) \sin\theta \cos\theta - \tau_{xy}(\cos^2\theta - \sin^2\theta) \qquad (2.2)$$

These equations may be written

$$\sigma_\theta = \tfrac{1}{2}(\sigma_x + \sigma_y) + \tfrac{1}{2}(\sigma_x - \sigma_y) \cos 2\theta + \tau_{xy} \sin 2\theta \qquad (2.3a)$$

$$\tau_\theta = \qquad\qquad \tfrac{1}{2}(\sigma_x - \sigma_y) \sin 2\theta - \tau_{xy} \cos 2\theta \qquad (2.3b)$$

This enables them to be taken into account simultaneously, by squaring and adding to eliminate the trigonometric functions:

$$[\sigma_\theta - \tfrac{1}{2}(\sigma_x + \sigma_y)]^2 + \tau_\theta{}^2 = [\tfrac{1}{2}(\sigma_x - \sigma_y)]^2 + \tau_{xy}{}^2$$

This equation is of the form

$$(\sigma - A)^2 + \tau^2 = B^2 \qquad (2.4)$$

which is the equation of a circle plotted with axes σ and τ, of radius

$$B = \sqrt{[\tfrac{1}{2}(\sigma_x - \sigma_y)]^2 + \tau_{xy}^2}$$

centred on the point $(A, 0)$ such that

$$A = \tfrac{1}{2}(\sigma_x + \sigma_y)$$

This is the Mohr circle, as shown in Figure 2.1b.

The plane on which σ_θ and τ_θ act is inclined at an angle θ, measured anticlockwise, to the plane on which σ_x and τ_{xy} act. To define these locations on the Mohr circle, it is necessary to adopt some convention about the sense of the shear stress. If clockwise shear is assumed to be positive, τ_{xy} has the negative value shown by $-$CD in Figure 2.1b. The σ component of the coordinates of the point D is OC, equal to σ_x. Similarly $\tau_{yx} = +$EF, and $\sigma_y =$ OE.

The principal stresses are the stresses acting on the planes where the shear stress is zero and are thus given by OS$_1$ and OS$_2$. The angle between the plane on which σ. acts and that on which σ_1 acts is seen from Figure 2.1b to be

$$\angle CAD = \tan^{-1} \frac{CD}{AC} = \tan^{-1} \frac{\tau_{xy}}{\tfrac{1}{2}(\sigma_x - \sigma_y)}$$

It should be noted that the angles in the Mohr circle are always double the angles in the diagram of the physical plane. For example σ_x and σ_y appear as the σ-coordinates of the points D and F situated at opposite ends of a diameter; AF is inclined at $180°$ to AD.

It can be seen that the stresses OS_1 and OS_2 represent direct stresses on planes where there is no shear stress. Such planes are defined as *principal planes*, and the direct stresses acting on them are *principal stresses*, specified as σ_1 and σ_2 with magnitudes defined so that $|\sigma_1|$ is always greater than $|\sigma_2|$.

Thus

$$\left.\begin{aligned}
\sigma_1 &= OS_1 = A + B = \tfrac{1}{2}(\sigma_x + \sigma_y) + \tfrac{1}{2}\sqrt{(\sigma_x - \sigma_y)^2 + 4\tau_{xy}^2} \\
\sigma_2 &= OS_2 = A - B = \tfrac{1}{2}(\sigma_x + \sigma_y) - \tfrac{1}{2}\sqrt{(\sigma_x - \sigma_y)^2 + 4\tau_{xy}^2}
\end{aligned}\right\} \qquad (2.5)$$

These are clearly also the greatest and least stresses acting in the system.

The following important results can now be seen directly:

(a) The plane across which the maximum shear stress acts is at an angle $2\theta = 90°$ to the plane on which the principal stress acts in the stress diagram. Consequently these planes intersect at $\theta = 45°$ in physical space.

(b) The maximum shearing stress

$$\tau_{max} = AH = B = \sqrt{[\tfrac{1}{2}(\sigma_x - \sigma_y)]^2 + \tau_{xy}^2} \qquad (2.6a)$$

(c) Since $AH = \tfrac{1}{2}S_1S_2 = \tfrac{1}{2}(OS_1 - OS_2)$, the maximum shearing stress is equal to half the difference between the principal stresses

$$\tau_{max} = \tfrac{1}{2}(\sigma_1 - \sigma_2) \qquad (2.6b)$$

(d) The normal stress on the plane of maximum shear is equal to the constant $A = \tfrac{1}{2}(\sigma_x + \sigma_y), = \tfrac{1}{2}(\sigma_1 + \sigma_2)$, the mean of the principal stresses.

The circle diagram is thus a powerful tool for obtaining desired results without resort to trigonometric equations of equilibrium. Other important uses will be described in later chapters. It is quite easy to draw the appropriate circle for a given stress system, and this helps in visualising changes in stress in different directions. The construction is particularly simple if the principal stresses are known in magnitude and direction.

2.1.1 Mohr's circle for two-dimensional stress, referred to principal axes

The principal axes are the directions of the principal stresses, and therefore are normal to the principal planes. If these are known, it is convenient to choose the x- and y-axes to coincide with them. Since they must be mutually perpendicular, it is in fact necessary to determine the direction of only one of them.

Then $\sigma_x = \sigma_1, \sigma_y = \sigma_2, \tau_{xy} = 0$ as Figure 2.2a.

The equilibrium equations (2.3) simplify to

$$\begin{aligned}
\sigma_\theta &= \tfrac{1}{2}(\sigma_1 + \sigma_2) + \tfrac{1}{2}(\sigma_1 - \sigma_2) \cos 2\theta \\
\tau_\theta &= \qquad\qquad + \tfrac{1}{2}(\sigma_1 - \sigma_2) \sin 2\theta
\end{aligned} \qquad (2.7)$$

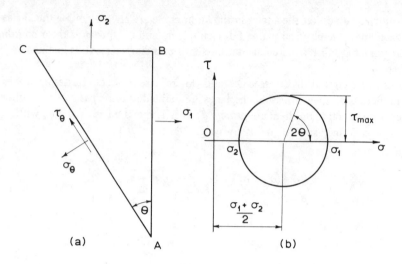

Figure 2.2 (*a*) The stress system referred to principal axes (*b*) The Mohr circle for this condition

whence
$$\left\{\sigma_\theta - \frac{\sigma_1 + \sigma_2}{2}\right\}^2 + \tau_\theta{}^2 = \left\{\frac{\sigma_1 - \sigma_2}{2}\right\}^2 \tag{2.8}$$

The stress circle in the (σ, τ) plane can thus be constructed as in Figure 2.2*b* immediately, from a knowledge of σ_1 and σ_2 only. The stresses on a plane at any angle θ to the plane on which σ_1 acts, will be given by the coordinates of the extremity of the radius vector at an angle 2θ, measured in the same sense as θ, from the σ axis.

A very simple example may be chosen to illustrate the use of this presentation. Others will be found in the exercises. In the tensile test $\sigma_2 = \sigma_3 = 0$. The circle passes through σ_1 and the origin. The maximum shear stress may be read directly:

$\tau_{max} = \frac{\sigma_1}{2}$, acting on a plane at 45° to the axis, as is well known.

2.2 Mohr's circle for three-dimensional stress

In a three-dimensional system there are three mutually perpendicular planes on which the shear stress is zero. The related principal stresses are σ_1, σ_2 and σ_3, and $|\sigma_1| > |\sigma_2| > |\sigma_3|$.

There are consequently three circles in the σ, τ diagram, encompassing respectively the stresses σ_1 and σ_2, σ_2 and σ_3, and σ_3 and σ_1 (Figure 2.3).

2.2.1 *Mohr's circles for stresses in plane plastic strain*
This condition is of special importance and will be considered later (p. 49). It will be shown that the Mohr circles are respectively of radius k, $\frac{1}{2}k$ and $\frac{1}{2}k$.

2.3 Yield criteria

The concept of principal stresses and the use of Mohr circles are very helpful, but it

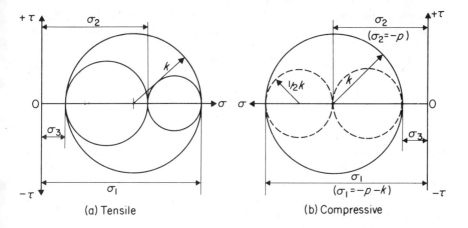

(a) Tensile   (b) Compressive

Figure 2.3 (*a*) The Mohr circles for three principal stresses (*b*) The Mohr stress circle for plane-strain conditions

is still necessary to formulate a statement of the combination of stresses that will produce plastic flow, otherwise known as a yield criterion.

In uniaxial tension or pure compression the yield stress is, in principle, easily defined. If the metal has previously been deformed to any known extent, subsequent yielding will occur as soon as the stress reaches the critical value Y, as shown by the simple stress–strain curve. With a real metal it is not quite so simple, since the onset of plastic flow is not sharply defined, but there is seldom serious doubt about the value.

It is not possible to perform separate yield tests for all stress systems, so some general criteria are used to relate the actual stresses to the simple tests. There are two criteria of major significance, due respectively to Tresca and von Mises. Both depend upon a recognition that plastic flow is essentially a shearing process; one postulating a critical shear stress, the other a critical shear-strain energy.

2.3.1 *Tresca maximum shear-stress criterion (1864)*
Tresca's criterion suggests that plastic flow occurs when the maximum shear stress reaches a particular value. In fact, under many conditions this criterion appears to predict yielding with sufficient accuracy. Since the maximum shearing stress is equal to half the difference between the maximum and minimum principal stresses (Figure 2.2), the criterion may be written

$$\tau_{\text{max}} = \tfrac{1}{2}(\sigma_1 - \sigma_3) = \text{constant} \tag{2.9}$$

It thus implies that yielding is independent of the magnitude of the intermediate principal stress σ_2, which is not strictly true.

2.3.2 *von Mises maximum shear-strain energy criterion*
In 1913 von Mises proposed a symmetrical quadratic condition:

$$(\sigma_1 - \sigma_2)^2 + (\sigma_2 - \sigma_3)^2 + (\sigma_3 - \sigma_1)^2 = \text{constant}$$

This includes all three principal stresses. Hencky (1924) interpreted this criterion as meaning that plastic flow occurs when the shear-strain energy reaches a critical value.

$$\frac{1}{6G}\{(\sigma_1 - \sigma_2)^2 + (\sigma_2 - \sigma_3)^2 + (\sigma_3 - \sigma_1)^2\} = \text{constant} = A \tag{2.10}$$

Here G is the rigidity modulus; $G = \dfrac{E}{2(1 + \nu)}$

The shear-strain energy is the elastic energy of distortion, and the criterion implies that the elastic energy associated with change in volume has no influence on yielding. Bridgman has confirmed experimentally that hydrostatic pressure has practically no effect on the stress system necessary to initiate plastic flow in metals. This should not be confused with the observation, also originally by Bridgman, that many materials which are normally brittle, such as marble, will flow plastically under high hydrostatic pressure. The superposition of a uniform compressive stress may suppress tensile failure but will not significantly affect the yield stresses.

It is now widely accepted that this criterion is more accurate, though it is sometimes convenient to use the Tresca criterion because of its simplicity.

2.3.3 *Relationship between tensile yield stress Y and shear yield stress k*

The yield criteria must obviously be applicable to any stress system. As the value of the constant A in equation 2.10 has not yet been specified, we are free to determine it from consideration of a simple tensile test. Within the gauge length of the tensile specimen, the stress system is a pure uniaxial tension, and yield is known to occur at the value Y.

Thus: $\sigma_1 = Y$, $\sigma_2 = 0$, $\sigma_3 = 0$, at the onset of plastic flow. Then the von Mises criterion gives

$$6GA = (\sigma_1 - \sigma_2)^2 + (\sigma_2 - \sigma_3)^2 + (\sigma_3 - \sigma_1)^2 = 2Y^2 \tag{2.11}$$

However, we might equally well have chosen to apply the criterion to a pure torsion test, in which yield occurs at a particular value of the applied shear stress, usually denoted by k. It can easily be shown that the principal stresses in a torsion test are equal in magnitude to the maximum shear stresses (the Mohr circle is centred on zero). Thus, at the onset of plastic flow in pure torsion: $\sigma_1 = +k$, $\sigma_2 = 0$, $\sigma_3 = -k$.

In this instance the von Mises criterion gives

$$6GA = k^2 + k^2 + 4k^2 \tag{2.12}$$

These values for A must be equal, since A is a constant and the criterion is known to be generally valid. This implies that, according to von Mises,

$$2Y^2 = 6k^2; \quad 2k = \frac{2}{\sqrt{3}}Y = 1 \cdot 155Y \tag{2.13}$$

It is convenient to express the result in terms of $2k$, rather than k, as will be seen in the next section.

If the Tresca criterion is applied to these two stress systems, a slightly different result is obtained. In pure torsion, yielding is predicted when

$$\tau_{max} = \tfrac{1}{2}(\sigma_1 - \sigma_3) = \tfrac{1}{2}(k + k) = k.$$

This follows also from the definition of k. In pure tension, however,

$$\tau_{max} = \tfrac{1}{2}(\sigma_1 - \sigma_3) = Y/2; \quad \sigma_1 - \sigma_3 = Y \tag{2.14}$$

Thus, according to Tresca, $\quad 2k = Y$ (2.15)

It may be noticed that when any two principal stresses are equal, both criteria reduce to the same equation. Thus if $\sigma_2 = \sigma_3$, von Mises criterion gives, from equation 2.11,

$$(\sigma_1 - \sigma_3)^2 + (\sigma_3 - \sigma_1)^2 = 2Y^2$$

or $\quad (\sigma_1 - \sigma_3)^2 = Y^2$ (2.16)

This is the same as the Tresca criterion, equation 2.14. The physical reason for this is that the stress system can be regarded as a combination of a uniaxial stress $(\sigma_1 - \sigma_2) = (\sigma_1 - \sigma_3)$ and a hydrostatic stress σ_2. Since the latter is known not to influence yielding, yield must occur at the uniaxial yield stress Y, and no criterion is required.

2.3.4 *Yield under plane-strain conditions*
It is also unnecessary to use a yield criterion for plane-strain conditions, where in fact yielding occurs due to pure shear, though this is not immediately obvious.

Plane-strain is defined as a condition in which (a) the flow is everywhere parallel to a given plane, say the (x,y) plane, and (b) the motion is independent of z. Thus one principal strain-increment, say $d\epsilon_2$, is zero. It follows that if there is no volume change $d\epsilon_1 = -d\epsilon_3$, ignoring elastic deformation, that is assuming an incompressible rigid-plastic material. The deformation is thus pure shear strain. It is assumed, as can be justified by an argument due to Hill, that pure shear strain is produced by pure shear stress. Yield consequently occurs in plane-strain at the shear yield stress k. The Mohr circle for plane plastic strain, with no strain-hardening, therefore always has the radius $\tau_{max} = k$. There may be a superimposed hydrostatic stress σ_2 which will alter the values of σ_1 and σ_3 but will not influence yielding. This is usually a compressive stress in metalworking. Under these conditions, as in Figure 5.2 of Chapter 5,

$$\sigma_1 = \sigma_2 - k, \quad \sigma_3 = \sigma_2 + k$$

Thus $\quad \sigma_2 = \tfrac{1}{2}(\sigma_1 + \sigma_3)$ (2.17)

and $\quad \sigma_1 - \sigma_3 = 2k$ (2.18)

The latter may be written

$$\sigma_1 - \sigma_3 = S,$$

which defines the yield stress in a plane-strain compression test, sometimes called the constrained yield stress. Using the von Mises relationship between k and Y (equation 2.13)

$$S = 2k = 1 \cdot 155Y$$

These equations are important in later developments of metalworking theory, since plane-strain conditions provide a simplification essential for slip-line field and most upper-bound techniques.

3

Determination of Drawing and Forging Loads by Consideration of Stresses

3.1 Introduction

The main objectives of metalworking theory are to predict metal deformation and the forces required to produce it. In addition, a knowledge of local stress and strain can help in predicting causes of failure in the final product. These factors govern the type of process chosen and the size of equipment required. The working loads and the energy consumed will also be greatly influenced by appropriate selection of the process parameters, including the pass schedules, lubrication, temperature, speed, and tool profile.

Many practical processes are too complex for full theoretical treatment, but even the empirical rules and formulae are more effectively applied with an understanding of their background. For the major basic processes of rolling, forging, extrusion and drawing it is possible to predict working loads with considerable accuracy.

In this chapter we shall discuss two methods of estimating metalworking loads by consideration of stresses. The fifth chapter will deal with analyses depending upon the flow of metal.

3.2 Work formula for homogeneous deformation

A general approach, applicable to simple tension or compression, and also to more complex processes such as wire-drawing, is to evaluate the work done in deforming a small element of the workpiece, and then to integrate this over the whole deforming region.

Thus, for uniaxial tension the principal stresses at any point are:

$$\sigma_1 = Y, \sigma_2 = 0, \sigma_3 = 0,$$

where Y is the instantaneous yield stress at the strain ϵ corresponding to the appropriate cross-sectional area A and length l. The increment of work done in increasing the length of the specimen by δl beyond this strain is given by the product of force and displacement:

$$\delta W = (YA)\delta l \tag{3.1}$$

The increment of work, per unit volume V, is

$$\frac{\delta W}{V} = \frac{\delta W}{Al} = Y\frac{\delta l}{l}$$

We may assume no volume change, and integrate this expression between the original length l_0 and the final length l_1:

$$\frac{W}{V} = \int_{l_0}^{l_1} Y \frac{dl}{l} = \int_{\epsilon_0}^{\epsilon_1} Y \, . \, d\epsilon \qquad (3.2)$$

This gives the well-known result that the work done per unit volume in homogeneous deformation is equal to the area of the stress–strain curve, between the appropriate strain values.

This may be evaluated directly from the dimension change, assuming an average yield stress $\overline{Y}$.

$$\frac{W}{V} = \overline{Y} \int_{l_0}^{l_1} \frac{dl}{l} = \overline{Y} \ln \frac{l_1}{l_0} \qquad (3.3)$$

Equation 3.3, often known as the work formula, gives a reasonable approximation for a metal which has been work-hardened before the tensile stretching, so that Y does not vary unduly in the process. It is less reliable for annealed material, where Y increases rapidly with strain, so it is then preferable to use equation 3.2, integrating the stress–strain curve graphically or numerically. This method can be applied to several practical operations.

3.2.1 *Work formula for wire-drawing*
The work done by the drawing force F in moving from the starting position, adjacent to the die, to the full length l_1 of drawn wire, is given by

$$W_1 = F l_1 \qquad (3.4)$$

Assuming homogeneous deformation, the work done in deforming the wire in the die is, from equation 3.3

$$W = V \overline{Y} \ln \frac{l_1}{l_0}$$

In the absence of friction these will be equal:

$$F = \frac{V}{l_1} \overline{Y} \ln \frac{l_1}{l_0}$$

Since $V = l_0 A_0 = l_1 A_1$ in plastic deformation, this may be written

$$F = A_1 \overline{Y} \ln \frac{l_1}{l_0} \qquad (3.5a$$

It is usual to consider reduction of area in wire-drawing, rather than increase in length, since change of area is the property required in practice. Using the constancy of volume again, equation 3.5a becomes

$$F = A_1 \overline{Y} \ln \frac{A_0}{A_1} \qquad (3.5b$$

The reduction of area r is given by

$$r = \frac{A_0 - A_1}{A_0} = 1 - \frac{A_1}{A_0}$$

Thus $F = A_1 \bar{Y} \ln \dfrac{1}{1-r}$ (3.5c)

The drawing stress σ_1 is consequently

$$\sigma_1 = \frac{F}{A_1} = \bar{Y} \ln \frac{1}{1-r}$$ (3.6)

This result forms the basis of many wire-drawing calculations, corrections being applied to take account of the influences of mechanical and frictional constraints.

3.2.2 *Example of application of work formula for drawing: determination of maximum possible reduction of area in one pass*

Wire-drawing is limited eventually by tensile failure of the drawn wire. For such a heavy pass, the maximum tensile stress will be nearly equal to its yield stress, because of the severe strain-hardening which the wire has experienced. Thus at the limiting reduction

$$\sigma_1 = Y_1$$

The rate of strain-hardening will be small, so that the mean yield stress $\bar{Y}$ will also be nearly equal to Y_1. The maximum reduction r_m is thus given by the conditions

$$\frac{\sigma_1}{Y_1} = 1; \quad \sigma_1 = \bar{Y} \ln \frac{1}{1-r_m} = Y_1 \ln \frac{1}{1-r_m}$$ (3.7)

Thus $\dfrac{1}{1-r_m} = e^{1\cdot0} = 2\cdot7$

$$r_m = 1 - \frac{1}{2\cdot7} = 0\cdot63$$ (3.8)

The maximum possible reduction with perfect lubrication would thus be about 63% or slightly more if the rate of strain-hardening is still appreciable. Internal distortion and friction reduce this limit, as will be seen in Chapter 6, but under favourable conditions wire may be drawn with reductions of area well over 50%.

3.2.3 *Extrusion of a bar*

The work formula can also be used to obtain a lower limit to extrusion pressure, assuming homogeneous deformation and zero friction. In extrusion, the force is applied to the original billet, of area A_0, not to the product whose area is A_1 as it was in the drawing example above. This force moves through a distance l_0 equal to the length of the billet and so does work

$$W_0 = (pA_0)l_0$$

This is equated to the work of homogeneous deformation

$$W = V\bar{Y} \ln \frac{l_1}{l_0} = V\bar{Y} \ln \frac{A_0}{A_1}$$

giving

$$p = \bar{Y} \ln A_0/A_1 \qquad\qquad (3.9)$$

We shall see later that this lower limit is a poor approximation for extrusion because the constraint factor is high for all useful extrusion ratios A_0/A_1.

It is possible to calculate a maximum reduction of area, as for drawing, based on the limit $p = Y$, which implies compressive yielding ahead of the die. This is important in open-die extrusion, used for some socket-head bolts and other fasteners, but in most extrusion it has no significance because the billet simply expands to fill the container and is then restrained from further increase in diameter.

3.3 Determination of rod- and wire-drawing load from local stress evaluation

A more accurate result can be obtained by considering the local stresses acting in the deforming region, including the effects of friction.

3.3.1 *Cylindrical rod drawing, with a conical die. (α, μ, Y constant)*
The equilibrium of a small element in the working zone is again considered. Figure 3.1 shows the stresses acting on a thin frustum, at a distance x from the virtual apex of the conical die.

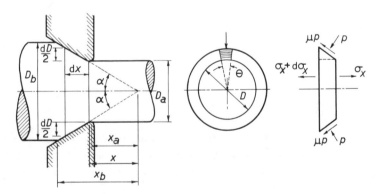

Figure 3.1 A diagram showing the stresses acting on an element of rod drawn through a conical die

There are three force components acting in the axial direction:

due to the change in longitudinal stress,

$$(\sigma_x + d\sigma_x)\frac{\pi}{4}(D + dD)^2 - \sigma_x\frac{\pi}{4}D^2;$$

due directly to the die pressure on the circumference,

$$p\left(\pi D \frac{dx}{\cos \alpha}\right)\sin \alpha;$$

due to the frictional drag at the circumference,

$$\mu p\left(\pi D \frac{dx}{\cos \alpha}\right)\cos \alpha.$$

Under steady drawing conditions, these must be in equilibrium. Thus, ignoring the products of infinitesimals,

$$\frac{\sigma_x D \; dD}{2} + \frac{D^2 \; d\sigma_x}{4} + pD \; dx \tan \alpha + \mu p D \; dx = 0$$

Since $dD = 2dx \tan \alpha$, this may be written

$$2\sigma_x \; dD + D \; d\sigma_x + 2p \; dD + 2\mu p \; dD \cot \alpha = 0$$

$$D \; d\sigma_x + 2[\sigma_x + p(1 + \mu \cot \alpha)] \; dD = 0 \qquad (3.10)$$

Radial equilibrium gives

$$\sigma_r(\pi D \; dx) = -p\left(\pi D \frac{dx}{\cos \alpha}\right)\cos \alpha + \mu p\left(\pi D \frac{dx}{\cos \alpha}\right)\sin \alpha$$

$$\sigma_r = -p(1 - \mu \tan \alpha)$$

It is usually permissible to ignore $\mu \tan \alpha$ in comparison with unity. Typical values are $\mu = 0 \cdot 05$, $\alpha = 6°$, $\mu \tan \alpha = 0 \cdot 005$. Then the state of stress is cylindrical, and the principal stresses are $\sigma_1 = \sigma_x$, $\sigma_2 = \sigma_3 = \sigma_r = -p$. As explained in Chapter 2, §2.3.3, when two principal stresses are equal, the system is equivalent to a uniaxial stress combined with a hydrostatic stress, so that yield occurs at the value Y. All yield criteria must give this result.

von Mises: $(\sigma_1 - \sigma_2)^2 + (\sigma_2 - \sigma_3)^2 + (\sigma_3 - \sigma_1)^2 = 2(\sigma_1 - \sigma_3)^2 = 2Y^2$

Tresca: $\frac{1}{2}(\sigma_1 - \sigma_3) = k = \frac{1}{2}Y$

Consequently in rod-drawing $\sigma_1 - \sigma_3 = Y$, so

$$\sigma_x + p = Y \qquad (3.11)$$

Combining this condition of yielding with equation 3.10, and writing $B = \mu \cot \alpha$,

$$\frac{d\sigma_x}{B\sigma_x - Y(1 + B)} = 2 \frac{dD}{D} \qquad (3.12)$$

This basic differential equation may be integrated directly if B and Y are constant.

$$\frac{1}{B}\ln [B\sigma_x - Y(1 + B)] = 2 \ln D + \text{constant}$$

$$B\sigma_x - Y(1 + B) = cD^{2B}$$

The constant of integration is found from the assumption that there is no longitudinal stress at the entry, as in single-hole drawing with no back-pull

$$\sigma_x = \sigma_{xb} = 0, \ D = D_b$$

$$c = -Y(1 + B)/D_b{}^{2B}$$

Thus
$$\frac{\sigma_x}{Y} = \frac{1 + B}{B}\left[1 - \left(\frac{D}{D_b}\right)^{2B}\right] \tag{3.13}$$

The drawing stress σ_{xa} is given by

$$\frac{\sigma_{xa}}{Y} = \frac{1 + B}{B}\left[1 - \left(\frac{D_a}{D_b}\right)^{2B}\right] \tag{3.14a}$$

In terms of the reduction of area,

$$r = \frac{\pi}{4}(D_b{}^2 - D_a{}^2)\Big/\frac{\pi}{4}D_b{}^2; \ r = 1 - \left(\frac{D_a}{D_b}\right)^2$$

$$\frac{\sigma_{xa}}{Y} = \frac{1 + B}{B}[1 - (1 - r)^B] \tag{3.14b}$$

The same equation can be used for drawing of strip, but the plane-strain yield stress S is then used in place of Y.

3.3.2 *Frictionless drawing of cylindrical rod (Y constant)*
If the coefficient of friction is zero, the parameter B is also zero, and equation 3.14 cannot be used. It is then necessary to revert to the differential equation 3.10, which becomes, with the condition $\mu = 0$,

$$D \, d\sigma_x + 2(\sigma_x + p) \, dD = 0$$

Eliminating p by use of the condition of yielding, equation 3.11

$$D \, d\sigma_x + 2Y \, dD = 0$$

This may be integrated if Y is constant:

$$\frac{\sigma_x}{Y} = -2 \ln D + \text{constant}$$

At entry, $\sigma_x = \sigma_{xb} = 0, D = D_b$, so

$$\frac{\sigma_x}{Y} = \ln\left(\frac{D_b}{D}\right)^2$$

The drawing stress is thus

$$\frac{\sigma_{xa}}{Y} = \ln\left(\frac{D_b}{D_a}\right)^2 = \ln\frac{1}{1 - r} \tag{3.15}$$

This result was also obtained in §3.2, equation 3.6, as the contribution of homo-geneous plastic-deformation. This is to be expected, since the stress-evaluation method takes no account of redundant work but does allow for the homogeneous deformation and the friction. It may be noticed that equation 3.15 is independent of the die angle. Indeed, the dies might equally well be curved, provided that there is perfect lubrication.

3.3.3 *Allowance for strain-hardening in rod-drawing*

Strain-hardening can be included by assuming a mean value of the yield stress, between entry and exit conditions, as in §3.2. This is satisfactory for pre-worked material or for second and subsequent passes, but for annealed wire a more accurate result is obtained by integration of equation 3.12 using a suitable equation of the type $\sigma = \sigma_0 \epsilon^m$, (1.4), preferably with an analogue or digital computer.

3.3.4 *Maximum reduction of area per pass in rod-, wire- and strip-drawing*

The maximum reduction of area in a single pass is found, as in §3.2.2, from the condition that the wire will fail in tension when the drawing stress reaches the yield stress of the drawn section. For the very heavily strained wire this will be approximately equal to the maximum tensile stress.

The limiting reduction is thus obtained using equation 3.14b.

$$\frac{\sigma_{xa}}{Y} = 1 = \frac{1+B}{B}[1-(1-r)^B]$$

For example, choosing typical values

$$\mu = 0.05, \alpha = 6°, B = \mu \cot \alpha = 0.476$$

$$1 = \frac{1.476}{0.476}[1-(1-r)^{0.476}]$$

$$(1-r)^{0.476} = 1 - 0.322; \quad 1 - r = 0.442$$

$$r \approx 0.56 \tag{3.16}$$

It is interesting to compare this result with the limit for strip-drawing, under the same conditions. Because wide strip is constrained during drawing by the undrawn elastic material entering the die, it is necessary to use the plane-strain yield stress S in place of Y in equation 3.14b, but the drawn strip is still limited by free yielding at Y.

Thus $\quad \dfrac{\sigma_{xa}}{S} = \dfrac{1+B}{B}[1-(1-r)^B]$

but $\quad \sigma_{xa} = Y = S/1.15$

$$0.870 = 3.101[1-(1-r)^{0.476}]$$

$$(1-r)^{0.476} = 1 - 0.280; \quad 1 - r = 0.50$$

$$r \approx 50\%$$

This is slightly less than for the round rod or wire, because the constraint increases the stress required.

In the absence of friction, equation 3.15 must be used instead of 3.14 to find the maximum reduction of area for wire or rod.

$$\frac{\sigma_{xa}}{Y} = 1 = \ln\frac{1}{1-r}$$

$$\frac{1}{1-r} = e^{1\cdot0} = 2\cdot72; \quad 1-r = 0\cdot368$$

$$r \approx 63\%$$

Thus the friction found in typical drawing operations does not very greatly influence the theoretical maximum reduction of area per pass. Because the metal strain-hardens, the yield stress of the drawn bar will exceed the mean value of the yield stress, which increases the possible reduction slightly. On the other hand, the contribution of redundant work increases the drawing stress but it is a small factor for normal die angles at these heavy reductions. The practical limit is in the vicinity of 60%, but passes are usually restricted to appreciably smaller reductions, often 35–45%, because of the deterioration in lubrication in very heavy passes and the consequent danger of pickup of drawn metal on the die.

3.4 Determination by stress evaluation of the load for close-pass drawing of a thin-walled tube

It is convenient at first to suppose that the diameter of the tube remains constant, and that the wall thickness alone is changed during drawing. There is then no hoop strain, and plane-strain conditions can be assumed. This is nearly true of many industrial passes, in which a large reduction is made in the wall thickness while the diameter is decreased by a small amount, just sufficient to allow easy insertion of the plug or mandrel before drawing. Large changes in diameter involve a high proportion of sinking which increases the amount of redundant work and reduces the efficiency. Close passes have negligible sinking.

3.4.1 *Close-pass plug-drawing with a conical die*
Figure 3.2 shows the stresses acting on an element of tube between the die and the plug.

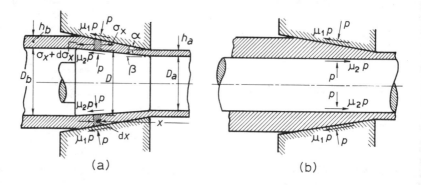

(a)   (b)

Figure 3.2 The stresses acting on an element of thin-walled tube in close-pass drawing (*a*) over a slightly tapered plug (*b*) with a moving mandrel

If the wall thickness h is small in comparison with the mean tube diameter D, which remains nearly constant, the determination of drawing stress proceeds as for plane-strain strip-drawing, except that the strip width w is replaced by the tube circumference. Assuming the die pressure p to be equal to the plug pressure, the axial components of the forces acting on the element are:

due to the longitudinal stress,

$$(\sigma_x + d\sigma_x)(h + dh)\pi D - \sigma_x h\pi D = (\sigma_x \, dh + h \, d\sigma_x)\pi D;$$

due to the die pressure

$$\int_0^{2\pi} p\left(\frac{dx}{\cos \alpha} \frac{D}{2} \, d\theta\right) \sin \alpha = p\pi D \tan \alpha \, dx;$$

due to the plug pressure,

$$-\int_0^{2\pi} p\left(\frac{dx}{\cos \beta} \frac{D}{2} \, d\theta\right) \sin \beta = -p\pi D \tan \beta \, dx;$$

due to the die friction,

$$\int_0^{2\pi} \mu_1 p\left(\frac{dx}{\cos \alpha} \frac{D}{2} \, d\theta\right) \cos \alpha = \mu_1 p\pi D \, dx;$$

due to the plug friction,

$$\int_0^{2\pi} \mu_2 p\left(\frac{dx}{\cos \beta} \frac{D}{2} \, d\theta\right) \cos \beta = \mu_2 p\pi D \, dx$$

Under steady drawing conditions, these must be in equilibrium. Thus

$$(\sigma_x \, dh + h \, d\sigma_x)\pi D + p\pi D(\tan \alpha - \tan \beta)dx + p\pi D(\mu_1 + \mu_2)dx = 0$$

Since the net wall-thickness change is

$$dh = dx \tan \alpha - dx \tan \beta,$$

the equation becomes

$$(\sigma_x \, dh + h \, d\sigma_x) + p \, dh \left(1 + \frac{\mu_1 + \mu_2}{\tan \alpha - \tan \beta}\right) = 0 \qquad (3.17)$$

With the parameter

$$B^*{}_{\text{plug}} = \frac{\mu_1 + \mu_2}{\tan \alpha - \tan \beta} \qquad (3.18)$$

this may be written

$$h \, d\sigma_x + [\sigma_x + p(1 + B^*)] \, dh = 0 \qquad (3.19)$$

which is of the same form as the equation for strip-drawing, appropriate allowance being made for the value of the parameter B for strip and B^* for tube. As in wire-drawing (§3.3.1), consideration of radial equilibrium suggests that the frictional contribution to the die pressure is small, and that the principal stresses can be taken as

$$\sigma_1 = \sigma_x, \quad \sigma_2 = -p$$

(This also justifies the assumption that die and plug pressures are equal.) Since in a close pass there is no change in diameter, these will be related by the condition of yielding in plane-strain, equation 2.18:

$$\sigma_1 - \sigma_2 = S = 1 \cdot 15Y; \quad \sigma_x + p = S$$

By substitution for p in equation 3.19,

$$\frac{d\sigma_x}{\sigma_x + (S - \sigma_x)(1 + B^*)} = -\frac{dh}{h}$$

$$\frac{d\sigma_x}{B^*\sigma_x - S(1 + B^*)} = \frac{dh}{h} \tag{3.20}$$

This equation is valid for any values of B^* and S, but the simplest solution is obtained if μ and S are constant or average values, and the die and plug have straight sides, so that α and β are constant. (In practical drawing the plug is usually cylindrical, so $\beta = 0$). Then, integrating directly,

$$\frac{1}{B^*} \ln \left[B^*\sigma_x - S(1 + B^*)\right] = \ln h + \text{constant}$$

$$B^*\sigma_x - S(1 + B^*) = ch^{B^*} \tag{3.21}$$

The constant of integration may be found from the entry conditions. Assuming no back-pull, $h = h_b$, $\sigma_x = \sigma_{xb} = 0$, and

$$c = -S(1 + B^*)h_b^{-B^*}$$

Equation 3.21 can thus be written

$$\frac{\sigma_x}{S} = \frac{1 + B^*}{B^*} \left[1 - \left(\frac{h}{h_b}\right)^{B^*}\right] \tag{3.22}$$

The drawing stress is the axial stress σ_{xa} at the exit, where $h = h_a$.

$$\frac{\sigma_{xa}}{S} = \frac{1 + B^*}{B^*} \left[1 - \left(\frac{h_a}{h_b}\right)^{B^*}\right] \tag{3.23}$$

The die or plug pressure is obtained from the condition $\dfrac{p}{S} = 1 - \dfrac{\sigma_x}{S}$.

3.4.2 Close-pass mandrel-drawing with a conical die
In plug-drawing, the frictional drag acts in the backward direction on both inside and outside of the tube. When a mandrel is drawn forward with the tube, however, the relative motion on the inside is reversed because the tube elongates while the

mandrel remains undeformed. The direction of the frictional force between mandrel and tube is therefore opposite to that between tube and die, as shown in Figure 3.2b. The stress equation and its solution are exactly the same as for plug-drawing except that the parameter B^* is changed to

$$B^*_{mandrel} = \frac{\mu_1 - \mu_2}{\tan \alpha - \tan \beta} \tag{3.24}$$

Thus if $\mu_1 = \mu_2$, as is often true, B^* takes the value zero. Under these circumstances the above integration cannot be used. The differential equation 3.19 with the value $B^* = 0$ becomes simply

$$h \, d\sigma_x + (\sigma_x + p) \, dh = 0$$

$$h \, d\sigma_x + S \, dh = 0$$

This may be directly integrated with the boundary condition $\sigma_{xb} = 0$ at $h = h_b$, giving

$$\frac{\sigma_{xa}}{S} = \ln \frac{h_b}{h_a} = \ln \frac{1}{1 - r} \tag{3.25}$$

This is the familiar expression for homogeneous deformation (3.6).

It is however possible for the friction coefficient μ_2 on the mandrel to exceed μ_1 on the die, and B^* is then negative. The analysis is otherwise unaltered, so the drawing stress can be less than that for frictionless drawing to the same reduction of area. The limiting reduction in area per pass is correspondingly increased.

3.4.3 *Plug-drawing with a circular-profile die*

One common type of wear during tube-drawing, particularly with relatively hard metals, is the formation of an annular depression or ring at the entry position. Dies of circular profile, symmetrical about the central plane, were once widely used as 'double-entry' dies which could be reversed in the die holder for further drawing after the ring had formed. This was not of course possible if wear or pickup occurred in the throat region, and the large entry angle of small-radius profiles tended to impair lubrication and to introduce inhomogeneity in the product. Straight-taper dies of small angle give better drawing and have generally superseded the double-entry die. Single-entry dies with circular profiles of larger radius are, however, quite satisfactory.

The basic differential equation is the same as that derived above for conical dies:

$$d(h\sigma_x) + p \, dh \left[1 + \frac{\mu_1 + \mu_2}{\tan \alpha - \tan \beta} \right] = 0 \tag{3.26}$$

However, the die angle α is now a trigonometric function of h, and the equation resembles that for rolling flat strip (4.3), the solution for which will be given in Chapter 4, equation 4.11.

For plug-drawing, if $\mu_1 = \mu_2$, as is commonly assumed,

$$\frac{\sigma_{xa}}{S} = 1 - \frac{h_a}{h_b} e^{2\mu(H_a - H_b)} \tag{3.27}$$

where $\quad H_b = 2\sqrt{\dfrac{R}{h_a}} \tan^{-1}\left(\sqrt{\dfrac{R}{h_a}} \cdot \alpha_b\right)$ $\qquad\qquad$ (3.28)

and $\quad H_a = 2\sqrt{\dfrac{R}{h_a}} \tan^{-1}\left(\sqrt{\dfrac{R}{h_a}}\,\alpha_a\right)$

3.5 Tube sinking

The process of sinking involves reduction of outside diameter, with no intentional change in wall thickness, by pulling the tube through a die, usually with a curved profile. The stresses can be analysed as above, but a modified value of the yield stress is used to allow for the complex stress system. The yield stress is expressed as mY, and the value of m is usually taken to be 1·10. This leads to an equation similar to that for drawing (3.14a):

$$\frac{\sigma_{xa}}{1\cdot 1 Y} = \frac{1+B}{B}\left[1 - \left(\frac{D_a}{D_b}\right)^B\right] \qquad\qquad (3.29)$$

The ratio D_a/D_b is raised to the power B, not $2B$ as in wire-drawing, because the area is approximately Dt, and the thickness t is unchanged in sinking, or slightly increased in practice.

3.6 Determination of forging load from local stress evaluation

The approach is basically the same as for drawing, starting from the force equilibriun of an element of the deforming metal, and then integrating over the whole billet.

3.6.1 *Plain-strain forging of well-lubricated thin strip*
Figure 3.3a shows the stresses acting at any instant on a thin, wide plate compressed between parallel overhanging platens. It is assumed that the horizontal stress σ_x is uniform across the section and is a principal stress. Then horizontal equilibrium of the forces acting on unit width of an element on the right of the centre-line requires that

$$(\sigma_x + d\sigma_x)h - \sigma_x h - 2\mu p\, dx = 0$$

On the left of the centre-line,

$$(\sigma_x + d\sigma_x)h - \sigma_x h + 2\mu p\, dx = 0$$

These equations may be simplified and combined:

$$h\, d\sigma_x \mp 2\mu p\, dx = 0 \qquad\qquad (3.30$$

The upper sign refers to the right-hand portion. Since σ_x is one principal stress, $-p$ is the other, and the two are related by the condition of yielding in plane-strain (equation 2.18)

$$\sigma_1 - \sigma_3 = S$$

$$\sigma_x + p = S = 2k; \quad d\sigma_x = -dp$$

Substitution in equation 3.30 gives a relationship between p and x:

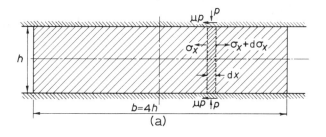

(a)

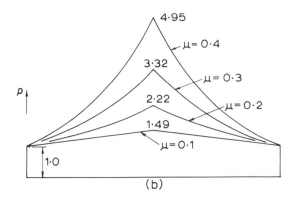

(b)

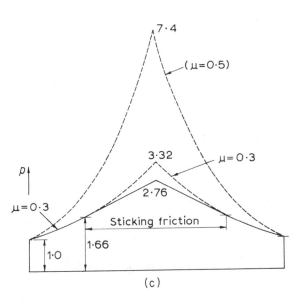

(c)

Figure 3.3 (*a*) The stresses acting on an element compressed under plane-strain conditions between parallel overhanging platens (*b*) The pressure distribution with low friction (*c*) The pressure distribution with sticking friction over the central region only ($\mu = 0.3$)

$$h\,dp \pm 2\mu p\,dx = 0$$

$$\frac{dp}{p} = \mp \frac{2\mu}{h}\,dx \qquad (3.31)$$

This can be integrated directly:

$$\ln p = \mp \frac{2\mu}{h} + \text{constant}$$

The constant of integration is found from the condition that the horizontal stress is zero at both edges, where $x = \pm b/2$. Thus at $x = b/2$,

$$(p)_{b/2} = c^- e^{\frac{-2\mu}{h}\frac{b}{2}} \quad \text{and} \quad (p)_{b/2} = 2k - (\sigma_x)_{b/2} = 2k$$

$$c^- = 2k\,e^{+\frac{\mu b}{h}}$$

Thus on the right-hand side of the centre-line, $x = 0$,

$$\frac{p}{2k} = e^{\frac{2\mu}{h}\left(\frac{b}{2} - x\right)} \qquad (3.32)$$

The constant of integration has the same value on the left-hand side, since

$$(p)_{-b/2} = c^+ e^{+\frac{2\mu}{h}\left(-\frac{b}{2}\right)} = 2k$$

The pressure thus increases inwards, exponentially from $p = 2k$ at both edges, as shown in Figure 3.3b. The maximum value, at the centre, is

$$\left(\frac{p}{2k}\right)_{\text{max}} = e^{\mu \frac{b}{h}} \qquad (3.33)$$

If μ is low, this may be written in approximate form

$$\left(\frac{p}{2k}\right)_{\text{max}} \approx 1 + \mu \frac{b}{h}$$

The mean pressure P on the platens is then

$$P \approx 2k\left(1 + \frac{1}{2}\mu \frac{b}{h}\right) \qquad (3.34)$$

Thus in forging thin strip between parallel platens, as in rolling, the pressure distribution shows a 'friction-hill'. There is, however, an important difference. In rolling, the conditions are steady; but in forging, the geometry changes continuously as the operation proceeds, and the contact with the platens increases. The load at any instant can be found by integration of equation 3.32, but the progressive increase in load cannot easily be determined, since it depends on the spread of the work-piece, which in turn depends on the dimensions and on the friction.

When the workpiece is thicker, there is again a friction-hill, but account must then be taken of the geometrical constraint, by the use of the slip-line field (§5.6).

3.6.2 *Plane-strain forging of thin strip with high friction*

If the friction is high, there is a limit to the shear stress at the interface, which cannot exceed the shear yield stress of the metal, $k = S/2$. If this sticking-friction regime extends over the whole interface, the equilibrium equation 3.30 should be written

$$h \, d\sigma_x \mp 2k \, dx = 0$$

It is often supposed that this equation can be integrated, assuming that σ_x and $-p$ are principal stresses, as before, but this clearly involves a gross assumption, since p is acting on the plane of maximum shear, at $45°$ to the principal planes. Making this assumption, the pressure increases linearly towards the centre as shown in Figure 3.3c. The equation for the mean pressure is

$$\bar{P} = 2k(1 + b/4h) \tag{3.35}$$

3.6.3 *Forging of a flat lubricated disc*

The stresses acting on a circular disc compressed in the axial direction are shown in Figure 3.4.

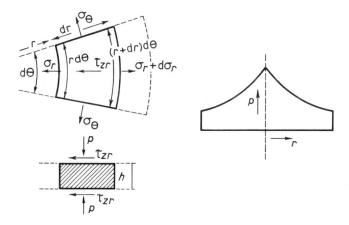

Figure 3.4 The stresses acting on an element of a forged disc

Assuming that σ_r and σ_θ are constant throughout the disc thickness, radial equilibrium requires that

$$(\sigma_r + d\sigma_r)h(r + dr) \, d\theta - \sigma_r hr \, d\theta - 2\sigma_\theta h \, dr \sin\frac{d\theta}{2} - 2\tau_{zr}r \, d\theta \, dr = 0$$

$$\sigma_r hr \, d\theta + \sigma_r h \, dr \, d\theta + d\sigma_r hr \, d\theta - \sigma_r hr \, d\theta - \sigma_\theta h \, dr \, d\theta - 2\tau_{zr}r \, d\theta \, dr = 0$$

$$\sigma_r h \, dr + d\sigma_r hr - \sigma_\theta h \, dr - 2\tau_{zr}r \, dr = 0 \tag{3.36}$$

It is reasonable to assume that σ_r, σ_θ and σ_z $(=-p)$ are the principal stresses, and it can be shown that the stress state is cylindrical, with $\sigma_r = \sigma_\theta$. Any yield criterion then gives (Chapter 2, §2.3.3)

$$\sigma_r - \sigma_z = Y; \quad \sigma_r + p = Y$$

Equation 3.36 thus becomes, with $\tau_{zr} = \mu p$ for sliding friction:

$$-h \, dp - 2\mu p \, dr = 0$$

$$\ln p = \frac{2\mu}{h} r + \text{constant}$$

The constant of integration may be found from the boundary condition that at $r = \dfrac{D}{2}, \sigma_r = 0, p = Y$, giving

$$\frac{p}{Y} = e^{\frac{2\mu}{h}\left(\frac{D}{2} - r\right)} \tag{3.37}$$

Comparison with equation 3.32 shows that the pressure distribution for forging a disc is identical with that for plane-strain forging of a block of breadth b equal to the diameter D of the disc, provided that due allowance is made for the yield stress. The value Y should be used for axially-symmetrical conditions, and S for plane strain.

4

Determination of Rolling Load and Power

Rolling presents special problems of analytical interest and is also an important industrial process. Flat rolling has been extensively studied.

4.1 Roll-pressure determination from local stress-evaluation

The procedure has a strong formal resemblance to that described for tube or strip-drawing, but there are important differences. In drawing, the die usually remains stationary, and a tension is applied to the drawn metal. The important working load is the applied tension. Rolling mills, on the other hand, usually have power-driven rolls which feed the strip through without any tension being necessary. The important load is the vertical constraining force on the rolls, corresponding to the die load in drawing. Intermediate conditions are also quite common, since a moderate tension between stands of a rolling mill reduces the roll load, improves the flatness of the strip, and gives a useful control of gauge. Idle rolls may, on the other hand, sometimes be used on a draw-bench for cold-forming small sections, and on a push-bench for hot-forming tubes on a mandrel. In the characteristic strip-rolling process, however, the peripheral velocity of the driven rolls exceeds that of the strip, which is consequently dragged in if the friction is high enough. As the strip is reduced in thickness it elongates and increases its linear speed until at the exit it is travelling faster than the rolls, and the friction acts in the reverse direction. There is a *neutral point* within the roll gap, at which the surface velocity of the strip equals the peripheral velocity of the rolls, there is no slip, and the direction of the friction force reverses. This is an important characteristic feature of rolling.

The assumptions used in evaluation of roll pressure in cold strip-rolling are:

Plane-strain conditions
Homogeneous deformation
Constant magnitude of the friction coefficient
Constant circular arc of contact
Neutral point within the arc of contact
Negligible elastic deformation

The analysis is reasonably straightforward but calculations of roll pressures can conveniently be performed directly from the basic differential equation using a small analogue computer.

4.1.1 *Derivation and general solution of the differential equation*

Longitudinal resolution of the forces acting on an element A, of unit width, in the deformation zone, on the exit side of the neutral point (Figure 4.1), gives:

35

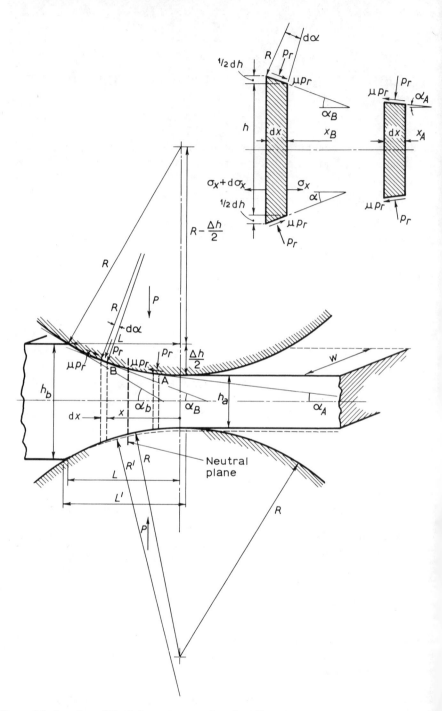

Figure 4.1 A section of the deformation zone in strip rolling, showing the stresses acting on two elements of strip, one on each side of the neutral plane. The broken-line profile shows the deformation of the rolls to a radius R' under load

$(\sigma_x + d\sigma_x)(h + dh) - h\sigma_x$ due to longitudinal stress

$2\left(p_r \dfrac{dx}{\cos \alpha}\right) \sin \alpha$ due to radial pressure on both rolls

$2\mu\left(p_r \dfrac{dx}{\cos \alpha}\right) \cos \alpha$ due to friction against both rolls

For steady rolling, these must be in equilibrium:

$$h \, d\sigma_x + \sigma_x \, dh + 2p_r \, dx \tan \alpha + 2\mu p_r \, dx = 0 \qquad (4.1)$$

The equilibrium of a similar element B, on the entry side of the neutral point, gives a similar equation, but with the frictional force in the opposite direction;

$$h \, d\sigma_x + \sigma_x \, dh + 2p_r \, dx \tan \alpha - 2\mu p_r \, dx = 0$$

It is convenient to combine these two equations:

$$h \, d\sigma_x + \sigma_x \, dh + 2p_r \, dx \tan \alpha \pm 2\mu p_r \, dx = 0 \qquad (4.2)$$

Here the upper sign refers to the exit side of the neutral point, and the lower sign to the entry side. Substituting $dh = 2dx \tan \alpha$,

$$h \, d\sigma_x + \sigma_x \, dh + p_r \, dh \pm \mu p_r \, dh \cot \alpha = 0$$

or $d(h\sigma_x) = -p_r(1 \pm \mu \cot \alpha) \, dh \qquad (4.3)$

This may be compared with equation 3.19, for strip-drawing. As for drawing it is possible to relate σ_x and p_r, using the yield criterion, because, to a close approximation,

$$\sigma_1 = \sigma_x, \text{ and } \sigma_3 = \sigma_y = -p$$

(The value of σ_y is found by resolution normal to the direction of rolling:

$$\sigma_y \, dx = -p_r \dfrac{dx}{\cos \alpha} \cos \alpha + \mu p_r \dfrac{dx}{\cos \alpha} \sin \alpha$$

$$\sigma_y = -p_r(1 - \mu \tan \alpha) \qquad (4.4)$$

Usually both μ and $\tan \alpha$ are small, e.g. $\mu = 0.07$, $\tan \alpha = 0.1$, and their product may be neglected in comparison with unity. Thus $\sigma_y \approx -p_r$; the radial pressure p_r is the same as the vertical pressure p, and the suffix may be omitted: $\sigma_y = -p$.) Substituting these values in the condition for yielding in plane-strain

$$\sigma_1 - \sigma_3 = 2k = S \qquad (2.18)$$

$$\sigma_x + p = S; \quad d(\sigma_x) = d(S - p) \qquad (4.5)$$

If the metal does not strain-harden, S is a constant; but usually it is necessary to allow for increase in S as the strip is thinned, from entry to exit. Thus, equation 4.3 becomes

$$d(h\sigma_x) = d(hS - hp) = -p(1 \pm \mu \cot \alpha) \, dh \qquad (4.6)$$

The radius of the rolls is assumed constant, and it is convenient to substitute for dh

in terms of the polar coordinates (R, α):

$$dh = 2(R \, d\alpha) \sin \alpha$$

Then $d(hS - hp) = -2Rp \sin \alpha (1 \pm \mu \cot \alpha) \, d\alpha$

In terms of the dimensionless ratio p/S,

$$\frac{d}{d\alpha}\left[hS\left(1 - \frac{p}{S}\right)\right] = -2Rp \sin \alpha (1 \pm \mu \cot \alpha)$$

$$hS \frac{d}{d\alpha}\left(1 - \frac{p}{S}\right) + \left(1 - \frac{p}{S}\right) \frac{d(hS)}{d\alpha} = -2Rp(\sin \alpha \pm \mu \cos \alpha) \tag{4.7}$$

A simplification, suggested by Bland and Ford in 1948, allows this equation to be integrated directly. Under most circumstances, the variation in roll pressure with angular position in the roll gap is much greater than the variation in yield stress. Moreover, the change in the product hS will be smaller still, since S increases as h decreases. Thus the term $\left(1 - \frac{p}{S}\right) \frac{d}{d\alpha} (hS)$ may usually be neglected in comparison with $hS \frac{d}{d\alpha} \left(1 - \frac{p}{S}\right)$. This approximation is not valid when the rate of strain-hardening is high, as it often is for annealed metal, nor when high back-tension is applied, which, as we shall see in equation 4.14, reduces the variation of p/S over the contact. For most practical rolling in second and subsequent passes, the error involved will be only a few per cent. Making this approximation, equation 4.7 becomes

$$hS \frac{d}{d\alpha}\left(\frac{p}{S}\right) = 2Rp(\sin \alpha \pm \mu \cos \alpha)$$

The angle of contact is also usually small, so further approximations may be made:

$$\sin \alpha \approx \alpha, \quad \cos \alpha \approx 1 - \frac{\alpha^2}{2} \approx 1$$

$$h = h_a + 2R(1 - \cos \alpha) \approx h_a + 2R \frac{\alpha^2}{2}$$

Then, $$\frac{d}{d\alpha}\left(\frac{p}{S}\right) = 2R \frac{p}{S} \frac{\alpha \pm \mu}{h_a + R\alpha^2} \tag{4.8}$$

$$\frac{d\left(\frac{p}{S}\right)}{\frac{p}{S}} = \frac{2\alpha \, d\alpha}{h_a/R + \alpha^2} \pm \frac{2\mu \, d\alpha}{h_a/R + \alpha^2}$$

Both sides of this equation may be integrated, to give a general solution:

$$\ln\left(\frac{p}{S}\right) = \ln(h_a/R + \alpha^2) \pm 2\mu \frac{1}{\sqrt{h_a/R}} \tan^{-1} \frac{\alpha}{\sqrt{h_a/R}} + \text{constant}$$

Introducing the symbol $$H = 2\sqrt{\frac{R}{h_a}} \tan^{-1}\left(\sqrt{\frac{R}{h_a}} \, \alpha\right) \tag{4.9}$$

$$\ln\left(\frac{p}{S}\right) = \ln\left(\frac{h}{R}\right) \pm \mu H + \text{constant}$$

Thus on the exit side of the neutral point,

$$\frac{p^{+}}{S} = c^{+}\frac{h}{R}e^{+\mu H} \tag{4.10a}$$

On the entry side,

$$\frac{p^{-}}{S} = c^{-}\frac{h}{R}e^{-\mu H} \tag{4.10b}$$

The values of the constants of integration may be found from the respective stress conditions at exit and entry.

4.1.2 *Rolling with no external tensions*
In the absence of front- or back-tensions, the longitudinal stresses at exit and entry must be zero; $\sigma_{xa} = \sigma_{xb} = 0$.

$$\frac{p_a}{S_a} = c^{+}\frac{h_a}{R}e^{\mu H_a}; \quad H_a = 2\sqrt{\frac{R}{h_a}}\tan^{-1}\sqrt{\frac{R}{h_a}}\,\alpha_a$$

but $\alpha_a = 0$, $\sigma_{xa} = 0$

Thus $H_a = 0$,   and, from equation 4.5, $p_a = S_a - \sigma_{xa} = S_a$,   so

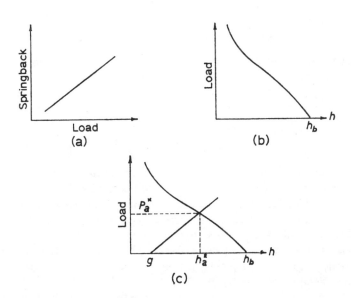

Figure 4.2 (*a*) Mill springback, which is the difference between the rolled strip thickness and the roll gap setting, plotted against load (*b*) The relationship between the final thickness h_a of strip rolled from a thickness h_b and the necessary roll load. This is often known as the plastic curve (*c*) Combination of mill modulus graph and plastic curve shows the intersection determining the actual gauge produced for a given initial roll gap, and strip thickness h_b

$$1 = c^+ \frac{h_a}{R}; \quad c^+ = \frac{R}{h_a}$$

At the entry:

$$\frac{p_b}{S_b} = c^- \frac{h_b}{R} e^{-\mu H_b}; \quad H_b = 2\sqrt{\frac{R}{h_a}} \tan^{-1} \sqrt{\frac{R}{h_a}} \alpha_b$$

Since $\sigma_{xb} = 0$, $p_b = S_b - \sigma_{xb} = S_b$, and

$$1 = c^- \frac{h_b}{R} e^{-\mu H_b}; \quad c^- = \frac{R}{h_b} e^{+\mu H_b}$$

Equations 4.10 may thus be written:

On the exit side $\quad \dfrac{p^+}{S} = \dfrac{h}{h_a} e^{\mu H}$ $\qquad\qquad\qquad\qquad$ (4.11a)

On the entry side $\quad \dfrac{p^-}{S} = \dfrac{h}{h_b} e^{\mu H_b} e^{-\mu H} = \dfrac{h}{h_b} e^{\mu(H_b - H)}$ $\qquad$ (4.11b)

The variation of roll pressure may be plotted as a function of angular position in the roll gap, from these equations.

The roll load is found by integrating the vertical pressure component over the contact area, using the flattened radius R' (equation 4.17)

$$\frac{P}{w} = \int p \, dx = \int pR' d\alpha = R' \int_0^{\alpha_N} p^+ d\alpha + R' \int_{\alpha_N}^{\alpha_b} p^- d\alpha \qquad (4.12)$$

$$= R'x \text{ (area of curves plotted from equations 4.11)}$$

The position of the neutral plane, α_N, is found from the intersection of the curves, or if a computer is used, from the condition that at α_N, $p^+ = p^-$.

The longitudinal stress at any position may readily be found from these equations, since

$$\sigma_x = S - p \; ; \quad \frac{\sigma_x}{S} = \left(1 - \frac{p}{S}\right) \qquad\qquad\qquad (4.13)$$

These graphs are often referred to in rolling as the *friction-hill*, because of their shape (as in Figure 3.3). Either can be so described, but the roll pressure is usually implied, since roll load is the more important feature. This relationship between friction and roll load arises because the frictional contribution to the longitudinal stress increases with distance inwards from entry and exit, and this provides increasing resistance to the expansion of vertical sections under the vertical load. The roll load required to produce a given deformation is thus increased by the presence of a longitudinal friction-hill.

4.1.3 Rolling with front- and back-tension
In most production mills, the strip is fed through several rolling stands in tandem. To keep the strip flat, and also to control gauge, it is usual to maintain a tension in

the strip between stands. Even single-stand mills usually employ power-driven coilers. Such tension has the further advantage of reducing the rolling loads, as may be seen by inserting the appropriate boundary conditions for front- and back-tensions, t_a and t_b, in equations 4.10.

At the exit: $\sigma_{xa} = t_a,$ $\alpha_a = 0,$ $H_a = 0$

The yield condition (equation 4.5) thus becomes

$$p_a = S_a - t_a$$

and the constant of integration in equation 4.10a is given by

$$\frac{p_a}{S_a} = 1 - \frac{t_a}{S_a} = c^+ \frac{h_a}{R} e^{\mu H_a} = c^+ \frac{h_a}{R}$$

$$c^+ = \left(1 - \frac{t_a}{S_a}\right) \frac{R}{h_a}$$

Similarly, at the entry,

$$c^- = \left(1 - \frac{t_b}{S_b}\right) \frac{R}{h_b} e^{+\mu H_b}$$

These constants correspond to those derived in the absence of tension, but are

multiplied by a factor $\left(1 - \frac{t}{S}\right)$. The two expressions giving the roll pressure are consequently reduced by the applied tensions:

$$\left. \begin{array}{ll} \dfrac{p^+}{S} = \left(1 - \dfrac{t_a}{S_a}\right) \dfrac{h}{h_a} e^{\mu H} & \text{(exit)} \\[3mm] \dfrac{p^-}{S} = \left(1 - \dfrac{t_b}{S_b}\right) \dfrac{h}{h_b} e^{\mu(H_b - H)} & \text{(entry)} \end{array} \right\} \tag{4.14}$$

These formulae may be expected to give reasonable accuracy for a large proportion of practical cold-rolling operations, but allowance should be made for roll flattening.

4.1.4 *Maximum reduction per pass*
The reduction per pass is limited by the condition that if the strip is to enter the roll gap unaided, the longitudinal component of the roll-surface friction must exceed that of the radial pressure, at the entry.

Referring to Figure 4.1, this can be written

$$\mu(p_r \, dA) \cos \alpha_b > (p_r \, dA) \sin \alpha_b \tag{4.15}$$

The maximum value, $\alpha_b{}^* = \tan^{-1} \mu$ is known as the *angle of bite*, or *gripping angle*. From Figure 4.1,

$$\tan \alpha_b = \frac{L}{R - \Delta h/2} = \sqrt{\left[\frac{R^2 - (R - \Delta h/2)^2}{R - \Delta h/2}\right]} \approx \sqrt{(\Delta h/R)}$$

since $\Delta h \ll R$.

The maximum reduction per pass is thus approximately

$$(\Delta h)_{max} = \mu^2 R \tag{4.16}$$

4.2 Allowance for roll flattening; limiting thickness

It was assumed above that the radius R of the rolls remains unchanged, and there is no complete theory that takes into account the elastic deformation of the rolls. As a useful approximation it has been suggested that the rolls remain circular in profile, but flatten to a larger radius.

4.2.1 *The Hitchcock equation*

Hitchcock has given an equation for the changed radius under load, making this assumption

$$R' = R \left(1 + \frac{c}{\Delta h} \frac{P}{w}\right) \tag{4.17}$$

where c is a constant depending on the elastic constants of the rolls. This arises from Hertz' theory of elastic deformation of two cylinders in contact: $\frac{1}{R} - \frac{1}{R'} = \frac{16(1 - \nu^2)P}{\pi E x_b^2}$. It has the value 0·022 mm²/kN ($3\cdot34 \times 10^{-4}$ in²/ton) for steel rolls. Thus for example, if $\frac{P}{w} = 4$ kN/mm (10 ton/in) and $\Delta h = 0\cdot88$ mm (0.033 in)

$$\frac{R'}{R} = 1 + \frac{0\cdot022}{0\cdot88} \times 4 = 1\cdot1$$

For harder strip, which would take a lower reduction in area under the same roll load, the roll flattening would be greater.

The deformed roll radius R' should be used in all accurate calculations of roll load. However, it is necessary first to find an approximate value of the load P to estimate R' from equation 4.17.

The simplest way to do this is to utilise the analogy between the compression in rolling and that in forging. The roll can be imagined as a forging platen of length L and width w, referring to Figure 4.1. Geometrically

$$R^2 = L^2 + (R - \Delta h/2)^2 \approx L^2 + R^2 - R\Delta h$$

$$L \approx \sqrt{(R\Delta h)} \tag{4.18}$$

If the mean yield stress is $\bar{S}$, the equivalent forging load can be written thus

$$P = \chi w L \bar{S} = \chi w \bar{S} \sqrt{R\Delta h} \tag{4.19}$$

where χ is a factor allowing for friction, often taken to be 1·2 for cold rolling.

4.2.2 *The limiting thickness for rolling thin strip*

With reference again to the analogy with forging, it can be seen that the forging or rolling load will increase as the ratio of width to thickness increases, as in equation 3.34. This will in turn increase the roll flattening and further increase the load.

Plate I A modern six-stand cold-rolling tandem mill, seen from the control pulpit.

Plate IIa A cluster mill rolling aluminium alloy sheet 1250 mm wide to a thickness tolerance of ±0.012 mm across the width and ±0.025 mm throughout the coil.

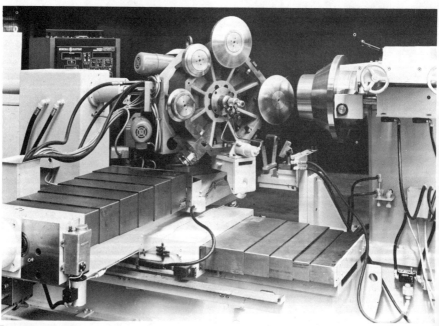

Plate IIb The roller and the forming-tool holder on a Leicomat computer-numerically-controlled flow-forming machine.

Eventually the whole of the expected reduction in thickness will be taken up by the elastic deformation of the rolls, especially with very hard strip.

This is observed in practice and the limiting thickness is found to be proportional to the coefficient of friction, the roll radius, and the hardness of the strip, and inversely proportional to the Young's modulus of the rolls. A useful formula for steel rolls is

$$h_{\lim} = 0.035\mu\,R\bar{S}\ \text{mm} \tag{4.20}$$

4.3 Roll bending and mill springback

The rolls will also deflect by bending and shear due to the centrally-applied load between the end supports. An extension of simple bending-beam theory provides an equation for finding the central deflection:

$$d = k_b\,\frac{Wl^3}{EI} + k_s\,\frac{Wl}{AG} \tag{4.21}$$

The values of the constants k_b and k_s depend on the relative dimensions of roll and strip, l is the effective length of the beam, W the roll load, E and G the elastic and shear moduli of the rolls and A the cross-sectional area of the barrel. For full-width strip, $k_b \sim 1.0$, $k_s \sim 0.2$, and for strip only half as wide as the rolls, $k_b \sim 0.5$, $k_s \sim 0.1$.

This bending will tend to produce strip that is thicker in the middle than at the edges, so the rolls themselves are cambered to ensure that the interface is approximately flat under the maximum load.

In addition to the elastic distortion of the rolls, the main framework of the mill will stretch under load. If the roll gap is g before the strip enters, the outgoing thickness h_a will be greater than this by an amount equal to the springback s

$$h_a = g + s \tag{4.22}$$

Since the mill frame is very long in comparison with the strip thickness, this must be calibrated and allowed for. An evaluation can be made graphically as in Figure 4.2, or s can be measured after each pass in the setting-up operation.

4.4 Mill power

4.4.1 *Roll torque*
It is possible to calculate the net circumferential force from the knowledge of the local pressures, given by equations 4.11, and the coefficient of friction. This is however inaccurate because the two frictional forces are in opposition (producing the friction-hill) so the net torque is the small difference between two numbers.

An alternative method is to consider the moment of the resultant vertical force about the axis. If the perpendicular distance from the line of action of the resultant to the axis is some fraction, λ', of the length L' of the chord of contact with the elastically-deformed rolls,

$$\text{torque} = \lambda'L' \times P \tag{4.23}$$

This neglects the contribution of horizontal forces, which deflect the resultant force slightly from the vertical. The fraction λ' is known as the *lever arm*.

$$\frac{T}{w} = \lambda' L' \frac{P}{w} = \lambda' L' R' \int_0^{\alpha_b} p \, d\alpha \tag{4.24}$$

$$(L' = R' \sin \alpha_b \approx \sqrt{R' \Delta h})$$

The lever arm has a value of about 0·5 in hot rolling, and about 0·45 for most cold rolling. The value of P can be found from the roll pressures (equations 4.11), or more simply using the semi-empirical equation 4.19.

4.4.2 *Mill power*

The power W_R supplied to each roll at an angular speed $\dot{\theta}$ is $T\dot{\theta}$ kN m/sec (kW) and in addition there will be friction at each of the roll-neck bearings. The load carried by each bearing is $\frac{1}{2}P$, giving a frictional drag $\frac{1}{2}\mu_n P$ and requiring a torque $\frac{1}{4}\mu_n Pd$, where μ_n is the coefficient of friction at the bearing, and d is the bearing diameter. Thus for two rolls, with four bearings, the total power will be

$$2W_R + 4W_N = 2T\dot{\theta} + \mu_n Pd\dot{\theta} \tag{4.25}$$

There will be losses in the motor and transmission, which may be allowed for by factors representing their efficiencies, η_m and η_t respectively.

The overall power requirement for the mill will thus be

$$W_M = \frac{1}{\eta_m \eta_t} (2T + \mu_n Pd) \dot{\theta} \text{ kW} \tag{4.26a}$$

In Imperial units, the speed is measured in revolutions per minute, N, and the torque is usually given in tons-inches, so the power is first converted to foot-pounds per second and then to horsepower, thus:

Horsepower for two rolls, with four neck bearings,

$$W_M = \frac{1}{\eta_m \eta_t} (2W_R + 4W_N) = \frac{1}{\eta_m \eta_t} (2T + \mu_n Pd) \frac{2\pi N}{60} \cdot \frac{2240}{12} \cdot \frac{1}{550} \tag{4.26b}$$

5

Basic Slip-line Field Theory

5.1 Introduction

The analysis of surface stresses allows for the contribution of friction, which may easily amount to 20% or 30% of the total working load. The results are in quite good agreement with the loads measured in practical metalworking, provided that the coefficient of friction is known and that the internal distortion of the workpiece involves the least possible shearing, compatible with the change of external shape. The problem of determining appropriate coefficients of friction will be considered in Chapter 8. The practical loads may however be much greater than those predicted, due to constraint imposed by the necessity for the metal to flow in a particular way. In general, the more curved the shear lines, the higher the pressure required to make the metal flow. The work done in overcoming this excess constraint cannot be found from the overall change in shape, and is known as redundant work. We shall see (§5.6.6) that it increases the load in hardness testing, for example, by a factor of nearly three, above that required for simple compression of a small cylinder. Factors of two or more are often encountered in extrusion.

Surface-stress analysis takes no account of redundant work, and there is in fact no general analytical theory. For the special condition where flow occurs entirely in one plane, with no deformation in the direction perpendicular to that plane (e.g. flow in the xy plane, with $\epsilon_z = 0$), a graphical type of solution can be obtained. This plane-strain condition is thus of considerable importance, though it does not often arise in practice. Where the practical geometry does produce approximately plane-strain deformation, as in small-tool forging of thin, wide strip (Figures 5.5 and 5.6), there is very close agreement with predicted results. The results of plane-strain theory can however prove very helpful in understanding practical processes involving axial symmetry (wire-drawing, bar extrusion etc), and more complex conditions. The graphical theory, known as slip-line field analysis, depends upon determination of the plastic flow pattern in the deforming workpiece.

Plastic flow in metals occurs predominantly by slip, on an atomic scale, along crystallographic planes. The details of the process of dislocation movement, which is the basic phenomenon of slip, have been extensively studied in recent years. Several comprehensive books are available for the reader interested in obtaining a deeper insight into the fundamental behaviour of deforming metals. For our present purpose, it is important to recognise only that plastic flow is essentially a shear process. In a real metal, slip occurs most easily on planes of close-packed atoms, and in the direction of the line of atoms which lies closest to the line of maximum shear stress. Metalworking, however, is concerned with metals containing very large numbers of crystals. It is thus, nearly always, reasonable to assume that a sufficient number will be favourably oriented for the general slip-direction to coincide with the direction of maximum shear stress.

For simplicity, it is usual to postulate a structureless, homogeneous, and isotropic material, in which slip always occurs precisely in the maximum shear-stress direction. This direction is consequently of importance in any consideration of metal flow. Once it is determined, the direction of plastic flow of the idealised material is known, and this gives a first approximation to the flow of a real metal. Allowance for anisotropy in real metals is very complex; this is unfortunate because all metals, though highly polycrystalline, tend to become anisotropic during deformation. The assumption of homogeneity is reasonably good, for most industrial metals; and the effects of structure are not usually important, except in metals with hexagonal crystal lattices (such as zinc, cadmium, magnesium and beryllium), which have only one active slip-plane in the crystal.

We shall confine our attention to the simple, idealised material. It is also convenient to consider first a material which does not work-harden, so that the value of the yield stress remains constant throughout the deformation. This is a poor approximation for annealed metal, but the slope of the stress—strain curve is quite small for most metals after a moderate deformation. Making these assumptions, we can evaluate plane-strain working loads, including the redundant work factor, by the use of slip-line fields.

5.2 Deformation in simple compression

It has been shown in Chapter 2 that the directions of maximum shear are inclined at 45° to the directions of the principal stresses (Figure 2.2). If a cube is compressed across two opposite faces, it can easily be shown experimentally that it will fail by shear on diagonal planes. Figure 5.1 shows a cylinder of 10% aluminium bronze

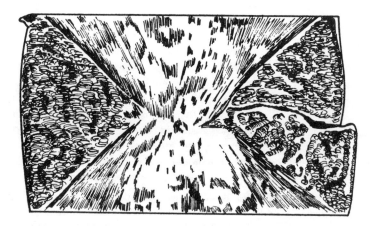

Figure 5.1 A tracing from a photograph of a 10% aluminium bronze cylinder which has been compressed to fracture. (*By courtesy of Dr. A. T. Male.*)

which has sheared along 45° cones, leaving a solid core in the form of a double cone, with smooth, bright sides. The same pattern is found in the standard compression test for concrete.

Metals which are more ductile start to deform in the same way, but the parts do not separate until the secondary tensile stresses have become much larger, after heavy deformation, which often obscures the pattern.

The general problem of three-dimensional deformation is still intractable, but for two-dimensional strain it is possible to predict working loads from consideration of slip-lines, which are lines showing the directions of maximum shear everywhere in the plastically-deforming body. We shall assume throughout this chapter that plane-strain conditions apply; namely that there is no strain in one principal direction so that $\epsilon_2 = 0$, and that the pattern of deformation is the same for all planes perpendicular to this direction.

If a wide strip is compressed between parallel flat-faced anvils of breadth b equal to the strip thickness h, the undeformed strip on each side of the anvils restricts the spread of the original width w. If w is greater than about $10b$, the lateral strain and the end effects may be ignored, so that plane-strain conditions apply. Figure 5.5 shows such a compression. Deformation starts by shearing along the diagonals, and the four blocks of metal I, II, III, IV start to move by sliding over one another as solid, undeformed bodies. This sliding coincides with the directions of maximum shearing stress, and it will be seen in §5.3 that deformation in plane-strain is a pure shear process, in which yield occurs when $\tau_{max} = k$.

The direct stress necessary to produce a shear stress k in this example is easily found. The two principal stresses will act at $45°$ to the direction of maximum shear stress, and so will be horizontal and vertical in Figure 5.5. The horizontal stress acting at any point on the line AC must be zero since there is no force acting on the rigid block II. The horizontal principal stress is thus $\sigma_3 = 0$. Since $k = \frac{1}{2}(\sigma_1 - \sigma_3)$, the vertical principal stress σ_1, acting on the surface AB of the anvil will be equal to $2k$. The indentation pressure is thus

$$q = \sigma_1 = 2k \tag{5.1}$$

This is the same as the yield stress $S = 2k$ which would be found if a tensile test could be conducted under conditions of plane-strain. It should be recognised, however, that the normal tensile test of round bar, or even of wide strip, does not involve the constraint of plane strain, and so gives the value Y. If the von Mises criterion is used, $Y = 2k/1.55$. The additional direct stress which is required to cause yielding in plane-strain, arises from the externally imposed necessity for the metal to flow in such a way that no lateral contraction occurs in tension, and no lateral spread in compression.

5.3 Stress evaluation using slip-lines

The elementary calculation given above shows the way in which a knowledge of the directions of maximum shear can be used, together with the magnitude of the shear yield stress, to determine a working load. This is the basis of slip-line field solutions. The slip-line field diagram can be considered as a map, showing the directions of maximum shear at every point in the deforming body. Figure 5.5 shows, therefore, a very simple slip-line field. Since shear must always be accompanied by complementary shear of equal magnitude and opposite sense, to preserve rotational equilibrium (§2.1), there will always be two mutually perpendicular directions of maximum shear at each point. A general map of these directions consequently consists of two sets of mutually orthogonal lines. In the simplest instance, these would all be straight and form a Cartesian network. They need not be straight however, and a network of straight radii and concentric circles, resembling a polar coordinate system, is frequently used. Both of these can be seen in Figure 5.7. Further developments utilise orthogonal networks in which the lines of both sets are curved (see Chapter 6, for example).

The spacing of the lines may be freely chosen. In straight regions it has no significance. Where the lines are curved, greater accuracy is obtained by drawing lines with small angular separation. Intervals of $5°$ usually give as high an accuracy as is useful, and $15°$ often suffices.

In the simple example of compression, given above, the stresses could be calculated directly in terms of the shear stress. In a more complex system, account must also be taken of a hydrostatic pressure which varies from point to point in the plastically deforming body. The significance of this can be appreciated by considering the Mohr circle, as follows.

Slip-line field solutions always refer to plane-strain, and for this condition, as was stated in Chapter 2, the principal stresses for an incompressible, ideally plastic material are related:

$$\sigma_2 = \tfrac{1}{2}(\sigma_1 + \sigma_3) \tag{2.17}$$

This has been shown, experimentally, to be very nearly true for a real metal. The Mohr stress circle for plane-strain conditions can thus be drawn with radius

$$\tau_{max} = \tfrac{1}{2}(\sigma_1 - \sigma_3) \tag{2.6b}$$

and centred on σ_2, in accordance with equation 2.17, as shown in Figure 5.2. Because the material is incompressible, plane-strain deformation with $d\epsilon_2 = 0$ implies that $d\epsilon_3 = -d\epsilon_1$ and the deformation must therefore be pure shear strain. It is assumed that this is produced by pure shear stress. Consequently yield will occur, as in any pure shear process, when the maximum shear stress reaches the value k. It is not necessary to use any yield criterion, because k is just the result of a pure shear test. Thus the radius τ_{max} of the Mohr stress circle for plane plastic strain is equal to k, and the principal stresses in Figure 5.2b are

$$\sigma_1 = \sigma_2 - k, \quad \sigma_3 = \sigma_2 + k.$$

These can be expressed in terms of a hydrostatic pressure $-p$, equal to σ_2:

$$\sigma_1 = -p - k, \quad \sigma_2 = -p, \quad \sigma_3 = -p + k \tag{5.2}$$

It is known (Chapter 2, §2.3) that a hydrostatic pressure does not affect yielding. The complete stress system in plane-strain is therefore pure shear with a superimposed hydrostatic pressure. (It is necessary to consider only the major stress circle, since we are interested only in the plane perpendicular to the direction of the intermediate principal stress σ_2.)

Thus in plane plastic strain, k is everywhere constant, for a non-hardening metal but p may vary. The stress system at any point can be completely determined if we can find the magnitude of p and the direction of k. The slip-lines show the direction

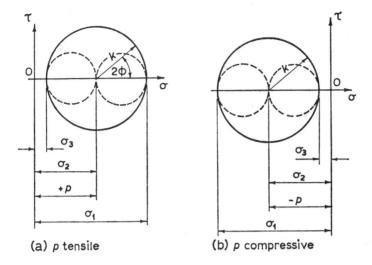

(a) p tensile   (b) p compressive

Figure 5.2 The Mohr stress circle for plane plastic strain, with maximum shear stress k. The superimposed hydrostatic pressure is given by $p = \frac{1}{2}(\sigma_1 + \sigma_3)$

of k at any point immediately. The changes in p can be deduced from the angular rotation of the slip-line between one point and another in the field, and the absolute magnitude of p is found by starting at some point on a boundary where p_0 is known from external conditions.

5.4 Determination of hydrostatic pressure from slip-line rotation. The Hencky equations

As we have seen (§5.3), at any point in the deforming body there will be two mutually-perpendicular directions of maximum shear stress, shown by the slip-lines. It is conventional to designate these lines α and β, such that, if they are regarded as a pair of right-handed axes of reference (like x and y), the line of action of the *algebraically greatest* principal stress lies in the first (and third) quadrant. It should be noted that the α- and β-lines may be curved, and that the stress of largest numerical value need not be greatest algebraically. It quite often happens that the stress of greatest magnitude is compressive and therefore negative, while the algebraically greatest stress is in fact zero. (See, for example, §5.6.5.) Let us suppose that the α-line, at some point P, is inclined at an angle ϕ, measured anticlockwise from the x-axis (Figure 5.3a).

The Mohr circle for the point P may be drawn (see Chapter 2, §2.2), assuming some value $-p$ for the hydrostatic compressive stress. If both principal stresses are compressive ($p > k$), σ_1 is given by the length OA. The stresses σ_x and σ_y may then be found from this circle. It must be remembered, as in Chapter 2, that the Mohr circle shows the planes on which stresses act. Direct stresses are perpendicular to their planes, while shear stresses are parallel. The plane $[Y]$, on which the stress σ_x acts, is thus at an angle $\left(\dfrac{\pi}{4} + \phi\right)$ measured clockwise from the plane $[1]$, on which σ_3 acts. Since angular rotation 2θ in the Mohr circle is double the rotation θ in the

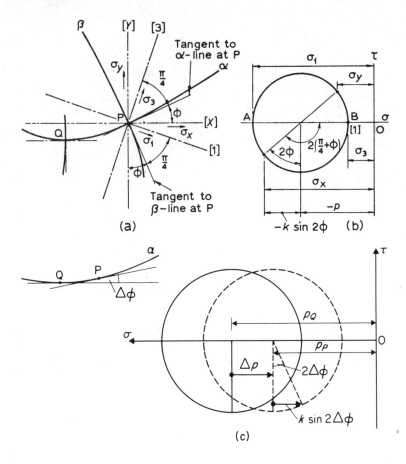

Figure 5.3 (*a*) The α and β slip-lines at points P and Q in the deforming body (*b*) The Mohr circle appropriate to the point P (*c*) The contributions to σ_α from displacement and rotation along the α-line

physical diagram, the circle shows σ_x at $\left(\dfrac{\pi}{2} + 2\phi\right)$ from the σ_3 direction, as in Figure 5.3*b*. The location of σ_y on the diagram can be found in the same way, and is on the opposite end of the diameter drawn from σ_x, since σ_x and σ_y are mutually perpendicular on the physical plane. The values of the stresses on the *x*- and *y*-planes can then be read directly from the coordinates of these points:

$$\sigma_x = -p - k \sin 2\phi$$

$$\sigma_y = -p + k \sin 2\phi \qquad\qquad (5.3$$

$$\tau_{xy} = k \cos 2\phi$$

It can be shown, by considering the equilibrium of a small element (Example 5.) that the gradients of the direct stresses along and perpendicular to a slip-line are zero, at any point on the slip-line. Thus

$$\frac{d\sigma_\alpha}{d\alpha} = \frac{d\sigma_\beta}{d\beta} = 0 \tag{5.4}$$

In Figure 5.3, the slip-lines were supposed to be at some angle ϕ to the x- and y-axes. These axes were not however specified in relation to any external system, and can be freely chosen. We may therefore suppose them to be such that at some other point Q the x- and y-axes coincide with the tangents to the α and β slip-lines, respectively, as in Figure 5.3a.

Then, at the point Q, equation 5.4 may be written

$$\left(\frac{d\sigma_x}{dx}\right)_Q = \left(\frac{d\sigma_y}{dy}\right)_Q = 0 \tag{5.4a}$$

Substitution from equations 5.3 shows that, at Q,

$$\frac{d}{dx}\,(p + k\,\sin 2\phi) = 0 = \frac{d}{dy}\,(p - k\,\sin 2\phi)$$

$$\tag{5.5}$$

$$\frac{dp}{dx} + (2k\,\cos 2\phi)\,\frac{d\phi}{dx} = 0 = \frac{dp}{dy} - (2k\,\cos 2\phi)\,\frac{d\phi}{dy}$$

But if the x- and y-axes are chosen to coincide with the tangents to the α- and β-lines at Q, then ϕ must be small in that region (at least for the distance involved in the differential). Thus, at or near Q, $\cos 2\phi \sim 1$. Making this approximation for the equation of the α-line, we see that the tangential derivative of $(p + 2k\phi)$ is zero at Q.

$$\frac{dp}{dx} + 2k\,\frac{d\phi}{dx} = 0 \quad \text{or} \quad \frac{d}{dx}(p + 2k\phi) = 0$$

Consequently $p + 2k\phi$ = constant along the α-line at Q. The point Q was chosen quite arbitrarily, and the x- and y-axes were then specified. Thus they could equally well have been specified for any other point, so that the relationship is valid at any point on the α-line:

$$p + 2k\phi = \text{constant}, C \tag{5.6}$$

This can readily be appreciated by reference to Figures 5.3a and 5.3c.

In passing from the point Q to the point P on the α slip-line the hydrostatic pressure changes by $+\Delta p$, so the circle changes to a new centre. Also the direction of maximum shear, tangential to the slip-line, rotates by an angle $\Delta\phi$ relative to the x-axis. This contributes a direct stress component $+ k\,\sin 2\Delta\phi$, so

$$\Delta\sigma_x = \Delta p + k\,\sin 2\Delta\phi \approx \Delta p + 2k\Delta\phi$$

This is, moreover, equally true if ϕ is measured from some other reference direction inclined at a constant angle ϕ' to the chosen axis Ox, since that would merely alter the value of the constant C.

The corresponding variation with y gives the relationship along a β-line. These two conditions,

$$p + 2k\phi = \text{constant, along an } \alpha\text{-line} \tag{5.7a}$$

$$p - 2k\phi = \text{constant, along a } \beta\text{-line} \tag{5.7b}$$

were first applied to metal deformation by Hencky in 1923, and are known as the Hencky slip-line equations. They had been formulated much earlier in the science of soil mechanics. (The reader may find it helpful to associate α and $+$ to remember these important equations correctly.)

The Hencky equations enable the hydrostatic pressure at any point in the deforming body to be determined from the curvature of the slip-lines, provided that the value of the constant is known. This is found from equilibrium conditions at one of the boundaries.

5.5 Stresses and slip-lines at boundaries of the plastic body

These conditions, as with all slip-line field theory, apply in plane-strain.

5.5.1 *Free surface*

The plastic zone sometimes extends to the free surface beyond the confines of the tool. We shall see that this occurs, for example, in the vicinity of a punch indenting a large block. (Figure 5.7.)

At a free surface, there can be no normal stress, so $\sigma_3 = 0$, assuming σ_1 compressive. Since $\sigma_3 = -p + k$ (equation 5.2), the hydrostatic pressure must then be equal in magnitude to the shear stress. This determines the major principal stress:

$$p = k; \quad \sigma_1 = -p - k = -2k \tag{5.8}$$

The directions of the slip-lines can also be found, from the condition that there can be no tangential stress at a free surface. The components of the shear stresses along the slip-lines, resolved parallel to the surface, must thus be equal, and consequently the slip-lines must meet a free surface at 45°. This follows also from the directions of maximum shear being at 45° to the principal stress directions.

It should be noted that there are two possible configurations, as shown in Figure 5.4a.

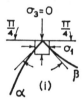

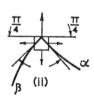

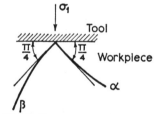

(a) Slip-lines at a free surface.
   (i) major principal stress compressive
      $p = k,\ \sigma_1 = -2k$
   (ii) major principal stress tensile

      $p = -k,\ \sigma_1 = +2k$

(b) Slip-lines at a frictionless interface.
      $\sigma_3 \neq 0,\ p \neq k$

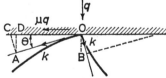

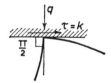

(c) Interface with Coulomb friction.

$$\theta = \tfrac{1}{2}\cos^{-1}\frac{\mu q}{k}$$

(d) Interface with sticking friction.

$$\theta = 0 \text{ or} \frac{\pi}{2}$$

Figure 5.4

The choice of α- and β-lines depends, as stated in §5.4, upon the convention that the direction of the algebraically greatest principal stress lies in the first quadrant between α and β.

5.5.2 *Frictionless interface*

Again, by definition, there can be no resultant shear parallel to the interface, so the slip-lines must meet the boundary at $45°$ (Figure 5.4b). There may be, and usually will be, a normal stress across the interface, so $\sigma_3 \neq 0$. The value of p is thus not usually equal to k.

5.5.3 *Interface with Coulomb friction (μ = constant)*

The resultant shear stress in an interface with Coulomb friction is equal to the product of normal stress q' and coefficient of friction μ. This is balanced by the resolved components of the forces on the slip-lines, which are inclined at some angle θ, respectively to the tangential and normal directions at the surface (Figure 5.4c). The value of θ may be found by resolution (Figure 5.4c), or from the Mohr circle.

The shear stress τ_{xy} on a plane inclined at $-\theta$ to the plane of maximum shear (the slip-line) can be read directly from the Mohr circle, at -2θ to the vertical vector giving τ_{max}.

$$\tau_{xy} = \tau_{max} \cos 2\theta = k \cos 2\theta \tag{5.9}$$

Equating this to $\mu q'$:

$$\cos 2\theta = \mu q'/k \tag{5.10}$$

This implies a knowledge of q' before the field can be drawn. In fact q' cannot be found until the field has been completed, so an iterative procedure is required. The first approach is made by determining q from a field drawn for a frictionless interface, and assuming $q' \approx q$. This is sufficiently accurate for the final solution in some instances, for example in strip-drawing.

5.5.4 *Perfectly-rough interface*

If the friction is so high that there is no interfacial movement, the metal will yield beneath the interface, when the tangential stress reaches the value k, its yield stress in pure shear. The applied frictional stress cannot therefore be greater than k. So when the friction is very high a special condition arises, with

$$\tau_{xy} = k \tag{5.11}$$

independent of the normal stress. This is known as 'sticking friction', and the coefficient of friction is then meaningless. Equation 5.9 shows that, for any condition,

$$\tau_{xy} = k \cos 2\theta$$

Thus, for sticking friction,

$$\cos 2\theta = 1; \quad \theta = 0 \tag{5.12}$$

Consequently, one slip-line meets the interface tangentially, the other normally, as in Figure 5.4d.

5.6 Application of the slip-line field to a static system. Plane-strain indentation with flat, frictionless platens

We shall consider first the application of slip-line fields to a simple example of forging. A load is applied to the platen or punch; when it reaches a particular value, the metal will yield slightly, leaving a permanent indentation. The problem is to determine this load, ignoring any changes which would occur if the punch sank further in. In the subsequent section we shall consider the significance of velocity, when the system is not statically in equilibrium.

This example is of importance in two common test procedures; the Ford plane-strain compression test and, by analogy, the Brinell hardness test.

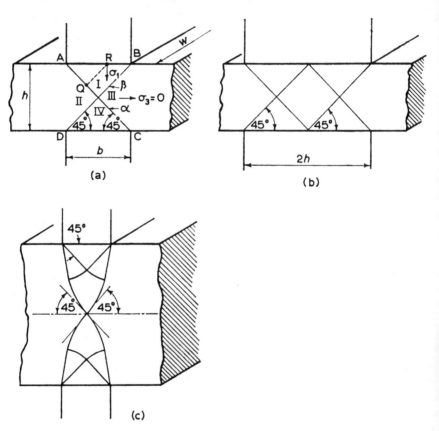

Figure 5.5 Plane-strain indentation. Simple slip-line fields for (*a*) $b = h$, (*b*) $b = 2h$, (*c*) $b < h$

Figure 5.5 shows a thin, wide strip, indented between two flat, rectangular platens, with as little friction as possible. If the strip is wide enough, say 10 times *b* or *h*, whichever is the larger, the lateral spread may be neglected. The conditions then approach plane-strain, and slip-line field theory can be applied.

The pressure σ_1 to produce yielding depends on the ratio of strip thickness to platen breadth.

5.6.1 *Strip thickness equal to platen breadth (h = b)*

Because the interface is assumed to be frictionless, the slip-lines meet it at 45°. We have already seen that the diagonals are slip-lines (§5.3), so the simple network shown in Figure 5.5a fulfils the boundary conditions. At a point Q on the slip-line AC, the horizontal principal-stress σ_3 must be zero, so that $p = k$. The vertical stress σ_1 will then be $-2k$. Between Q and R, the β slip-line is straight, so $\phi = 0$ and, as we have seen, the Hencky equation ($p - 2k\phi$ = constant along a β-line) shows that the hydrostatic pressure remains constant along a straight slip-line. The hydrostatic pressure p at R is thus also equal to k, and $\sigma_1 = -2k$ at the platen surface.

For this simple example it is not, of course, necessary to use the slip-line field equations, and we have already derived the result from first principles (§5.2). The same approach can be used for platen breadths which are integral multiples of the strip thickness.

5.6.2 *Platen breadth an integral multiple of strip thickness (b/h = 2, 3, 4 etc.)*

The field can be constructed from an integral number of units corresponding to Figure 5.5b, and the lines are all straight, giving the same result: $\sigma_1 = -2k$.

5.6.3 *Platen breadth greater than strip thickness, but b/h not integral*

The boundary conditions still demand that the lines meet the interface at 45°. Slip-lines must always intersect orthogonally, and the field must be symmetrical about the centre-line.

To fulfil these conditions, and to ensure that the field transforms steadily as the ratio h/b changes from 1 to $\frac{1}{2}$, the slip-lines must be curved. This means that the overall indentation pressure will be greater than when the simple shear pattern is possible. Green has provided a solution, which shows that the pressure distribution is then not uniform across the platen face, even though the friction is zero. The average pressure passes through maximum values between integral b/h ratios, but the greatest increase for $b/h > 1$ ($h/b < 1$) is only 4% (Figure 5.6).

5.6.4 *Strip thickness greater than platen breadth (h/b between 1 and 10)*

The field again involves curved slip-lines, and the pressure rises rapidly with decreasing relative platen breadth.

5.6.5 *Single-punch indentation of a semi-infinite block (h/b ~ ∞)*

a) Construction of the slip-line field. When the block is very thick, the zones of plastic deformation do not extend completely across the block, and the problem becomes essentially that of single-sided indentation by one punch. Beyond a value $b \sim 10$, changes in geometry by alteration of die breadth have no further influence.

This may be considered in detail with reference to Figure 5.7.

The conditions immediately below the die are the same as in Figure 5.5a. Because the die is assumed frictionless, the slip-lines must meet it at 45°. A triangular region ABF can thus be drawn, as before. However, it would not be possible for the metal to move physically, if this were the full extent of the plastic zone. It is fully constrained laterally and beneath by the rigid metal, and can only flow upwards at

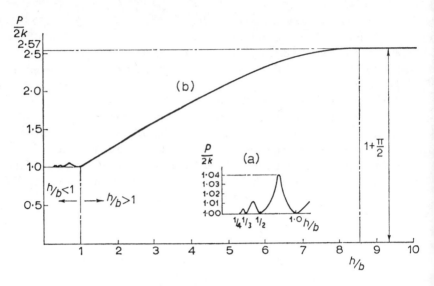

Figure 5.6 (a) Variation of p with h/b for values b/h > 1 (b) Variation of p with h/b for values h/b > 1

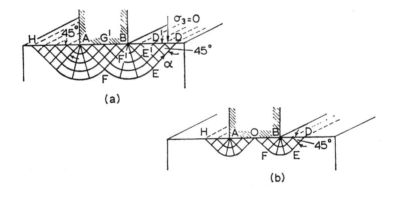

Figure 5.7 Indentation of a very thick block by a single flat punch (a) Slip-line field suggested by Prandtl (b) Slip-line field suggested by Hill

the sides of the punch. This suggests that the plastic zone must be extended to the free surface along AH and BD.

The slip-lines must meet this surface also at 45°, and they must always be straight since the pressure cannot build up beneath a free surface, so another triangular network can be drawn, in the vicinity of B. The simplest way of connecting these two zones is to use a fan centred on B. It is useful to remember that fans can always be drawn round singularities, that is around points where there is no specified normal to the surface. The field so constructed at B defines the position of D, and the full solution is obtained by completing the left-hand side symmetrically.

Hill has pointed out that this solution, due to Prandtl, would involve a considerable amount of distortion of the metal before the plastic region had spread sufficiently to fill the postulated zone. Moreover, the velocity distribution in the triangle ABF is indeterminate. Prandtl assumed that the triangle formed a rigid nose or dead-zone, which moved downwards with the punch. This is found to occur when the friction is high, for example in hot piercing, and also represents fairly well the physical behaviour of annealed metal which strain-hardens rapidly. For the assumed conditions of low friction and constant yield stress, Hill proposed a solution in which the region beneath the indenter is divided into two parts (Figure 5.7b). Metal from the zone OBF flows along the slip-lines within OFED to the free surface at the right. Metal from OA flows to the left. The flow of metal is therefore everywhere determinate. Both solutions lead to the same value for the indentation pressure, which is calculated using the Hencky equations, starting at a suitable point of known known stress.

(b) *Stress determination from the slip-line field.* The presure on the punch may easily be found by following the slip-lines in Figure 5.7a, starting at the free surface BD. There can be no stress normal to the surface in this region, so σ_3 is equal to zero and $p = k$, (equation 5.2). The slip-line ED is an α-line, because the algebraically greatest principal stress is $\sigma_3 = 0$, the other principal stress being compressive and therefore negative according to the usual convention. The appropriate Hencky equation for DE is thus, taking DE as the reference direction from which ϕ is measured,

$$p + 2k\phi = \text{constant} = k \tag{5.13}$$

Because the line DE is straight, $\phi = 0$, and p is constant from D to E. The pressure p_E at E is thus also equal to k. Between E and F, however, the slip-line is curved, and the tangent rotates clockwise, until at F it makes an angle $\frac{\pi}{2}$ with DE. The angle ϕ, measured anticlockwise according to convention, therefore changes by $-\frac{\pi}{2}$ between E and F. Substituting this in equation 5.13 gives the pressure at F:

$$p_F + 2k\phi = p_F + 2k\left(-\frac{\pi}{2}\right) = \text{constant} = p_E = k.$$

or $p_F = k(1 + \pi)$

It will be seen that *as an α-line curves clockwise, the stress magnitude increases.* This is a convenient way of selecting an α-line rapidly in any field. The converse is true of β-lines. The pressure remains unchanged along the straight lines FA and FB, so the pressure p_G at any point G' on the punch face is also equal to $k(1 + \pi)$. The major principal stress at G', acting in the vertical direction, is consequently given, according to equation 5.2, by

$$\sigma_1 = p_G + k = k(2 + \pi) = 2k\left(1 + \frac{\pi}{2}\right) \tag{5.14}$$

It is convenient to express the stress in terms of the dimensionless ratio $\sigma_1/2k$, where $2k$ is, as we have seen (equation 2.18), the yield stress in simple plane-strain compression, whether the maximum shear-stress or maximum shear-strain energy criterion is used.

Slip-lines drawn anywhere in the plastic zone will be parallel to these lines and give the same result, so the indentation pressure P is uniform across AB, and is given by:

$$\frac{P}{2k} = 1 + \frac{\pi}{2} = 2 \cdot 57 \qquad (5.15)$$

Thus the geometrical constraint on the flow increases the load required to cause yielding by a factor 2·57.

This can be verified experimentally. The whole variation of yield pressure with width/thickness ratio (Figure 5.6) has been shown to follow closely the predictions of slip-line field theory. This provides, in fact, the most detailed correlation currently available. The striking cyclic variation of the pressure required to initiate incremental yielding was in fact observed independently, and was at first attributed to experimental errors. The theory deals only with small changes in deformation at any particular stage because the overall geometry alters if large deformation is imposed. It is possible, by using a digital computer, to predict the effects of sequential increments of strain and thus to apply slip-line fields to progressive forging in large passes, but this will not be discussed here.

These results, like all slip-line field solutions, apply strictly to plane-strain conditions only. It should however be emphasised that the slip-line field solutions can also be used to suggest the type of deformation and stress variation to be expected, even when there is considerable departure from plane-strain. Cylindrical strain, where there is axial symmetry, is an important example, which occurs in extrusion of round bars, wire-drawing and elsewhere. We shall see in §6.5.3 how the slip-line field solution has been used to suggest a formula into which two empirical constants can be inserted for estimation of rod-extrusion pressure. The Brinell hardness test is an axially-symmetrical process resembling the indentation just considered. The true analogue would be a flat-ended cylindrical punch, but the results are only slightly modified when a ball is used, provided that the radius of the ball is large in comparison with that of the indentation.

5.6.6 *The Brinell Hardness Test*

In the Brinell test, a hard steel sphere is pressed into a softer metal under a given load. The diameter of the plastic indentation left, after removal of the sphere, is a measure of the hardness of the deformed metal. The Meyer hardness of the indented metal is found by dividing the load by the projected area of the indentation, and is expressed in kilograms per square millimetre. The Brinell hardness is similarly obtained, but relates to the curved surface area, which for most practical conditions is only very slightly different. Tabor has shown that the hardness H is closely related to the yield stress Y in homogeneous deformation, and for many metals

$$\frac{H}{Y} \approx 2 \cdot 8 - 2 \cdot 9 \qquad (5.16)$$

This is a somewhat greater ratio than that due to the constraint in a comparable plane-strain indentation (equation 5.15), confirming the occurrence of such large factors in a common operation. The relationship (5.16) is very useful for rapid estimation of yield stress or degree of work-hardening of stock material, without destroying any of the metal. It can be used, for example, in approximate prediction of working loads. Conversions to other units are given in equation 1.21.

5.7 Velocity of metal-flow. Hodographs

The configuration of the slip-line field implies certain related velocities of metal flow at all points in the deforming region. These must be compatible with the incompressibility of the metal and also with any imposed velocity-boundary conditions.

The field can be checked algebraically, using Geiringer's equations, or more conveniently by constructing a hodograph. This is a diagram in which the velocity of any element in the deforming metal is represented by a vector from the pole or origin to a specific point. Every zone bounded by slip-lines has its corresponding point in the hodograph.

5.7.1 *Construction of a hodograph*

To construct a hodograph from a given slip-line field, it is convenient to divide the field into discrete zones and to assume that the velocity remains constant throughout any one such zone, labelled 1, 2, 3, etc. as in Figure 5.8. The hodograph is

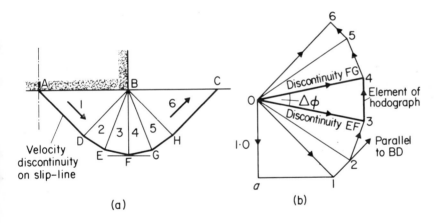

Figure 5.8 (*a*) Slip-line field (*b*) Hodograph

started by drawing a velocity vector 0*a* from the pole 0 to represent the velocity of descent of the punch, usually taken as 1·0. Because the metal is incompressible and all metal in the first zone ABD has the same velocity, there must be continuity of velocity across AB, though the metal can slide outwards along AB. The vertical component of the velocity in zone 1 is therefore 1·0.

A further necessary condition is that there can be no discontinuity in the velocity component normal to the slip-line AD. If such a discontinuity did exist, the metal would pile up against AD or leave a void, neither of which is permitted.

As there is no velocity at all in the rigid metal below AD, the absolute velocity in zone 1 must be parallel to the line AD. This, like all absolute velocities, is represented by a vector from the pole 0.

The velocity in zone 1 is thus given by the vector 01 in the hodograph, whose length is determined by its vertical component 1·0. The triangle of velocities 0a1 then shows that the velocity tangential to AB is given by the vector a1.

The concept of tangential velocity discontinuities is basic to this construction. There can never be a normal velocity discontinuity across a slip-line. Tangential velocity discontinuities are assumed to occur on all slip-lines for construction purposes, though they may degenerate to infinitesimally small magnitude on some lines, such as BE, BF, etc. if very small angular displacements are considered.

To continue the construction, the point 2 in the hodograph is found by drawing a vector from 1 parallel to BD, to represent the assumed tangential velocity discontinuity along BD. The absolute velocity in zone 2 must be parallel to the boundary with the rigid metal made by the slip-line DE, represented by the chord DE or the mean tangent, and therefore given by the vector in the direction 02. This intersects the vector 12 to locate the point 2.

Similarly the velocity in zone 3 is parallel to EF and is reached by a tangential discontinuity along the line BE, and so on for zones 4 and 5.

The final velocity in zone 6 must be parallel to the boundary HC against the rigid metal. The whole block BCH therefore moves in this direction with the velocity given by 06. Such a deformation pattern can actually be observed in some alloys of low ductility but usually the discontinuity is spread out by strain-hardening effects. It is associated with the piling-up of metal around a hardness indentation.

As stated above, if the angles B̂ED, etc. are chosen to be very small the peripheral line 16 in the hodograph becomes a smooth arc with no finite tangential discontinuities on BE, BF, etc. However, the large velocity discontinuity all along AD–HC remains, with magnitude 01.

It is a general property that if there is a velocity discontinuity along a slip-line, its magnitude must remain constant over the whole line. Otherwise the condition of volume constancy would be violated.

5.7.2 *Orthogonality of the slip-line field and hodograph*

It will be observed that the hodograph has a marked resemblance to the slip-line field, but the fan region is rotated through $\pi/2$.

It is a general principle that all elements of the hodograph are orthogonal to the corresponding elements of the slip-line field. Consider for example the element of slip-line FG and the zone 4. The absolute velocity in zone 4 is given by the vector 04 in the hodograph, parallel to the discontinuity on FG. However, the element of the hodograph corresponding to FG is the line 34. This is approximately at right angles to 04 and in the limit as $\Delta\theta \to 0$ it becomes orthogonal to 04 and therefore to FG, which becomes the tangent at F.

This should not be allowed to cause confusion and it can be ignored until needed. In §6.6 for example, we shall improve the accuracy of the simple hodograph by considering the average velocity in a given zone, recognising that the assumed discontinuities on BE, BF, etc. arise only because finite zones were postulated. The average velocity in zone 2 can then be represented by the vector to the mid-point of the line 12 in the hodograph, and the mean velocity in BFG by the vector to the mid-point of 34. The true curved slip-line can then be used.

6

Applications of Slip-line Field Theory. Forging, Drawing, and Extrusion

6.1 Slip-line fields for plane-strain compression between parallel platens with sticking friction

We assume that the platens overhang the workpiece, which distinguishes the process from punching. The construction of the slip-line field and hodograph provides an example of the general problem of extending fields from a centred fan.

6.1.1 Construction of the slip-line field. $b/h = 3.6$

Since sticking friction has been assumed, the slip-lines must meet the platen surface at $0°$ and $90°$ (see Chapter 5, §5.5.4). They must also meet the central plane at $45°$, to avoid a resultant shear on the plane of symmetry. These conditions are fulfilled by two equal circular fans centred on the corners A and B, each having a radius $h/(2 \sin 45°)$, as in Figure 6.1a.

For ease of description, these fans may be divided into $15°$ segments, though $5°$ would give better accuracy. In Figure 6.1, the radii AC_1 and $BC_1{}'$ are extended to the right by curves intersecting orthogonally and at $45°$ to the central plane, at D. The tangent to the slip-line AC_1D must therefore rotate clockwise by $15°$ between C_1 and D. To find the position of D it is easier to draw the chord C_1D rather than the true curve. This chord will be parallel to the mean of the tangents at C_1 and D, and is therefore drawn from C_1 at $7\frac{1}{2}°$ to the direction AC_1.

Similarly a chord is drawn from C_2 at $7\frac{1}{2}°$ to the direction AC_2, to cut another drawn from D at $52\frac{1}{2}°$ to the central plane. Their intersection determines the point D_1.

To find the position of D_2, a chord is drawn from D_1 at $15°$ to the direction of the chord DD_1, since both chords will be inclined at $7\frac{1}{2}°$ to the tangent at D_1.

The points E, E_1 and F are located in the same way. If the platen breadth has the value chosen, $b = 3.6h$, F will be the centre-point. The field must always be symmetrical about the central plane, and also about the centre-line of the platens. To complete the field, the intersections are joined by smoothed curves, which will clearly be more accurate if $5°$ intervals are chosen.

The region bounded by the platen and the slip-line $C_3D_2E_1FE_1{}''D_2{}''C_3{}''$ remains rigid and moves with the platen. It can be regarded as a dead nose on the tool. If the platen breadth is increased to $b = 4.56h$, the field can be extended so that D_3 becomes the limit of the plastic zone and the central rigid zone is bounded by $D_3E_2F_1G$, and its reflection. The solution may be extended in the same way, however wide the platens; at intermediate values of the ratio b/h the centre-line will fall

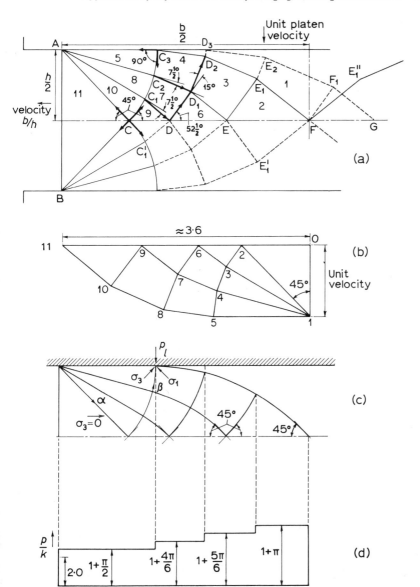

Figure 6.1 An approximate slip-line field solution, using a 15° network, for compression between overlapping platens with sticking friction. (*a*) The initial stages in construction of the field, for *b* = 3·6*h* (*b*) The hodograph construction for one quarter of the field (*c*) The final smoothed slip-line field (*d*) The pressure distribution

on a slip-line at an intermediate angle, but there will always be a rigid zone in the centre of each platen.

6.1.2 *Construction of the hodograph*

The compatibility of the chosen field with the velocity boundary conditions is verified by constructing the hodograph. This is most easily done by drawing chords to find the intersections, corresponding to the approximate slip-line field, and then joining these by smoothed curves.

The velocity solution is started at the central point F. Each platen is assumed to move towards the central plane with unit velocity, represented by a vertical line of unit length drawn from 0 in Figure 6.1b. As metal from the rigid zone adjacent to the upper platen crosses the boundary E_1F in the vicinity of F, it is sheared parallel to the slip-line, and so at 45° to the central plane. Its absolute velocity must subsequently be horizontally outwards, by reason of symmetry, so the appropriate velocity triangle is 012, with the angle $\angle 012 = 45°$.

The next region to consider is to the left of E_1. As metal from the rigid zone crosses D_2E_1, it is sheared with a velocity discontinuity equal in magnitude to that experienced by metal crossing E_1F since these are two portions of the same slip-line. There can be no change in the tangential velocity discontinuity along a slip-line. The line 13 can therefore be drawn parallel to E_1D_2 and equal in length to 12, in Figure 6.1b. As the element of metal, having crossed D_2E_1 into the mesh 3 of the slip-line field proceeds further and crosses EE_1 into 2, it will be sheared parallel to EE_1 and take the final velocity of all particles in mesh 2, represented by 02. The velocity change 32 should therefore be parallel to EE_1 in an accurate (small intercept) diagram.

To the left of the point D_2, metal crossing C_3D_2 from the rigid zone into the mesh 4 will be sheared parallel to C_3D_2 again with a velocity discontinuity equal to 12. This is represented by the line 14 parallel to C_3D_2. The element of metal may then cross D_2D_1 into mesh 3, being subjected to a parallel velocity discontinuity 43. If it subsequently crosses D_1E into mesh 6, its absolute velocity must again be horizontal. This discontinuity is represented by the line 36, parallel to D_1E and intersecting the horizontal from 0 in 6.

The metal between C_3 and A is not part of the rigid zone attached to the platen but it must move downwards with the platen, so all particles in the mesh 5 have unit vertical velocity-component, represented by 01. An element crossing C_3C_2 from 5 into 4 will experience a velocity discontinuity represented by the line drawn from 4 parallel to C_3C_2, since all particles in mesh 4 have the velocity 04. This gives the position of 5 which could also have been found by considering AC_3 an extension of the slip-line FC_3 for which the velocity discontinuity is everywhere equal to 1–2

The rest of the hodograph is constructed in the same way, considering one mesh at a time, until the position of 11 is found. The velocity at the boundary ACB must be compatible with the velocity of the rigid metal to the left, and so must be horizontally outwards and of magnitude b/h (multiplied by the platen velocity, which was assumed to be unity). The length 0–11 should therefore be equal to 3·6 in Figure 6.1b. If the diagrams are drawn accurately to scale, this will be found to be correct, confirming the validity of the slip-line field.

6.1.3 *Stress-determination from the slip-line field ($b/h = 3·6$)*

When the chosen field has been shown to be compatible with the stress and velocity boundary conditions, the stresses in the plastic zone may be evaluated using the Hencky equations (Chapter 5, §5.4).

The solution is started at the boundary ACB, where the horizontal principal stress σ_3 is equal to zero. Because the vertical stress σ_1 is compressive, σ_3 is algebraically greater than σ_1, and AC must be an α-line. The pressure p_C acting upon it is given by

$$\sigma_3 = -p_C + k = 0; \quad p_C = k$$

Using the Hencky equation 5.7b, the pressure acting on AC_3 is given by

$$p_{C_3} - 2k\frac{\pi}{4} = p_C = k; \quad p_{C_3} = k\left(1 + \frac{\pi}{2}\right)$$

This is constant over the portion AC_3 of the slip-line AF, which is straight and parallel to the platen surface. The vertical stress P acting over AC_3 is thus equal to the hydrostatic pressure

$$P_{AC_3} = p_{C_3} = k\left(1 + \frac{\pi}{2}\right) \tag{6.1}$$

This may be seen from the Mohr circle, as the direct stress on the plane of maximum shear, or by considering the equilibrium of a cube element of side l parallel to a slip-line

$$-Pl = (\sigma_1 l \cos 45°) \cos 45° + (\sigma_3 l \sin 45°) \sin 45°$$

$$P = -\tfrac{1}{2}(\sigma_1 + \sigma_3) = \tfrac{1}{2}(p + k + p - k)$$

The pressure at D_2 is found from the 15° clockwise rotation $(-\pi/12)$ of the α slip-line, using equation 5.7a

$$p_{D_2} + 2k\left(-\frac{\pi}{12}\right) = p_{C_3}; \quad p_{D_2} = k\left(1 + \frac{4\pi}{6}\right)$$

Similarly,

$$p_{E_1} + 2k\left(-\frac{\pi}{12}\right) = p_{D_2}; \quad p_{E_1} = k\left(1 + \frac{5\pi}{6}\right)$$

$$p_F + 2k\left(-\frac{\pi}{12}\right) = p_{E_1}; \quad p_F = k(1 + \pi) \tag{6.2}$$

The principal stresses and hence the vertical stress-component acting on the boundary C_3F can thus be found at each point along it. The mean vertical stress acting on the rigid zone boundary must be equal to the mean platen pressure over this region, so the latter can be evaluated, although it is not possible to calculate local pressures in the rigid zone. The pressure distribution is shown in Figure 6.1d.

6.1.4 *General solution for sticking friction with parallel platens (b > h)*
If the platens are wider than the value $b = 3\cdot6h$ chosen in the above section, the plastic zone in contact with the platens will extend inwards to D_3, E_3 and so on. The slip-line field is continued by the same procedure as before and Hill has shown

that the average pressure over the platen can be represented with sufficient accuracy by the equation

$$\frac{P}{2k} = \frac{3}{4} + \frac{b}{4h} \text{ when } b > h \tag{6.3}$$

This equation predicts somewhat lower average pressures than equation 3.35 which was derived from stress evaluation, but the difference becomes less significant as the ratio b/h becomes large and friction dominates the result.

If b is less than h, the operation can conveniently be considered as punching or indentation, which will be discussed in §6.3.

6.2 Compression with intermediate friction values

A slip-line field can be built up with the boundary condition that the slip-lines meet the platen surface at angles given by

$$\cos 2\theta = \frac{\mu q'}{k}$$

assuming a starting value of q' first. The field resembles the solution found for sticking friction in Figure 6.1 but the hodograph is found not to conform to the velocity boundary-conditions except when b/h is integral. A solution has been obtained in a different manner by Prandtl, and with a computer program by Li.

6.3 Slip-line field solutions for plane-strain indentation or punching

If the platen breadth is small in comparison with the thickness of the workpiece, the forging pattern of the deformation is altered, and the process can be considered separately as one of indentation. Again the slip-line field is valid for infinitesimal displacements only.

6.3.1 *Indentation with a flat punch (h > b)*

The field is again constructed with a right-angled triangular zone beneath the indenter, as in Figure 5.7, but the fans centred on the corners, or singularities, do not continue towards the free surface. Instead they are extended, by the method described in §6.1.1 until they intersect symmetrically at the centre-line (Figure 6.2). This involves less curvature and the pressure is lower than for the semi-infinite block.

There is however no simple starting point for stress calculation, so it is necessary to use the condition that the average lateral stress acting across the plastic zone boundary is zero.

We assume that the hydrostatic pressure at F has some value p_F, to be determined. Then the pressure at E, along the α-line FA, is given by the Hencky equation (5.6), recognising that the tangent rotates by $\Delta\phi$ clockwise, and therefore negatively between F and E.

$$p_E + 2k(-\Delta\phi) = p_F; \quad p_E = p_F + 2k\Delta\phi \tag{6.4}$$

The mean pressure across EF is thus

$$\bar{p}_{EF} = p_F + k\Delta\phi$$

Similarly $p_D = p_E + 2k\Delta\phi$; $\bar{p}_{DE} = p_F + 3k\Delta\phi$.

From D to A the line is straight, so

$$\bar{p}_{DA} = p_D = p_A = p_F + 4k\Delta\phi \tag{6.5}$$

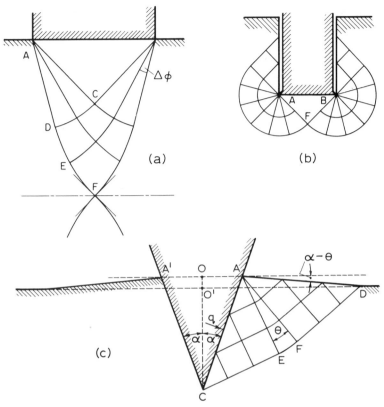

Figure 6.2 Slip-line fields for indentation of a wide strip (*a*) Two flat punches, $b < h < 8\cdot7b$ (*b*) Flat punch, $h \sim \infty$. Deep groove (*c*) Smooth wedge, $h \sim \infty$

The stress normal to a slip-line is equal to the hydrostatic pressure, as may be seen from the Mohr circle, Figure 5.2, being the direct stress acting on the plane of maximum shear. The stress parallel to the slip-line is, of course, the shear yield stress k. The pressure acts outwards on the rigid metal, and the metal flows downwards, exerting a downward shear force on the rigid metal. The force components normal and tangential to the section EF are consequently as shown:

$$F_{\mathrm{T}} = \mathrm{EF}\,wk$$

$$F_{\mathrm{N}} = \mathrm{EF}\,w\bar{p}_{\mathrm{EF}}$$

The horizontal force component acting on the rigid metal is thus, for this sector,

$$F_H = F_N \sin(\pi/4 + \Delta\phi/2) - F_T \cos(\pi/4 + \Delta\phi/2)$$

$$= EF \cdot w (p_F + k\Delta\phi) \sin(\pi/4 + \Delta\phi/2) - EF \cdot wk \cos(\pi/4 + \Delta\phi/2),$$

giving the horizontal stress, on the area $EF \sin(\pi/4 + \Delta\phi/2)w = EFw$,

$$(\sigma_H)_{EF} = (p_F + k\Delta\phi) - k \cot(\pi/4 + \Delta\phi/2).$$

Similarly

$$(\sigma_H)_{DE} = (p_F + 3k\Delta\phi) - k \cot(\pi/4 + 3\Delta\phi/2)$$

$$(\sigma_H)_{AD} = (p_F + 4k\Delta\phi) - k \cot(\pi/4 + 2\Delta\phi)$$

The nett horizontal force must be zero, since it is unopposed, so

$$(\sigma_H)_{EF} \cdot \widehat{EF} \cdot w + (\sigma_H)_{DE} \cdot \widehat{DE} \cdot w + (\sigma_H)_{AD} \; \widehat{AD} \cdot w = 0 \tag{6.6}$$

The only unknown in this equation is the pressure p_F, which can therefore be found.

The Hencky equations are then used to find p_D along the α-line, as above, and p_C along the β-line. The pressure acting along CA is uniform and equal to p_C, so the principal stress $(\sigma_1)_{CA} = -(p_C + k)$. This acts at $\pi/4$ to the line CA and thus normal to the platen face, giving the indentation pressure P.

In more general terms for a smoothed slip-line, the pressure p_G at some point G, where the tangent has rotated by $-\phi'$ from its datum at F, will be given by

$$p_G = p_F + 2k\phi'$$

The horizontal component of the force acting normal to an element ds of the slip-line will be

$$(p + 2k\phi') \, ds \sin(\pi/4 + \phi')$$

The horizontal component of the tangential force will be

$$-k \, ds \cos(\pi/4 + \phi')$$

assuming unit width normal to the plane.
Thus

$$\int_0^h \sigma_x \, dy = \int_0^s (p + 2k\phi') \sin(\pi/4 + \phi') \, ds - k \int_0^s \cos(\pi/4 + \phi') \, ds \tag{6.7}$$

which can be equated to zero to find p_F.

6.3.2 *Deep penetration by a flat punch*
If the flat-faced punch, with suitable clearance at the sides, is envisaged at the bottom of a deep groove, as in Figure 6.2b, the stress boundary conditions will be the same as for initial penetration. A possible slip-line field is thus of the type shown, which closely resembles Figure 5.7a, except that the fan regions centred on the punch corners are developed through $180°$. The pressure for deformation at the foot of a deep groove is therefore greater than that for initial deformation (equation 5.15) and is given by

$$P = 2k(1 + \pi) = 4 \cdot 14 \times 2k \tag{6.8}$$

As mentioned in Chapter 5, this solution is appropriate to a rough indenter, and the area ABF can be considered as a dead zone or nose on the punch.

6.3.3 *Wedge-indentation of a semi-infinite block*

When a smooth wedge-shaped indenter enters a semi-infinite block, the metal is displaced upwards so that $\triangle ADO' = \triangle ACO'$. The pressure is given by

$$P = 2k(1 + \theta) \tag{6.9}$$

6.4 Drawing of strip, wire and rod

6.4.1 *Strip-drawing*

The slip-line field for strip-drawing shown in Figure 6.3 closely resembles that for forging with a narrow platen, shown in Figure 6.2*a*.

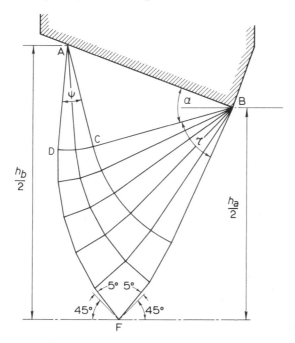

Figure 6.3 The slip-line field for strip-drawing through wedge-shaped dies with finite friction

There are two significant differences. The die surface is inclined at a small angle α, probably $12°$, and the triangular zone adjacent to the die meets the surface at an angle θ determined by the friction coefficient, using the equation

$$\cos 2\theta = \mu q'/k \tag{5.10}$$

There is a complication in this, since q' must be assumed before the field can be drawn. The usual practice is to draw the field for zero friction ($\theta = \pi/4$) and calculate the die pressure q, which is then assumed to be equal to q', the die pressure including the friction contribution. The field is then redrawn and a more accurate value of q' obtained.

The calculation follows the same pattern as for forging (§6.3), assuming no back-pull and therefore no nett horizontal force over AF. The nett horizontal force is calculated over BF to find the mean drawing stress or the drawing force.

The results show that the redundant work factor f can be represented by the curve found for forging (Figure 5.6) if h is replaced by the mean arc of separation of the dies, c, and b by the die contact length d. Geometrically, $c/d = (2 - r)/r \cdot \alpha$, and a useful approximation is

$$f = 0.70 + 0.26 \, c/d \qquad (6.10)$$

6.4.2 *Wire- and rod-drawing*

Examination of the deformed section in a partly-drawn rod suggests that the slip-line field shown in Figure 6.3 can be assumed, without great error, to be applicable to a diametral section of a rod.

The calculation of the hydrostatic pressure at F, and hence of all the stresses, proceeds in the same way, except that forces are considered to act on the conical surfaces of each sector, not simply on a uniform width w as in plane strain. This clearly gives preponderance to the forces contributed at large radius, especially over AD. Fortunately this is the region which most nearly approaches plane strain (zero circumferential strain) and hence introduces least inaccuracy, but it should be recognised that the method is not rigorous.

The results of such analysis, together with experimental measurements, lead to a simple formula for the drawing stress for wires, based on the stress analysis (§3.3, equation 3.14) and a correction ϕ for redundant work.

$$\sigma_{xa} = \phi \bar{Y} [(1 + B)/B] \, [1 - (1 - r)^B] \qquad (6.11a)$$

where $\quad \phi = 0.88 + 0.78 \dfrac{D_b + D_a}{D_b - D_a} \dfrac{1 - \cos \alpha}{2 \sin \alpha} \approx 0.87 + \dfrac{1 - r}{r} \cdot \sin \alpha \qquad (6.11b)$

If α is large and r is small, the redundant work factor may become large. The deformation pattern will then change, in a manner analogous to the indentation pattern, resulting in a bulge of metal forming ahead of the die, and in extreme instances this will be scalped off, leaving a very damaged surface.

6.5 Plane-strain extrusion

Direct extrusion, which is more common than inverted extrusion, involves a container, closed at one end by the die, and at the other end by a close-fitting plunger (more usually a close-fitting pressure pad on the end of a mandrel), as in Figure 6.4a. The billet is squeezed by application of pressure to the plunger, causing metal to flow steadily out through the die. As extrusion proceeds, the plunger moves towards the die, and the billet slides forward against the inner wall of the container. This frictional contact, of poorly-defined magnitude, can be avoided by holding the billet stationary in a container which is closed at one end and forcing a close-fitting die against the free end of the billet (Figure 6.4c). As the extrusion proceeds, the die moves forward into the container, and the extruded metal flows backwards through the die and the hollow pressure-stem. In this inverted form of extrusion, there is no relative movement between billet and container, and consequently no frictional contribution. We shall consider this simpler condition first.

Plate III A hydraulically-driven screw press, developing 90MN force for closed-die forging, and at least 110 MN impact force.

Plate IV A Quintus hot isostatic press for making aircraft parts, operating at a temperature of 1260°C and a pressure of 200 MPa.

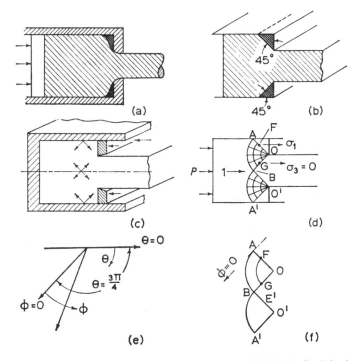

Figure 6.4 (*a*) The dead-metal zone in direct extrusion of a bar (*b*) The idealised dead-metal boundary assumed (*c*) The slip-lines defined by boundary conditions in plane-strain inverted 50% extrusion (*d*) The complete slip-line field (*e*), (*f*) The reference line for measurement of ϕ, chosen to coincide with the tangent to the α-line AB, at A

It is convenient to assume that the die is at rest, and that the billet and container move towards it with unit velocity (Figure 6.4*d*).

6.5.1 *2:1 Inverted extrusion; 180° die*

From the boundary conditions for a frictionless interface (§5.5.2) we know that the slip-lines must meet the frictionless container wall at 45° (Figure 6.4*c*). The centre-line of the billet is an axis of symmetry, and can have no resultant shear component along it, so the slip-lines must meet the centre-line also at 45°. To proceed further, we consider the flow pattern in a real extrusion with a 180° die. It is known that a 'dead-metal' zone forms in the corner between container and die (Figure 6.4*a*). Flow takes place by intense shear over the surface of this region. The billet skin flows into the interface, and in some circumstances, for example when the billet is coated with graphite so that welding is prevented, the dead zone may be physically separated from the end of the billet after the extrusion. The boundary is usually curved at each extremity against container and die orifice, but reasonably straight over most of its length. As an approximation, we may make the simple assumption that the dead zone is bounded by a straight line at 45° to the axis (Figure 6.4*b*). In fact, the exact position of this line does not greatly affect the result. This assumption provides the first slip-line AO, which meets the wall at 45° as required by the boundary conditions. Recalling the example of §5.6.5, it can be seen that two radial fans centred on O and O' would complete the field (Figure 6.4*d*).

It is now necessary to examine this field to see whether it satisfies the necessary velocity conditions, by drawing the hodograph.

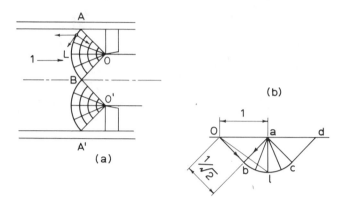

Figure 6.5 (*a*) The slip-line field as in Figure 6.4 (*b*) The corresponding hodograph for 50% inverted extrusion

In Figure 6.5*a*, any particle of metal to the left of the boundary AB is assumed to move in the extrusion direction with unit velocity. This is represented by a vector 0a of unit length drawn from the origin in the hodograph, Figure 6.5*b*, parallel to the physical velocity. It is assumed that there is a velocity discontinuity along the boundary slip-line AB. The hodograph eventually shows this to be a valid assumption. A particle crossing AB in the vicinity of A will undergo a sudden shearing parallel to the tangent to AB at the point of crossing. For a particle crossing very near to A, this change in velocity will be represented by a vector drawn from the point a, parallel to the tangent at A. After crossing the discontinuity, the element will be constrained to slide parallel to the assumed dead-metal boundary, so that its absolute velocity must be represented by a vector from 0 parallel to the line AO. This will intersect the vector from a in the point b.

Since the velocity discontinuity along AB has constant magnitude, equal to ab over the whole slip-line, a particle crossing AB at any other point will experience a velocity change parallel to the tangent at the point of crossing and equal in magnitude to ab. Thus at L, for example, the tangent is vertical and the velocity triangle is 0al.

In the vicinity of B, the tangent is at 45° to the centre-line, so the discontinuity is ac and the absolute velocity within the plastic zone is 0c. The particle then traverses the plastic region and finally emerges from it by crossing the boundary slip-line BO, when it again experiences a sudden shear or velocity discontinuity parallel to BO, represented by a vector in the direction cd. The final velocity in the rigid metal to the right of BO must be in the extrusion direction, represented by the vector 0a produced. The intersection of cd and 0d gives the final absolute velocity vector 0d. It is clear from Figure 6.5*b* that 0d = 20a, so that the final velocity has magnitude 2, showing that the chosen slip-line field is thus compatible with the velocity for 2:1 extrusion.

The extrusion pressure is readily calculated. There is no force on the extruded bar, so $\sigma_3 = 0$ on BO. Consequently, from equations 5.2, $-p_{BC} + k = 0$, $p_{BC} = k$.

The circumferential lines such as BA rotate clockwise into higher pressure (near A) so the Hencky equation 5.7a for an α-line is used. The rotation from B to A is clockwise, therefore negative, so

$$p_{AC} + 2k(-\pi/2) = p_{BC} = k; \quad p_{AC} = k(1 + \pi)$$

Using equations 5.2 again

$$(\sigma_1)_{AC} = p_{AC} + k = 2k(1 + \pi/2) \tag{6.12}$$

The principal stress σ_1 acts, of course, at 45° to the slip-line AC and thus normal to the die. The result resembles that for indentation (equation 5.14), but the extrusion pressure P on the billet acts over twice this area, so

$$2P = 1 \cdot \sigma_1 = 2k(1 + \pi/2); \quad P/2k = 1 \cdot 29 \tag{6.13}$$

6.5.2 *Extrusion with larger reductions in area*

Most extrusion involves reduction of area ratios much greater than 2. For large ratios, the field still starts with a fan centred on the die outlet and intersecting the centre-line at 45°. This is then extended by the method of drawing chords (§6.1.1) until the requisite boundary frictional conditions are satisfied. Examples are shown in Figure 6.6.

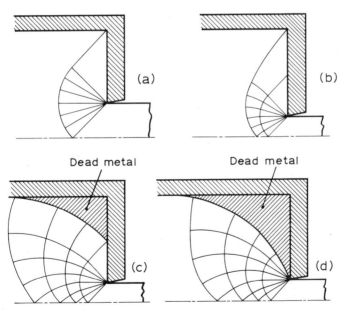

Figure 6.6 Slip-line fields for extrusion through a square die (*a*) Frictionless die and container ($r = 2/3$) (*b*) Frictionless die and container ($r > 2/3$) (*c*) Frictionless die with sticking friction at the container walls, showing a dead-metal zone (*d*) Sticking friction at the die and container

6.5.3 *Extrusion through unsymmetrical and multi-hole dies*

It is difficult to extend the theory to complex geometries, but a number of examples of extrusion through unsymmetrically-placed single-hole dies, dies with oblique faces, stepped dies, lateral orifices, and multiple-hole dies, have been examined by Johnson and his colleagues. They have proposed slip-line fields and verified them by hodographs, and have also shown that many of these problems can conveniently be handled by the upper-bound technique.

For practical purposes, the pressure for longitudinal extrusion is determined mainly by the total reduction of area, the mean die angle, and the friction. A useful approximation to the extrusion pressure can usually be obtained by assuming an equivalent simple extrusion condition, and evaluating the effect of these parameters for this model. Thus, for example, it has been shown that the extrusion pressure for simultaneous extrusion of four bars, with good lubrication, is practically the same as that for a single central bar with the same total reduction of area. A useful formula is

$$P/Y = 0.8 + 1.5 \ln A_1/A_2 \tag{6.14}$$

6.6 Metal-flow streamlines in extrusion

Consider the simple 2:1 extrusion once again, as in Figure 6.7.

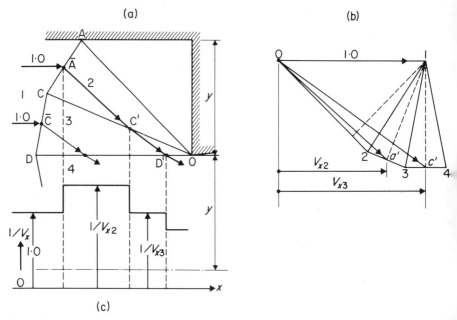

Figure 6.7 (*a*) A simplified representation of part of the slip-line field for 2:1 extrusion (*b*) The corresponding part of the hodograph (*c*) A plot of the reciprocal of velocity through each zone

An element approaching the mid-point $\bar{A}$ of the entry slip-line AC has velocity 1·0, which changes abruptly by a velocity discontinuity parallel to AC, so that it travels with the mean velocity $0a'$ of the sector AOC, shown in the hodograph,

Figure 6.7*b*. This is somewhat more accurate than the simpler assumption made previously that the velocity in AOC is represented by 01 and changes discontinuously to the velocity 02 for the region COD. The element experiences a further discontinuity on passing at C′ into the sector COD, after which it travels with mean velocity 0c′ until it reaches D′, on the line OD.

The horizontal components of these velocities can be found from the hodograph, as $(\bar{V}_x)_{AOC}$ and $(\bar{V}_x)_{COD}$.

From these values, it is possible to calculate the time required to traverse each sector, since

$$V_x = \frac{dx}{dt} \; ; \quad t_{12} = \int_{x_1}^{x_2} \frac{dx}{V_x} \qquad (6.15)$$

Thus $\quad (\Delta t)_{AOC} = (\Delta x)_{AOC}/(\bar{V}_x)_{AOC}$

This can be calculated or found graphically from the area of a $1/V_x$ plot against x, as shown in Figure 6.7*c*. The time to cross the second sector is correspondingly

$$(\Delta t)_{COD} = (\Delta x)_{COD}/(\bar{V}_x)_{COD} \qquad (6.16)$$

and the total time required to reach any selected distance x, within or beyond the plastic zone, can be calculated. After passing the exit boundary, the element will continue with the steady velocity 2·0, for a 2:1 extrusion.

All other elements approach the entry boundary with velocity 1·0, and the element approaching $\bar{C}$ must of course travel with the velocity 0c′ in the sector COD, just as the first element did after crossing at C′. The time it takes to cross the sector COD is thus found in the same way.

A graph can then be plotted as in Figure 6.8*a* for each element, crossing at $\bar{A}$, $\bar{C}$, etc., showing the total time required for each to travel to any distance x from a starting line in the undeformed metal.

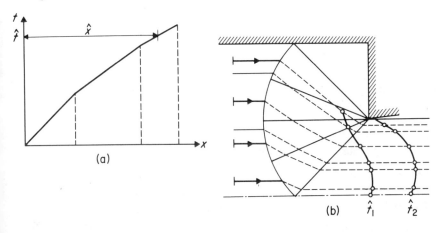

(a)

(b) $\hat{t}_1$ $\hat{t}_2$

Figure 6.8 (*a*) A graph showing the time for a given element of metal to reach a distance x, measured along the axis (*b*) Flow lines and the distortion of a transverse line after passing through the die

Finally, the intercepts $\hat{x}$ for some chosen time interval $\hat{t}$ can be replotted onto the flow lines to show the positions reached by each one.

When correctly plotted, with small angular intervals, these distortion patterns agree closely with those found experimentally using split billets with an inscribed grid.

6.7 Slip-line fields for axial symmetry, and for strain-hardening material

There is no rigorous slip-line field theory for axial symmetry, but approximations can be made. The simple method of assuming the slip-line field on a diametral section to be closely similar to the plane-strain field has been found useful, as indicated in §6.4.2. Another assumption that has often been used is that the circumferential stress is equal to one of the meridional principal stresses. Other, more complicated, suggestions have been made, none of which are strictly accurate.

Strain-hardening is most easily accounted for in force calculations by assuming a mean yield stress, based on the work concept

$$2k = \frac{1}{\epsilon_2 - \epsilon_1} \int_{\epsilon_1}^{\epsilon_2} 2k \; d\epsilon \tag{6.17}$$

Strain-hardening does however influence the flow, and attempts have been made to include it in the basic analysis. Figure 6.9 shows an experimentally-derived field for work-hardening (annealed) metal.

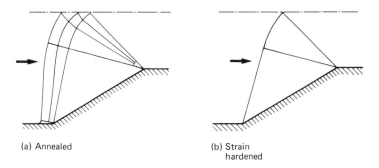

(a) Annealed   (b) Strain hardened

Figure 6.9 An experimental slip-line field for extrusion of annealed metal, compared with a theoretical field assuming no hardening

6.8 Slip-line fields for metal cutting

Although ordinary lathe-cutting appears simple, it is a difficult process to analyse, because there are steep strain, velocity and temperature gradients in each of three dimensions. It is usual to simplify the geometric conditions by considering orthogonal cutting, in which the chip formation involves flow in one plane only, and the tool is set at right angles to this plane, across the workpiece. These conditions can be produced by shaping, on the edge of a plate, or by cutting in a helical path on the end of a tube.

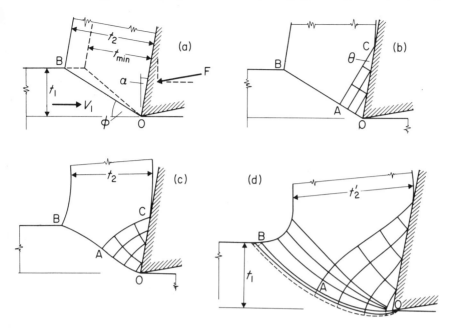

Figure 6.10 Plane-strain models of chip or swarf formation (*a*) Minimum energy, straight shear plane (*b*) Simple slip-line field with rake-face friction (*c*) Slip-line field allowing chip curl (*d*) Inclusion of strain-hardening on the shear plane

Figure 6.10 shows a simplified model of chip formation that is often used. Shear is assumed to occur on the single discontinuity OB, inclined at the shear-plane angle ϕ to the direction of tool motion in a shaping operation. The resultant force F is as shown, almost horizontal. The angle ϕ is supposed to adjust to a position determined by the principle of minimum energy, to be discussed in Chapter 7, §7.7.

It is found that cutting also involves significant deformation adjacent to the rake face of the tool OC, in Figure 6.10*b*, which can be allowed for by a region of slip-line field with the lines meeting OC at a friction angle θ, as in Figure 5.4*c*. Further development of this field allows for chip curl by introducing a reflex curvature of the shear plane BAO, as in Figure 6.10*c*. This field implies a reduction in the angle θ as the tool edge is approached.

Because of the large strain involved in cutting, strain-hardening can be very important, especially for annealed stock. The principal effect of this is to broaden the shear plane into a band, as shown in Figure 6.10*d* and further discussed in Chapter 7, §7.7. Calculation of forces is usually less informative than the analysis of chip shape in metal cutting. In practice, wear is the dominant feature.

7

Upper-bound Solutions

7.1 The principle of upper-bound analysis

Slip-line field solutions are very accurate if the assumed conditions are satisfied. They are however rather time-consuming and it is often satisfactory to use a simple, quick, but admittedly approximate bounding technique. The upper-bound method involves only the conditions that have to be fulfilled by the strain increments or velocities, and does not concern itself with stress equilibrium.

In an *upper-bound* solution, the plastically-deforming body is supposed to be divided into simple zones, usually triangular, which remain rigid but are separated from their neighbours by lines of tangential velocity discontinuity. The implied pattern of velocities must be compatible with the externally-imposed conditions, as verified by drawing a hodograph.

The applied load is assumed to advance with some fixed velocity, which may be taken as unity, thereby performing work at a fixed rate. If there are no other losses, this is exactly balanced by the rate of performing work by shearing on all the discontinuities.

If the length of a discontinuity is s, the shearing force F acting over it will be, for unit width in plane strain,

$$F = ks \cdot 1 \cdot 0$$

since the shear yield stress k is the same everywhere. If the magnitude of the velocity discontinuity is u, the rate of performing work by the force F will be

$$Fu = kus$$

The total rate of performing work *internally* is thus

$$\frac{\mathrm{d}W}{\mathrm{d}t} = \Sigma kus \qquad (7.1$$

The rate of performance of work *externally* by an applied pressure P acting on an area $1 \cdot 0a$ at velocity $1 \cdot 0$ is simply Pa.

Equating these:

$$Pa = \Sigma kus \qquad (7.2$$

There will be many possible velocity fields, but the one most likely to operate will be the one requiring the least load. Once the metal starts to deform there is no way in which the load can rise to the level needed to operate some more resistive mode.

Consequently, the load deduced from any arbitrary field that satisfies velocity but not stress conditions is either fortuitously correct, or larger than the real load.

Several different configurations can be tried, as in Figures 7.1 and 7.2, the best solution being the one that predicts the lowest load.

In practice this method is easy to use, and it is advantageous to know that the predicted load will be at least sufficient to perform the operation. Consideration of stress equilibrium alone, without regard to velocity will give a *lower bound*, which is always less than the real value.

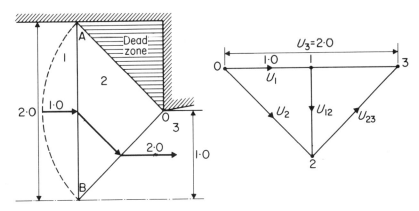

Figure 7.1 A simple upper-bound shear field and hodograph for 2:1 extrusion

7.2 An upper-bound solution for 2:1 extrusion

It is assumed that the shear pattern can be represented by the three lines AB, AO and OB, bearing in mind the slip-line field, shown by the broken line, as in Figure 6.5.

The hodograph is drawn by assuming that an element of the metal approaches the boundary shear-line AB with unit velocity and then experiences a tangential discontinuity 12, to make the absolute velocity in zone 2 parallel to the dead zone boundary AO. It finally leaves the plastic region to enter the exit zone 3 across the discontinuity BO, represented by 23 in the hodograph. The exit velocity is horizontal and equal to 2·0, as required by the 2:1 extrusion ratio, so this field satisfies the velocity boundary conditions.

The rate of performing work on the three shear lines is

$$\left(\frac{dW}{dt}\right)_{\text{int}} = k\Sigma us = k(u_{12}\text{AB} + u_2\text{AO} + u_{23}\text{BO}) \tag{7.3}$$

Direct measurement or calculation gives the required values:

$$\left(\frac{dW}{dt}\right)_{\text{int}} = k(1 \times 2 + \sqrt{2} \times \sqrt{2} + \sqrt{2} \times \sqrt{2}) = 6k \tag{7.4}$$

If the extrusion pressure is P, the rate of performing work on the billet is

$$\left(\frac{dW}{dt}\right)_{\text{ext}} = P \times \text{AB} \times 1\cdot0 = 2P$$

Equating these,

$$P = 3k, \quad \text{or} \quad P/2k = 1.5 \tag{7.5}$$

This is, as may be anticipated, greater than the slip-line field prediction that $P = 2k \times 1.29$, as in equation 6.13.

It is instructive to work out the pressure for the field shown in Figure 7.2, with its hodograph.

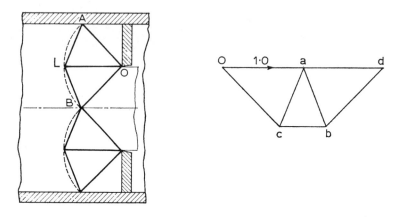

Figure 7.2 An alternative upper-bound shear field and hodograph for 2:1 extrusion

The extrusion pressure will be found to be

$$P/2k = 1.33 \tag{7.6}$$

This is still greater than the slip-line field value, but closer to it.

In general, the predictions from upper-bound solutions become closer to the accurate value as the fields themselves resemble more closely the slip-line field. (Try sub-dividing AOL and LOB once more, as in Example 7.2.)

The advantage of the upper-bound method is seen more clearly by using a single-triangle field for calculation of the pressure for extrusion with a large ratio, as in Figure 6.6d, compared with the slip-line field calculation.

7.3 An upper-bound solution for indentation

Figure 7.3 shows a suitable field for indentation, together with its hodograph, whose construction can be followed by reference to the slip-line field and hodograph of Figure 5.8. It should be noticed that, as stress equilibrium is not considered, it is not necessary for the shear lines to intersect at $\pi/2$. To emphasise this, and also to simplify the calculation, equilateral triangles are chosen here.

From the field shown in Figure 7.3b, if AB = a, all the lines AC, etc. will also be of length a. In the hodograph, Figure 7.3c, the velocity discontinuities along AC, etc. are all equal to 0b, namely $1/\cos 30° = 2/\sqrt{3}$, but the shear velocity at the punch face AB is $1 \times \tan 30° = 1/\sqrt{3}$.

If we suppose that there is sticking friction along AB, the shear stress there will be equal to k, as on all the other lines. The rate of performing work in shear is then

$$\left(\frac{dW}{dt}\right)_{int} = \Sigma kus = kABu_{AB} + k(ACu_{AC} + CBu_{CB} + CDu_{CD} + BDu_{BD} + DEu_{DE})$$

$$= ka . \frac{1}{\sqrt{3}} + 5ka . \frac{2}{\sqrt{3}} = \frac{11ak}{\sqrt{3}}$$

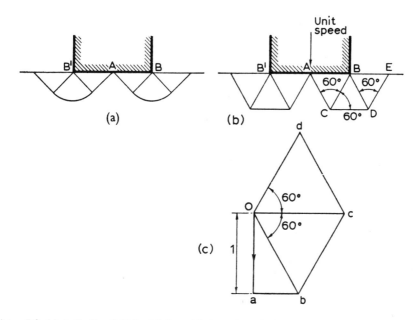

Figure 7.3 (*a*) A slip-line field for lubricated indentation of a large block (*b*) An approximate representation by straight lines to give an upper-bound solution consisting of equilateral triangles (*c*) The hodograph relating to (*b*)

Equating this to the rate of performing work by the indenter,

$$\left(\frac{dW}{dt}\right)_{ext} = Pa . 1.0,$$

$$P = 11k/\sqrt{3}, \quad P/2k = 3.18 \tag{7.7}$$

It is interesting to note that for frictionless conditions the term relating to shear on AB would be eliminated, but the rest of the solution would be unchanged.

Then $P = 10k/3; \quad P = 2.89$ \hfill (7.8)

In the slip-line field solution, the result $P/2k = 2.57$ is obtained whether there is friction at the die face or not (§5.6.5). However, the field shown in Figure 5.7a is more appropriate for high friction, with the whole triangular zone ABF acting as a dead nose on the tool. When the upper-bound field is changed to resemble Figure 5.7a rather than Figure 5.7b, the predicted pressure is lower. If the dead zone is represented by an equilateral triangle based on the whole of BB' instead of on the half AB in Figure 7.3b, and the rest of the field is correspondingly enlarged, the pressure found by the upper-bound method is again $P = 2k \times 2 \cdot 89$, as for the frictionless indentation.

This demonstrates that the choice of field is important, and again shows that the slip-line field can provide important clues to the type and extent of upper-bound field to select.

7.4 An upper-bound solution for deep punching

Deep punching with a flat-faced indenter involves a dead zone or nose in front of the punch, whether or not there is lubrication, as shown in Figure 6.2b. This may

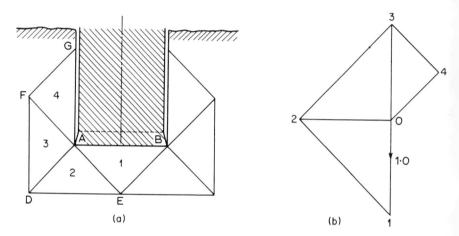

Figure 7.4 (a) An upper-bound solution for deep piercing (b) The hodograph

be represented by the isosceles right-angled triangle ABE in Figure 7.4. The upper-bound solution then predicts a pressure

$$P/2k = 5 \tag{7.9}$$

which may be compared with the value $(1 + \pi)$, or $4 \cdot 14$, given by the slip-line field, equation 6.8.

7.5 Upper-bound solutions for compression with smooth platens

Bearing in mind the slip-line field for compression of thin wide strip between smooth flat platens (Figure 5.5), a simple upper-bound solution may be drawn as i▸ Figure 7.5. If the platens are assumed to move inwards with unit velocity, the velocity along CH is given by $u_{CH} \sin \theta = 1$, which is also the velocity along CB, BA▸

and so on. The hodograph is thus as shown in Figure 7.5b. Using equation 7.1, the rate of performance of work in the deformation is

$$\frac{dW}{dt} = \Sigma kus = k(ABu_{AB} + BCu_{BC} -----)$$

The length s_{AB} is $s_{AG}/\cos\theta$, so

$$\frac{dW}{dt} = ku_{AB}\, \Sigma s_{AG}/\cos\theta = k\,\frac{1}{\sin\theta}\,\frac{b}{\cos\theta} \tag{7.10}$$

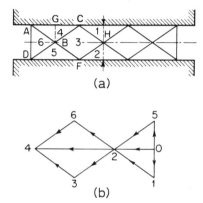

(a)

(b)

Figure 7.5 (*a*) An upper-bound solution for plane-strain compression between smooth flat platens (*b*) The hodograph

The rate of performance of work by the applied pressure P is

$$\frac{dW}{dt} = Pb\,.\,1$$

Equating these values,

$$Pb = \frac{kb}{\sin\theta\cos\theta} \quad \text{or} \quad \frac{P}{2k} = \frac{1}{\sin 2\theta} \tag{7.11}$$

The pressure passes through minimum values, equal to $2k$, when $\sin 2\theta = 1$, or when $\theta = \pi/4$, which occurs when the ratio b/h is integral, as in the slip-line field solution (Figure 5.6).

7.6 Application of upper-bound technique to axial symmetry

The upper-bound method for axial symmetry has been developed by Kudo from his technique for obtaining upper-bound solutions to plane-strain problems for which no slip-line fields exist. The plane-strain method may be illustrated for the previous simple example of strip extrusion to 50% reduction through square dies. The slip-line field solution has already been discussed in Chapter 6, §6.5. For the upper-bound solution, the billet is divided into rectangular units, whose sides are assumed to move with constant speed in directions normal to their respective planes (Figure 7.6*a*).

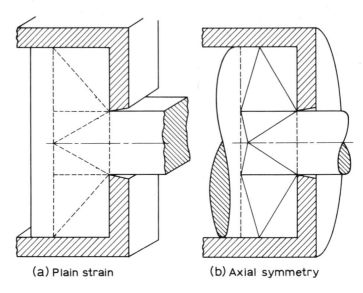

(a) Plain strain   (b) Axial symmetry

Figure 7.6 (*a*) Plane-strain extrusion with square dies, considered by the upper-bound method. The billet is divided into rectangular units, (*b*) Division of a billet into cylindrical regions for estimation of an upper-bound load in extrusion of round bar

The energy dissipated in the deformation of each unit is calculated, including the work done in shearing over sticking-friction interfaces where appropriate. The best combination of dimensions for the rectangles is the one which gives the least total energy dissipation. Velocity fields within these rectangles are then selected, again to give the least possible energy dissipation. The method requires some skill and practice, and the reader is referred to the original paper for examples.

For problems involving axial symmetry, the approach is similar, but the billet is divided into cylindrical regions instead of rectangles, as in Figure 7.6*b*.

These units may again be divided by triangular velocity fields chosen for least energy dissipation.

7.7 A simplified approach to metal cutting

A highly-simplified but useful interpretation of metal cutting can be obtained by an upper-bound approach.

The shear field is based on Figures 6.10*a* and 6.10*b*. It is assumed that chip formation occurs by simple shear along OB, in Figure 7.7, but there is a region OC along which work is done against friction. Instead of assuming a coefficient of friction, it is more appropriate to use some fraction β of the maximum shear stress to represent the mean frictional stress. The value of β then lies between the limits 0

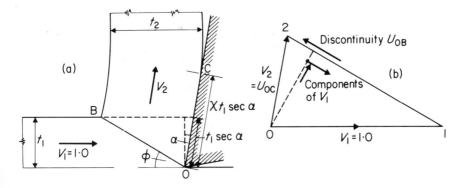

Figure 7.7 (*a*) Pure shear deformation on a single plane, as in an idealised machining operation (*b*) The associated hodograph

for perfect lubrication and 1 for sticking friction, usually being close to 1. The contact length OC is not known, but for the purpose of the analysis it is assumed to be some multiple χ of the depth of cut (or feed rate in lathe cutting) t_1, often known as the undeformed chip thickness, projected onto the tool face. Thus the relevant lengths are

$$OC = \chi t_1 \sec \alpha, \quad OB = t_1 \operatorname{cosec} \alpha \tag{7.12}$$

The hodograph is drawn to find the rate of performing work on those shear lines. An element of the workpiece approaches the shear plane with velocity 1 and is then sheared parallel to OB to move parallel to the rake face, with velocity O2. The velocity discontinuity on OB is seen from Figure 7.7*b* to be the whole of the line 1–2.

The rate of performing work by shear is thus

$$\left(\frac{\mathrm{d}W}{\mathrm{d}t}\right)_{\text{int}} = \Sigma kus = k \, OB \, u_{OB} + \beta k \, OC \, u_{OC} \tag{7.13}$$

The values of the velocities can be determined from the hodograph, with a little manipulation as in Example 7.11, in the form

$$u_{OB} = \frac{\cot \alpha}{\sin \phi + \cos \phi \cot \alpha}; \quad u_{OC} = \frac{\sin \phi}{\cos(\phi - \alpha)} \tag{7.14}$$

Substituting 7.12 and 7.14 into equation 7.13, and rearranging:

$$\left(\frac{\mathrm{d}W}{\mathrm{d}t}\right)_{\text{int}} = k\left[\frac{t_1 \cos \alpha}{\sin \phi \, \cos(\phi - \alpha)} + \frac{\beta \chi t_1 \sin \phi}{\cos \alpha \, \cos(\phi - \alpha)}\right] \tag{7.15}$$

The principle of least action suggests that the system will tend to adjust to an extremum value. If we make the further assumption that the only variable is the shear-plane angle ϕ, this implies that

$$\frac{\partial}{\partial \phi}\left(\frac{\mathrm{d}W}{\mathrm{d}t}\right)_{\text{int}} = 0$$

and hence

$$\frac{\partial}{\partial\phi}\left(\frac{\cos\alpha}{\sin\phi\cos(\phi-\alpha)} + \frac{\beta\chi\sin\phi}{\cos\alpha\cos(\phi-\alpha)}\right) = 0 \tag{7.16}$$

though in fact neither β nor χ are externally imposed, so accurate results are not to be expected. By carrying out the differentiation and simplifying, the condition 7.16 becomes,

$$\cos\alpha\cos(2\phi-\alpha) - \beta\chi\sin^2\phi = 0 \tag{7.17}$$

from which the value of ϕ can be found in terms of α and $\beta\chi$. The nature of the energy minimum can be appreciated from the graphical plot shown in Figure 7.8a.

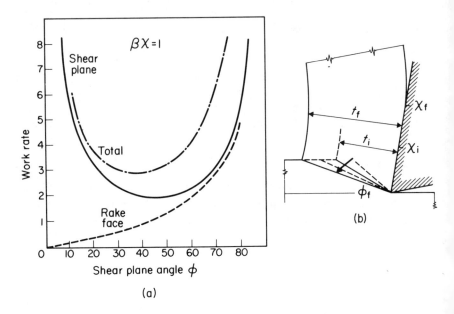

Figure 7.8 The theoretical energy required for cutting, as a function of shear-plane angle

It is widely accepted, on experimental evidence, that there is a zone of sticking friction near the nose of the tool. To a good approximation this can be taken to extend over the whole of the region visibly smeared with workpiece material on the tool, from which χ can be inferred, and for which $\beta = 1$. The small contribution of shear work in the adjacent narrower band of elastic contact can usually be neglected

This simplified model provides semi-quantitative explanations of several major features of metal cutting. With a brittle material such as magnesium, or tellurium—copper, the swarf appears as broken chips, shearing on a fairly straight line at an angle close to the predicted value ϕ_0 for zero friction. The condition for this is, substituting $\beta = 0$ in equation 7.16

$$\cos\alpha\cos(2\phi-\alpha) = 0; \quad 2\phi_0 = 90 + \alpha \tag{7.18}$$

In other words, ϕ bisects the angle between the tool face and the direction of cutting. No values of ϕ greater than this are found; the swarf is always thicker than t_1.

A major function of lubrication is found to be the reduction of contact length OC, and hence χ, rather than a reduction in coefficient of friction. A small sticking-friction zone, sometimes with a dead zone known as a built-up edge, can still be found in the presence of a lubricant. Reduction in χ increases the angle ϕ, and reduces the force.

Although the model assumes constant shear stress, it is possible to extend it to include strain-hardening. Qualitatively, it can be seen that it will require more energy to continue shear along OB (Figure 7.7) after a small strain-increment has hardened this zone. It may in fact require less energy to cause shear along a slightly longer path, at an angle $\phi - \Delta\phi$, in the unhardened material. The shear plane will therefore, on the minimum energy principle, tend to descend to lower values of ϕ as hardening proceeds, as shown in Figure 7.8b. This can be followed in some detail in both hot and cold machining. With annealed stock, the shear plane may become almost horizontal ($\phi \sim 0$), leading to flat-based discontinuous chips of the type found with mild steel at low speeds.

Speed itself tends to reduce the shear strength of the shear plane because of the local heat generated, so the spread of the plane into a zone is reduced. This in turn reduces the pressure on the rake face, the shear-plane angle is increased, and the overall cutting force falls with increase in speed.

8

Some Suggested Experimental Studies

Metalworking is essentially practical, and a knowledge of theory is greatly enhanced by experimental work, without which it is difficult to appreciate the advantages and limitations of the analytical methods. The following brief account is intended to provide a selection of illustrative experiments and to suggest various interesting additional studies. The instructions are not fully detailed, as the dimensions and materials will depend upon the available equipment, but it is hoped that sufficient information is given for the desired results to be obtained even with relatively modest plant. A 20 tonne hydraulic ram and a 5 kW geared motor provide useful power units with which most processes can be demonstrated.

8.1 Flat rolling

Objective: To use a precision cold-rolling mill in a controlled way to produce strip to a close thickness-tolerance efficiently, without exceeding a prescribed roll load.

Basic equipment: A power-driven rolling mill whose rolls are 100 mm in diameter and 150 mm in length is very suitable, but even a hand-operated mill with 25 mm diameter rolls can be used if fitted with appropriate load cells and a roll-position indicator.

Auxiliary equipment: A hardness tester or other means of measuring yield stress, such as the sub-press shown in Figure 1.1, is required. Hardness testing is easier and quicker.

Materials: For the 100 mm mill, an annealed copper strip, 75 mm wide and 10 mm thick is suitable. A length of 0·5 m should suffice to obtain steady readings.

Theoretical background: The procedure is based on the analogy between rolling and forging, equation 4.19,

$$P = \chi w L \bar{S} = \chi w \bar{S} \sqrt{(R \Delta h)}$$

The friction factor χ is evaluated after each pass and then used predictively for the next. In this way it will automatically also make allowance for roll flattening.
  Yield stress is found from hardness values, using equation 1.21.

Experimental method and measurements: For the first pass, it is necessary to measure the hardness, or yield stress, and to estimate a value of the mean yield stress $\bar{S}$ in the forthcoming pass. As this will not be accurate, a high value of χ is postulated, say 1·5. A suitable value of the reduction Δh is then calculated for a value of P close to the permitted maximum. Accuracy improves as rolling proceeds. If this exceeds the maximum bite (equation 4.16), a lower value must be chosen.
  The strip is next rolled at a speed low enough to obtain steady readings of the

load, probably 10 m/min. The thickness and hardness of the rolled strip are then measured, the latter conveniently on an off-cut. Equation 4.19 can thus be re-calculated with the known values to find the value of χ appropriate to the pass just completed. This is then used to estimate Δh for a chosen value of P in the next pass. A small calculator can easily be used, programmed if desired.

In setting the roll gap g, it is necessary to allow for the elastic distortion of the mill housing and bearings, which is known as the springback s, equation 4.22.

This springback is linear after the initial bedding-down load has been exceeded, but it is advisable to plot a graph of s against load as rolling proceeds.

The procedure of estimating a roll pass to find Δh, hence h_2 and g, then rolling and calculating χ again from the pass for use in estimating Δh for the next pass, is repeated as often as may be necessary until the final thickness is approached. By that stage, a high degree of control will have been obtained, but to make the last pass, Δh will usually differ from the value for maximum load. It is advisable to split the final pass into two halves so that accurate information on χ and s is available from the penultimate pass, of roughly equal magnitude, for calculation of the last pass.

General result: It is usually possible for a team of students, having no previous acquaintance with a rolling mill, to produce strip to a tolerance of ±0·02 mm using this method, keeping close to the prescribed maximum load (preferably less than the actual cut-out load of the mill) for most of the passes. A repeat can be made to improve the efficiency of the schedule if desired.

8.2 Additional experiments on rolling

(1) If rolls of other radius are available, the effect of R can readily be demonstrated, both on roll load and on limiting thickness (equations 4.19 and 4.20).

(2) If the coefficient of friction is known for the material and lubricant, the validity of equation 4.12 for roll load can be checked for a selected pass. An approximate value for μ can be found by slightly chamfering the end of the strip and pushing it gently (with a stick, not an arm) into the roll gap. The gap is slowly increased until the rolls will just bite. Equation 4.16 is then used.

(3) It is very interesting to compare the rolling schedules in this way for Al 4% Cu precipitation-hardening alloy in the annealed (450°C furnace cooled) and solution-treated (water quench from 500°C) conditions. The latter is not suitable for rolling.

(4) The plastic curve for rolling from a given thickness (Figure 4.2b) can be found and the effects of friction and yield stress examined.

8.3 Drawing a slip-line field from a deformed grid pattern

This method has many applications. It can most conveniently be applied first to a simple forging of a rectangular block with b/h ratio 2, for which the slip-line field is well-known.

Objective: To etch a grid on the surface of a sectioned aluminium block and to reduce the slip-line field after deforming the block by about 4%.

Basic equipment: Metallographic polishing equipment, preferably using a hard pad with 1 μm diamond dust as the final stage. Etching and simple 'photo-resist' technique facilities. Photographic enlargement or projection microscope.

Materials: Commercially-pure aluminium, hardened by rolling to about 20%.

Theoretical background: For the 2:1 forging ratio, the slip-line field of Figure 6.1 type is appropriate. The sticking-friction condition is simulated by degreasing the block carefully with benzene or acetone.

The circles of the grid deform into ellipses, and the directions of maximum shear strain will be at 45° to the major axis of the ellipse for a small deformation.

Experimental method: It is important first to produce an accurate grid on a smooth polished face of the workpiece. Various methods have been tried, including the insertion of radioactive or coloured wires, scribing the surface and rolling or printing ink grids. The most satisfactory method involves photographic reproduction of a grid and subsequent acidic etching. Details of a suitable technique are as follows:

A specimen, preferably of strain-hardened aluminium, is deformed to within a few per cent of the desired final shape and size. If the aluminium has been strained by more than 20% before use, it will be almost non-hardening in a small subsequent deformation. The sample is then cut in the plane to be examined and the two faces are polished flat and parallel. The greater the care taken at this stage, the better the result will be. Accuracy better than 0·01 mm should be sought. Final polishing with 1 μm diamond powder on a hard disc gives a good finish. Soft polishing pads should not be used or accuracy will be lost, especially at the edges.

One of these faces is then prepared for the photographic process. It is degreased by immersion in 5% NaOH solution and then in 35% HNO_3, after which it is washed in distilled water and dried at room temperature. A mixture of commercial 'metal-etching reagent' or 'photo-resist' emulsion and thinner, at about 2:1 ratio, is then spread thinly and uniformly over the surface. This is best done by spinning the specimen, if it is reasonably symmetrical, at say 250 rad/m for 30 seconds, or by blowing a moderate stream of air across an irregular surface. This should be done in a dark room under yellow or red light.

The coated specimen is then dried in dust-free air at room temperature for 15 min and baked in an oven at 120°C for a further 10 min. When it has cooled to room temperature a photographic negative of the grid is placed on it and held in tight contact. The emulsion is then exposed to a 300 watt ultraviolet lamp, through the grid negative, for 3 min.

The emulsion is next developed in a commercial developer for 2 min, washed and dried at 120°C again for 10 min. It can then be handled, with considerable care in open daylight again. When it is cool, the exposed metal in the grid pattern is gently swabbed with wet cotton wool soaked in 10% NaOH solution. The fine lines of hardened emulsion are still very delicate and must not be damaged at this stage. When the etching is judged to be sufficiently deep, the specimen is washed with water and dried in warm air.

Either circular- or square-mesh grids may be used. Circular grids have the advantage that they deform into ellipses whose major and minor diameters give a direct

Plate Va A 200-ton horizontal double-ended deep-drawing and ironing press, producing 193 mm diameter x 1190 mm long aluminium cylinders in a two-stage drawing operation from a preformed cup.

Plate Vb A Davey horizontal extrusion press of medium capacity (1500T) producing aluminium glazing bars.

Plate VIa A Verrina hydraulic 4-roll bending machine, forming a tubular shell from steel sheet 80 mm thick.

Plate VIb A pair of single-stand high-speed wire drawing Bull Blocks, single-draft in the foreground and twin-draft behind, arranged for independent operation or linked 3-die continuous operation.

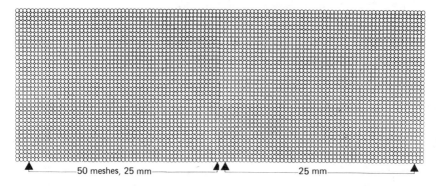

Figure 8.1 A grid suitable for use in the photo-resist etching technique. The diameter of the etched mesh should be about 0·5 mm

measure of the local strain. The centres of the circles can be used as reference points for a computer input matrix. A useful grid is reproduced in Figure 8.1.

When the specimen has been prepared, it is carefully reassembled with its polished companion and held in close contact during a deformation of about 4%. It is found that this allows the deformed elliptical meshes to be measured satisfactorily without introducing large enough overall strain to distort the slip-line field pattern unduly. If the etched surface is held tightly against the counterface, using a suitable jig in plane-strain or by close fitting in an axisymmetric die, the highly-strained regions distort and mark the polished counterface, giving an easily-recognised pattern of the most highly-strained regions.

The deformed grid is examined either by photographic enlargement or preferably at 100 x magnification in a digitised projection microscope. The major and minor axes are measured and their directions recorded for each mesh. These directions, for moderate deformation, coincide with the directions of principal strain-increment. They are plotted on a large-scale (20x) map and short lines at 45° to each axis are added. These show the local directions of maximum shear strain, assumed to coincide with the directions of maximum shear-strain rate and maximum shear stress, for the isotropic aluminium.

An experimental slip-line field can then be constructed by superimposing a square grid of comparable mesh size and transferring these directions. A line is first drawn in any square, somewhere well inside the boundaries of the specimen, right across the square in the direction of maximum shear stress. This line is then continued right across the next square, changing direction according to the 45° lines from the nearest ellipse. The process is continued until a boundary is reached, and the line is then completed in the opposite direction, after returning to the starting point. Sufficient other lines are then drawn in, using the same method, until the slip-line pattern is evident.

Usually the slip-lines so drawn do not obey all the rules of slip-line field geometry over the whole surface. In particular, they are likely to diverge near a singularity and not to remain orthogonal in high-strain regions, probably because of the finite deformation needed to recognise the ellipses. Nevertheless they can often be smoothed and adjusted to conform to ideal incremental conditions quite easily.

The agreement with theoretical solutions, where known, is good.

Friction conditions can be varied by using benzene degreasing or silicone fluid for high friction and PTFE tape or lead or indium foil for low fricton. Lanolin and other common lubricants can of course also be used.

8.4 Additional experiments on slip-line field patterns

(1) The same result can be obtained more simply and quickly but with somewhat less accuracy by using a grid impressed on plasticine.

This can be made in the form of a square mesh by using a grooved roll passed over the flat surface of the plasticine once in the longitudinal direction and then once in the transverse direction. 1 mm line spacing is appropriate. The depth should be controlled by guides or, very conveniently, by mounting a grooved mild-steel roller on the arbor of a milling machine.

A useful alternative that sometimes produces clearer results is to roll in one direction on one mating surface and in the cross-direction on the other.

Circular grids have advantages, and can easily be produced by making a matrix of uniform holes of controlled shallow depth in a perspex plate, which is then pressed onto the plasticine. Unless the holes are shallow, the grid may not be uniform. Such a plate is quickly made on a numerically-controlled miller.

Talc is a good lubricant for plasticine and should also be used as a separating agent between the surfaces. Lower friction can be obtained on the edges by using a household detergent.

(2) A special type of wax mixture (Indramic 7534, resin and kaolin) forms a brittle surface skin that will crack along lines of severe shear, thus outlining the plastic zone. Very close similarity to the boundary of a slip-line field can be obtained in forming, drawing and extrusion models. Details are given by Wanheim.

8.5 Extrusion

The split-billet technique can be used for a wide range of experiments on extrusion.

Objective: To examine flow patterns in extrusion and to correlate them with slip-line fields.

Basic equipment: A 200 or 400 tonne press is excellent, but many useful experiments can be made with plasticine models, using either rectangular (plane-strain) or cylindrical containers.

Materials: Commercially-pure aluminium usually contains enough impurities to reveal flow-lines and deformation zones clearly after etching, as well as being suitable for grid marking.

Theoretical background: The slip-line fields for simple extrusion are discussed in §6.5. These can be verified, for the frictional conditions shown in Figure 6.6, and for various area reductions.

The plastic-zone boundaries for axisymmetric extrusions can be compared with their plane-strain analogues and with the slip-line fields. Other fields for unsymmetrically-placed die orifices or multiple orifices are available or can be constructed following the general principles of §6.5.

Experimental method: The billets are made in two halves with a flat polished interface, on one side of which a grid is marked as described in §8.3. Alternatively, a
pattern of parallel grooves can be rolled onto one half and a similar pattern, at right
angles to the first, on the other. The flow and distortion lines then appear on the
respective sides.

A simpler method can be used if measurements are not required. A solid partially-
extruded billet is sectioned and polished in the usual metallographic way. It is then
deeply etched for 30 seconds in an aqueous solution containing about 15% HNO_3,
2·5% HF. The surface is then repolished with 0·3 μm alumina. The etching and
polishing sequence is repeated until a high contrast is obtained after the final
polishing.

Plasticine models with imprinted grids correlate well with the results from strain-
hardened aluminium.

8.6   Additional experiments on extrusion

(1) These techniques, using split billets, are especially interesting when applied to
extrusion-forging and other more complex processes.

A sequence of changes in flow pattern can be followed if a billet is forged
between a smooth flat platen and one containing a central orifice (see *Principles of
Industrial Metalworking Processes*, p. 270). Aluminium or plasticine may be used.

(2) A useful demonstration model can be made for use on an overhead projector. A
model billet is cast in a suitable mould using double-strength table jelly of light
colour, with a number of transverse cotton threads embedded in it. This should be
about 20 mm thick, and shaped to fit a perspex extrusion chamber fitted with dies
giving several area reductions and die angles. With a little experimentation the jelly
can be partially extruded, and the threads take up the deformation pattern. This is
readily visible on the projection screen.

8.7   Forging and section rolling

(1) Many forging experiments can be undertaken of the type described under
Extrusion, §8.5, and using the deformed mesh technique of §8.3.

It is particularly informative to perform ring compression tests, to determine
both the average coefficient of friction and the flow-stress curve.

The latter may be compared with the results obtained with a plane-strain compression test, described in §1.3.

(2) The deformation patterns in the forging of complex sections can be determined
on split billets as described in §8.3 and §8.6.

(3) It is possible to consider the transverse flow of metal in rolling as analogous to
that in forging of a similar profile. Though this is not exact, useful information can
be obtained. The technique is a little more difficult because the workpiece is not confined, so the halves of a split billet will separate. Satisfactory results can however be
obtained by sectioning the billet transversely and holding the two parts firmly in a
rectangular window-type opening cut in a steel plate that is sufficiently thin to pass
between the rolls without touching them. For example, a 25 mm rod can be rolled

into a T section in a 5 mm restraining frame whose position is adjusted between passes.

8.8 Wire-drawing

Objective: To plan an efficient sequence of passes on a wire-drawing bench for given dimensional requirements.

Basic equipment: It is convenient to use a straight chain- or hydraulic-bench to draw 10 mm bar. The effects of the inevitable die land or throat radius become important as size is reduced, and the accuracy of measuring dimensions is also poorer. To illustrate the theory, there is no need to operate at high speeds. A drawing speed of 6 m/min is satisfactory and allows short specimen rods to be used.

A load-measuring device is essential. The simple and robust Bourdon-tube type of load cell is very reliable and occupies little space behind the die.

Die profiles can be ascertained on wax replicas, using a projection microscope.

Hardness measurement or flow-stress determination is necessary (Chapter 1).

In the absence of a drawbench, useful experiments can be done at low speeds using any pulling device, including a tensile testing machine or a low-geared motor. (See Examples 3.2 and 3.5.)

A swaging machine is very useful.

Materials: Mild steel (0·1% C) is suitable for many experiments. It should be available as 0·5 m lengths at 10 mm diameter, in an annealed condition.

It is convenient to grit-blast the surfaces uniformly to a fine matt finish.

A set of WC–Co dies giving sequential 20% reductions of area down to 1 mm diameter is suitable. These should have about 12–16° included angle and no intentional throat land. A definite small radius at the throat is desirable (0·2 mm).

A second set of dies of a selected intermediate diameter, say 5 mm, but internal angles varying from 8° to 30° is useful.

Theoretical background: The theory of drawing is discussed in §3.3 and §6.4. Equation 6.11 is used in this experiment.

$$\sigma_{xa} = \phi \bar{Y} \frac{1+B}{B} [1 - (1-r)^B]$$

$$\phi = 0\cdot87 + 0\cdot78 \frac{D_b + D_a}{D_b - D_a} \frac{1 - \cos \alpha}{2 \sin \alpha}$$

Experimental method and calculation: The stock material is annealed and pickled to remove scale, or preferably annealed in vacuum. It is then uniformly and lightly grit-blasted, if possible, to produce a uniform fine matt surface. This encourages lubricant throughput and avoids the danger of pickup without the necessity for phosphating. Otherwise, the rods should be lightly abraded with emery paper in the circumferential, not longitudinal, direction.

The ends then have to be pointed or swaged so that they will pass through the die into the grip. If no swaging machine is available this will need to be done carefully by hand with a file and a hammer. Particular care should be taken with the shoulders, where lubrication is most likely to fail. These should again be grit-blasted before drawing.

The rods can be lubricated by hand with a drawing soap, paste or grease, and then drawn at about 6 m/min with as smooth a start as possible.

The value of μ is calculated from equation 6.11 for each pass, either programming a calculator for an iterative solution, or performing a few iterations manually.

General Results: From these values, a new schedule with other constraints can be prepared, for example requiring wire at 5 mm and 3 mm as well as 1 mm exactly (±0·02). (See Example 3.7.)

The results usually indicate that a double 20% pass (36% total) is possible. This can be tried, with care, by omitting one die in the sequence.

The effects of die angle on forces can be demonstrated with the constant-reduction set of dies showing the optimum.

8.9 Additional experiments on drawing

(1) A similar set of experiments can be undertaken with tubular stock, of similar external dimensions. The effects of a moving mandrel, gripped with the swaged tag, or of a fixed plug, held on a back stop, can be studied.

(2) A plane-strain analogue of tube-drawing can be set up using strips of section 6 mm x 1 mm. It is then fairly easy to measure die separating forces as well as plug-bar and main drawing tensions.

8.10 Metal cutting

Objective: To demonstrate the effect of cutting speed upon the forces and chip formation in lathe cutting.

Basic equipment: A screw-cutting lathe capable of machining 50–100 mm diameter stock at surface speeds between 0·05 and 2·5 m/s.

Auxiliary equipment: A tool-post dynamometer capable of measuring forces up to about 2 kN. This can conveniently be of a cantilever type with displacements measured by dial gauges or preferably electronic transducers.

A separate quick-stop unit is useful but not essential. This can be made by pivoting the tool holder in a robust frame fitting on the cross-slide. The tool rests on a brittle shear pin, which can conveniently be made from 5 mm diameter quenched 0·4% C steel with suitable narrow saw slots on the under side. A sliding plunger above the tool can be hit smartly with a hammer to fracture this pin, allowing the tool to pivot down into a bed of clay. The chip root area can then be cut out, sectioned, polished and etched to show the deformation and built-up edge, if any.

Materials: 50–100 mm bars of soft iron, mild steel (0·1% C) and a free-cutting steel, used in the hot-rolled condition.

Tungsten–titanium carbide tools ground with 6° rake angle, 6° clearance angle and set to 0° approach angle. A fixed nose radius of about 0·8 mm is desirable.

Theoretical background: The simplified theory of §7.7 is appropriate. Equation

7.17 and Figure 7.8 show that the shear-plane angle is strongly dependent upon the product $\beta\chi$. This represents the drag force on the rake face, or the energy expended by shearing there. The cutting force and the chip thickness will consequently be closely associated with the contact on the rake face, which can be altered by speed, lubrication and material properties.

Experimental method and measurements: The stock is machined without coolant, at say 0·16 mm/rev feed, 1·25 mm depth of cut, and the forces in the cutting direction and normal to it are recorded at various speeds. The average chip thickness can be measured with a micrometer or by weighing.

Quick-stop sections should be taken at the highest available speed and at about 0·5 m/s.

The area of sticking friction or of built-up edge can be estimated roughly by visual inspection in a low-power microscope. The total area of contact can be made more visible by depositing a thin film of soot on the tool before the test.

General results: The cutting force falls rapidly with speed for soft iron but is much higher than for mild steel, with or without a free-cutting additive. This is associated with a longer tool-face contact and a lateral spread of the chip.

Free-cutting mild steel requires low force and is little affected by speed. Plain mild steel shows a dip in the force curve at about 0·5 m/s, associated with the formation of a built-up edge and a thinner chip.

8.11 Additional experiments on cutting

(1) The reduction in forces and in chip thickness with fatty-chlorinated and other lubricants can be studied. It is instructive to compare the effects of a jet of oxygen or a jet of nitrogen directed at the tool interface. At low speeds, in dry conditions, the oxygen reduces tool-face contact and reduces forces. Even atmospheric oxygen has a significant effect.

(2) The wear of a high-speed steel tool can be studied by examining the flank scar. More sensitive measurements are possible using implanted radioactive ions.

(3) Similar experiments with non-ferrous alloys are interesting. Beryllium-copper often gives a shear-plane angle close to the zero-friction value (equation 7.18) and magnesium produces discontinuous chips at a similar angle. The effects of strain-hardening are best demonstrated using rolled strips of copper or aluminium in a shaping operation.

(4) Tool rake angle is important and its effects on forces, chip thickness and surface roughness can be seen.

Examples

Use the stress-strain data of the Chapter 1 examples where appropriate. When it is necessary to assume constant yield stress, use suitable mean values.

Chapter 1

1.1 The following data were obtained in a tensile test using a 15 mm diameter mild steel specimen with a 50 mm gauge length:

Load:	42·05	41·85	47·43	51·32	54·80	57·59	59·98	62·28	63·77 kN
Length:	51·18	51·59	52·37	53·16	53·92	54·71	55·50	56·29	57·05 mm

Load:	64·86	66·16	69·35	70·74	70·55	68·95	58·69	48·33 kN
Length:	57·83	58·62	61·95	68·78	71·12	71·52	72·31	72·64 mm

Plot the stress–strain curve in terms of
  (a) nominal stress and strain
  (b) true stress and logarithmic strain
What would be the yield stress of this material after compression by 20% reduction of area?

1.2 The following data were obtained in plane-strain compression tests on (1) annealed 60/40 brass and (2) the same material after cold rolling to 41% reduction of area. The platens were 5·0 mm broad and were well lubricated. The initial dimensions of the test piece were chosen to be about 40 mm wide and 5 mm thick.

(1) Load:

0	5	50	70	80	89	100	120	149	175	199 kN

Thickness:

5·00	5·00	4·88	4·62	4·47	4·29	4·09	3·61	2·51	1·17	0·66 mm

Width:

39·4	39·4	39·4	39·4	39·4	39·4	39·6	39·6	40·1	41·4	42·2 mm

(2) Load:

0	75	120	130	135	140	145	150	170 kN

Thickness:

5·61	5·59	5·46	5·05	4·60	4·04	3·43	2·51	1·30 mm

Width:

36·3	36·3	36·3	36·5	36·5	36·6	36·6	37·1	38·1 mm

Plot the stress–strain curves of these specimens using true stress and (a) nominal strain, (b) logarithmic strain.
What is the yield stress of the material after 80% reduction of area?
How could the accuracy of the results be improved?

1.3 Plot the true stress–logarithmic-strain curves for 0·15% C steel, for commercial purity aluminium, and for high-conductivity copper from the following data:

(a) Mild steel
Load:

0	10	20	41	60	81	100	120	141	150	159	170 kN

Thickness:

5·16	5·16	5·16	5·10	5·05	4·90	4·52	3·99	3·18	2·74	2·29	1·80 mm

Width:

37·3	37·3	37·3	37·3	37·3	37·5	37·5	37·8	38·1	38·1	38·3	38·6 mm

(b) Aluminium
Load:

0	5	10	12	14	16	18	20	22	24	26	28 kN

Thickness:

5·18	5·18	5·13	5·08	5·00	4·93	4·80	4·65	4·39	4·09	3·73	3·38 mm

Width:

40·1	40·1	40·2	40·2	40·4	40·5	40·6	40·6	40·7	40·8	40·9	41·1 mm

(c) Copper
Load:

0	20	30	40	50	60	65	70	75	80	85	90 kN

Thickness:

5·03	4·80	4·62	4·47	4·19	3·84	3·63	3·40	3·20	3·02	2·84	2·59 mm

Width:

38·6	38·6	38·6	38·8	38·8	38·9	39·1	39·4	39·4	39·6	39·8	40·1 mm

The equipment used is the same as in Example 1.2.

1.4 What would be the total strain experienced by a block compressed under ideal conditions in five successive passes, each giving 20% reduction of area?

1.5 What would be the yield stress of the block after five successive 20% passes, assuming the material to be the same as that tested in Example 1.2?

1.6 Plot a graph showing the relationship between ϵ_c and e_c, or r, up to 98% reduction of area.

1.7 Approximate to the true-stress–natural-strain curve found in Example 1.2 (a) by a linear hardening law, (b) by an exponential law. What errors are involved in those approximations for passes from 0 to 42% reduction of area, 0–18%, 18%–42% and 42%–64%?

1.8 The hardness of a cold-rolled strip is found to be 193 in a Brinell test. What is its approximate yield stress in N/mm²?

1.9 Suggest suitable dimensions for a plane-strain compression test apparatus to be used on 6 mm thick 0·2% C steel, assuming that the stress–strain curve resembles that of Example 1.3 but that the yield stress may be about 10% higher. A 500 kN press is available.

Chapter 2

2.1 In a plane-stress system $\sigma_x = 750$ N/mm², $\sigma_y = 150$ N/mm², $\sigma_z = 0$ and $\tau_{xy} = 150$ N/mm². What are the magnitudes and directions of the principal stresses?

2.2 Show that the normal stress on the planes of maximum shear is equal to the mean of the principal stresses
(a) from first principles
(b) by constructing the Mohr circle

2.3 A compressive stress of 150 N/mm² is applied between opposite faces of a 250 mm steel cube. Determine the normal forces on the other two pairs of faces that would prevent the cube from expanding by more than 0·050 mm.
For steel $E = 207$ kN/mm², $\nu = 0·3$.

2.4 What are the directions and magnitudes of the maximum shear stresses in Example 2.1?

2.5 If $\sigma_x = 450$ N/mm², $\sigma_y = 450$ N/mm², $\sigma_z = 0$ and $\tau_{xy} = 150$ N/mm², what are the principal stresses and the maximum shear stresses?

2.6 If the stress system of Example 2.1 just causes yielding, what is the uniaxial yield stress Y of the material, according to (a) the Tresca criterion, (b) the von Mises criterion?

2.7 If the same material is used as in Example 2.6, would the stress system of Example 2.5 cause plastic flow? Would the material yield if $\sigma_x = 450$ N/mm², $\sigma_y = 450$ N/mm², $\sigma_z = 450$ N/mm² and $\tau_{xy} = 150$ N/mm²?

2.8 The yield stress of a tensile specimen machined from a 500 mm wide, 5 mm thick copper strip is found to be 340 N/mm². The strip is further rolled, with an applied tension of 250 kN. What roll pressure would just cause deformation, ignoring any friction effects?

Chapter 3

3.1 A 2·50 mm diameter annealed brass wire is drawn to 2·15 mm diameter. Calculate the approximate minimum drawing load. What would this be if the wire had been annealed at 3·20 mm diameter and drawn to 2·50 mm before this pass?

3.2 A 7·5 kW electric motor is geared to a draw-bench speed of 0·1 m/s. What would be the maximum size of round steel bar that could be drawn under ideal conditions in a pass reducing its diameter by 1·60 mm?

3.3 A copper wire is annealed at 2·12 mm diameter. What is the smallest diameter to which it could theoretically be drawn in (a) one pass; (b) three passes?

3.4 A nickel-silver ribbon 10 mm wide and 0·50 mm thick is drawn to 0·30 mm thick through dies of 20° included angle. The hardness of the drawn strip is found to be 165 V.P.N. Estimate the drawing load and the die pressure, assuming $\mu = 0·08$. If all the work done appeared as heat, what would be the temperature rise in the strip?

3.5 An annealed steel strip 10 mm wide and 0·40 mm thick is drawn to 0·30 mm thick through dies of 24° included angle, at 2·0 m/s. What is the total work expended in drawing a 50 kg coil, assuming $\mu = 0·10$? If the efficiency of the drawbench drive is 85%, what would be the input current to the driving motor on a 230 volt main? What would be the cost of electricity at 2·2p per unit (kWh)?

3.6 Compare the force required to draw 25 mm x 6 mm copper strip to 45% reduction of area with that required for an equal reduction on round bar of the same cross-sectional area, using (a) 12° included-angle dies, (b) 30° included-angle dies, if $\mu = 0·07$. Redundant work may be neglected.

3.7 Annealed brass wire is to be drawn from 6 mm diameter to 1·5 mm with an intermediate annealing at about 3 mm. Suggest a suitable drawing schedule for a wire-drawing machine with a maximum pull of 4·5 kN. The dies may be ground to any angle, but the best available lubricant gives $\mu = 0·04$.

3.8 Determine the total equivalent strain in copper wire drawn from the annealed condition at 3 mm diameter to 0·075 mm using a die of 20° included angle, with (a) the theoretical maximum reduction in each pass, (b) 19% reduction of area in each pass.

3.9 Compare the drawing loads for plug- and mandrel-drawing of annealed mild-steel tube from 50 mm internal diameter and 2·5 mm wall thickness to 49 mm I.D. x 1·8 mm. Assume that the included angle of the die is $2\alpha = 30°$ and that $\mu = 0·10$.

3.10 Suggest a tandem die arrangement to allow tubes to be drawn with 65% reduction of area in one pass.

3.11 Suggest a plug-drawing schedule for reducing 50 mm O.D. x 6 mm mild steel tube to 12 mm O.D. x 0·9 mm, and calculate the size of equipment required, assuming reasonable values of the necessary parameters. The strain should not exceed 80% between annealing processes.

3.12 What is the maximum size of stainless steel tube that can be drawn by 25% reduction of area in a close pass on a draw-bench with 200 kN pull? Assume $S \approx 0·75$ kN/mm².

3.13 Approximately what power is required for a draw-bench driven by a geared motor of overall efficiency 85%, to be used in drawing annealed copper tube from 40 mm O.D. x 3 mm to 30 mm O.D. x 2·4 mm with a conical die of 24° included angle and a suitable floating plug, at a speed of 1·6 m/sec? Assume zero plug-bar force.

3.14 Estimate the force required for sinking a 100 mm O.D. x 12 mm mild steel tube to 90 mm O.D., using a die with semi-angle 15°, and a lubricant giving $\mu = 0.05$.

3.15 To remove scale, a hot steel bloom 3 m long, 0·7 m wide and 0·7 m thick is compressed longitudinally by 5%. If the yield stress is 60 N/mm², what capacity press is required? What load would be necessary to perform the operation if the bloom were allowed to cool to room temperature first?

3.16 Evaluate the press capacity necessary for forging a 1 m long cylindrical bloom to hexagonal section with approximately 300 mm side, if the yield stress is initially 75 N/mm² but increases to 120 N/mm² at the end of the operation. Assume (a) that the bloom is partially lubricated so that $\mu = 0.3$, (b) that there is no lubrication. What maximum pressures would be expected?

3.17 What load is required to forge a 300 mm long 600 mm diameter cylindrical steel billet to 80% of its original length between flat platens (a) at room temperature with good lubrication ($\mu = 0.05$), (b) at 900°C where $Y = 60$ N/mm² but there is sticking friction?

3.18 Approximately what forging load would be required to transform a 1 m long, 1 m diameter cylindrical bloom into a square section of equal area in a hydraulic press? $Y = 60$ N/mm².

Chapter 4

4.1 What would be the approximate roll load necessary to reduce 2 m wide, 2·50 mm thick aluminium sheet to 2·00 mm thick in one pass at room temperature, using 350 mm diameter rolls?

4.2 If the pass in Example 4.1 were increased from a draft 0·50 mm to 0·75 mm, what influence would there be on the roll load?

4.3 If the maximum roll capacity is 1 MN, suggest a suitable rolling schedule for the operation described in Example 4.1. Could a similar schedule be prepared if the material were mild steel instead of aluminium?

4.4 (a) An annealed mild steel strip 2·50 mm thick is rolled to 2·00 mm in one pass and then to 1·50 mm. What is the mean yield stress in the second pass? What error would be involved in assuming the yield stress constant at its final value?
(b) If the strip is further rolled to 1·25 mm, what would be the mean yield stress for this pass, and by how much would it differ from the final yield stress?

4.5 What roll load is necessary to roll 150 mm x 6 mm copper strip, previously rolled 30%, with 20% reduction of area using 350 mm diameter steel rolls? What roll load would be necessary in a further 20% reduction-of-area pass? What would be the maximum deflection of the roll surface, assuming Hitchcock flattening?

4.6 What roll load is required to roll 500 mm x 2·50 mm mild steel strip, previously rolled 30%, to 2·40 mm thick with 350 mm diameter steel rolls? What is the Hitchcock flattening (a) in the absence of tensions, (b) with front tension equal to 150 N/mm² and back tension equal to 75 N/mm²? What is the thinnest gauge to which this strip can be rolled without tensions on this mill?

4.7 A mill housing is 3 m high and is designed for a maximum tensile stress of 12 N/mm². Calculate the elastic extension of the housing under full load.

4.8 Suggest a suitable size and power of rolling mill for production of 750 mm wide 0·40 mm thick mild steel sheet in two passes from annealed sheet 0·80 mm thick.

4.9 Estimate rolling schedules for cold annealed copper and mild steel strips from 400 x 3·00 mm to 400 x 2·40 mm with 150 mm diameter rolls on a 4-high mill, if the roll load may not exceed 1000 kN. Find the ratio of the power requirements for the two materials.

Chapter 5

5.1 Show, by considering the equilibrium of a small element in the plastic zone, that

$$\frac{\partial \sigma_x}{\partial x} + \frac{\partial \tau_{yx}}{\partial y} = 0 \text{ and } \frac{\partial \sigma_y}{\partial y} + \frac{\partial \tau_{xy}}{\partial x} = 0.$$ Hence, using the fact that k is constant along a slip-line,

show that $\dfrac{\partial \sigma_\alpha}{\partial \alpha} = 0 = \dfrac{\partial \sigma_\beta}{\partial \beta}$.

5.2 The yield stress of an ideal rigid-plastic material in plane-strain compression is 600 N/mm². If a block of this material is subjected to a hydrostatic compression of 450 N/mm², what principal stresses would just cause plastic flow? What is the magnitude of the shear stress on a plane inclined at 20° to one principal plane?

5.3 Show by consideration of two pairs of α-lines and β-lines, using the Hencky equations, that the angle between two slip-lines of one family, where they are cut by a slip-line of the other family, is constant along their length.

5.4 The coefficient of friction for lubrication of mild steel is found to be $\mu = 0·04$ for soap and $\mu = 0·11$ for an oil. At what angles would the slip-lines be inclined to the tool–workpiece interface when using each of these lubricants?

5.5 Sketch the distribution of hydrostatic pressure 10 mm beneath a long 75 mm wide, flat indenter which is loaded so that plastic flow just occurs in a very thick block.

5.6 An experimental inverted extrusion with tellurium lead is planned to reduce a 75 mm wide x 12 mm thick billet to 75 mm wide x 6 mm thick, using a square die. What capacity press will be needed? Assume that $S = 25$ N/mm². What effect does the length of the billet have on the pressure?

5.7 Write a short account of the purpose of slip-line field theory. What is its significance in practical metalworking? What assumptions are necessary to slip-line field theory but not to the stress-evaluation method?

Chapter 6

6.1 Draw a slip-line field and hodograph for plane-strain compression of a flat billet whose cross-section is 1 m x 165 mm. Assume (a) zero friction and (b) sticking friction.

6.2 What pressure would be required for the compression of Example 6.1?

6.3 A series of 8 straight-sided parallel grooves 6 mm wide with 6 mm separation is to be formed along a thick aluminium blank 100 mm wide and 300 mm long. If a suitable forging tool is used in a hydraulic press, what initial force would be necessary? How much would this increase by the time the punch had penetrated to a depth of 6 mm? Assume that the blank has previously been forged, so that the yield stress is sensibly constant at 150 N/mm².

6.4 What force would be necessary to form 8 grooves of 60° included angle to the same depth in the blank of Example 6.3?

6.5 Draw two graphs showing the redundant work factors for strip-drawing and for wire-drawing, in terms of appropriate geometrical parameters. Re-draw these graphs to show the redundant work factors as functions of die angle for various reductions of area between 10% and 60%.

6.6   What are the optimum die angles for strip-drawing and wire-drawing with 30% reduction of area if $\mu = 0.04$? How is the power requirement affected by departure from the optimum? (For strip-drawing the redundant work factor is $f\left(\dfrac{c}{d}\right) = f\left(\dfrac{2-r}{r}.\ \alpha\right)$, negligible for 2° and 5° but equal to 1·38 for 14°. The influence of strain-hardening may be ignored.)

6.7   Draw the slip-line field and the hodograph for 20% reduction of area of non-hardening wide strip with dies of semi-angle 20°, assuming $\mu = 0.10$. What redundant strain is involved? (It is necessary to evaluate q by drawing the field for $\mu = 0$ first.)

6.8   If the ductility of homogeneously-deformed brass can be expressed in the form

$$el\% = 42 \exp(-7.5\epsilon)$$

determine the ductility of a 25 mm × 3 mm brass strip drawn to 25 mm × 2·4 mm using dies of 20° semi-angle, ignoring the influence of friction. Compare this with the ductility when drawn to the same reduction of area under ideal conditions. Assume a redundant work factor $f\left(\dfrac{2-r}{r}.\ \alpha\right) = 1.53$.

6.9   Estimate the average temperature rise of the strip in Example 6.8, assuming the frictional heating to be equal to the heat loss by convection.

6.10   Draw the slip-line field for 2:1 extrusion with a 150° included-angle die, (a) with zero friction (b) with dead zone formation.

6.11   Draw the hodographs for 2:1 extrusion with a 150° included-angle die (a) with zero friction and, using the slip-line fields of Example 6.10 (b) with dead zone formation.

6.12   What would be the maximum possible extrusion ratio for cold plane-strain extrusion of aluminium ($\overline{S} = 250$ N/mm²) through a frictonless 120° die using a 2500 kN press taking 150 × 25 mm billets? (It is convenient to draw the slip-line field to a scale giving the final strip thickness $h_2 = 50$ mm, so the diagram occupies a space about 300 mm high and 250 mm wide.)

6.13   Draw the slip-line field for 10:1 plane-strain direct extrusion (a) with a frictionless 180° die and (b) with a dead zone. (The second diagram occupies about 300 × 300 mm if the first strip thickness is chosen to be represented by $h_2 = 50$ mm.)

6.14   Draw the slip-line field and hodograph for 4·3:1 extrusion through a frictionless square die, and from these draw the flow-lines of metal passing through the plastic zone.

6.15   Draw a slip-line field and hodograph for 3:1 extrusion with a frictionless 180° die, using 10° intervals in the slip-line field. Superimpose the metal flow-lines on the slip-line field.

6.16   Estimate the pressure required to extrude aluminium curtain rail of I section 12 mm high with 6 mm wide flanges, all 1·6 mm thick, from 25 mm diameter bar stock.

6.17   Estimate the largest possible extrusion ratio for cold extrusion of 25 mm diameter, 3 mm-wall mild-steel tube in a 10000 kN press.

Chapter 7

7.1   Evaluate the pressure for 2:1 extrusion, using the shear field and hodograph of Figure 7.

7.2   Evaluate the pressure for 2:1 extrusion, using a shear field similar to that shown in Figure 7.2, but subdividing each fan AOB into four equal sectors.

7.3   Sketch a suitable upper-bound solution for high-friction, plane-strain extrusion with a ratio 10:1, bearing in mind the slip-line fields shown in Figure 6.6, and your solution to Example 6.13. Calculate the extrusion pressure from this field.

7.4 Estimate the pressure required for indentation, using an upper-bound solution based on Figure 5.7*a*. How could a more accurate result be calculated?

7.5 Estimate the pressure required to compress a billet with width: height ratio 3·6:1, using upper-bound fields for (a) zero friction, (b) sticking friction.

7.6 Suggest an upper-bound solution for indentation with a wedge of 60° included angle. What pressure would be required (a) with perfect lubrication and (b) with sticking friction?

7.7 Suggest an upper-bound solution for strip-drawing, based on the slip-line field shown in Figure 6.3. Calculate the drawing force for (a) zero friction, (b) sticking friction and (c) a shear stress $\tau = 0 \cdot 1k$ acting on the die face.

7.8 Plot the metal flow and distortion for 10:1 extrusion with high friction, using an upper-bound field based on your solution to Example 6.13.

7.9 If the angles of two unsymmetrical dies in a 2:1 extrusion are respectively 40° and 20°, find the angle at which the product may be expected to leave the die exit, and estimate the extrusion pressure using both a slip-line field and an upper-bound solution.

7.10 Suggest an upper-bound solution for backward extrusion of a can with wall-thickness equal to one quarter of the outer radius. Calculate the pressure needed.

7.11 Show, using the hodograph in Figure 7.7, that the shear velocity u in an orthogonal cutting operation can be expressed in terms of the shear-plane angle ϕ and the rake angle α as $u = \sin \phi \sec (\phi - \alpha)$.

Solutions

Chapter 1

1.1 (a) The nomimal stress s is found by dividing the load P by the original cross-sectional area, $A_0 = 176 \cdot 7$ mm² for each value given. The nominal strain e is found from $e = (l - l_0)/l_0$.

(b) The true stress σ is found by dividing each load value P by the actual cross-sectional area A at that stage of the test. Because the volume remains constant in plastic deformation (at $V_0 = 8836$ mm³), $A = A_0 l_0/l$, and $\sigma = Pl/8836$ N/mm², up to the maximum stress.

The logarithmic strain $\epsilon = \ln l_1/l_0$, equation 1.1.

At 20% reduction of area by compression, $\epsilon = \ln \dfrac{A_0}{A} = 0 \cdot 223$, and the appropriate yield stress is $0 \cdot 492$ kN/mm².

This assumes that the true stress is identical for yielding in tension and in compression.

1.2 (1) The true stress is found by dividing the load P by the area of contact, which is the product of the strip width w and the platen breadth b. For example, at $P = 149$ kN, $\sigma = 149/(5 \cdot 0 \times 40 \cdot 1) = 0 \cdot 743$ kN/mm². It is quite common to assume no change in strip width, which would predict a stress $\sigma' = 0 \cdot 756$ kN/mm² in this instance. It is instructive to plot both in this example.

The nominal strain is $(h_0 - h)/h_0$; for example at $P = 149$, $h = 2 \cdot 51$, $\epsilon = 0 \cdot 498$. The true strain is $\epsilon = \ln h_0/h$, which at $P = 149$ is $0 \cdot 689$. At 80% reduction of area, $\epsilon_c = \ln 1/(1 - e_c)$ $= \ln 5 \cdot 0 = 1 \cdot 61$. From the curve $S \approx 0 \cdot 86$ kN/mm² so $Y \approx 0 \cdot 75$ kN/mm².

The accuracy could be improved by taking more readings in the range $150 - 200$ kN, which covers a large range of strains. It will be noticed that at the end of the test the h/b ratio has become small: at $P = 175$, $h/b = 0 \cdot 234$; at $P = 199$, $h/b = 0 \cdot 132$. The last point will therefore be high, because of friction on the platens. These should strictly be changed for narrower ones and the coefficient of friction μ evaluated, from equation 1.12. An allowance can however be made by assuming a reasonable value of μ. Thus, from equation 3.34

$$\bar{p} = 2k \left(1 + \tfrac{1}{2} \mu \frac{b}{h} \right)$$

For the last point of the curve, assuming $\mu = 0 \cdot 02$ or $0 \cdot 05$,

$$\frac{\bar{p}}{2k} = 1 + \tfrac{1}{2} . \mu . 7 \cdot 6 = 1 \cdot 08 \text{ or } 1 \cdot 20$$

bringing the true stress to $0 \cdot 87$ or $0 \cdot 79$ instead of $0 \cdot 94$ kN/mm². Similar corrections can also be applied to the measurements at 175 and 149 kN.

(2) The true stress and true strain are evaluated as above, but the stress–strain curve should be plotted from an initial strain $\epsilon_{01} = \ln 1/(1 - 0 \cdot 41) = 0 \cdot 528$. It will be found that this curve superimposes quite closely on that obtained from the data of part 1 of this example, particularly when allowance is made for friction in both, assuming $\mu = 0 \cdot 02$. With this correction the yield stress at 80% reduction is found to be $S \approx 0 \cdot 80$ kN/mm².

1.3 The graphs are plotted in the same way as in the preceding example. They will be needed in later examples.

1.4 The separate passes are:
$1 - 0 \cdot 8$; $0 \cdot 8 - 0 \cdot 64$; $0 \cdot 64 - 0 \cdot 512$; $0 \cdot 512 - 0 \cdot 410$; $0 \cdot 410 - 0 \cdot 328$.
Thus $r_{05} = 0 \cdot 672$.

Considering logarithmic strain, each pass imparts

$$\epsilon_{01} = \ln 1/(1-e_C) = \ln 1/0.8 = 0.223$$

The total strain is $\epsilon_{05} = 5$, $\epsilon_{01} = 1.116$;

$$1/(1-e_C) = \exp(1.116) = 3.05; \quad e_C = 0.672$$

For complex schedules the logarithmic strain is more convenient, and it is useful to prepare a conversion graph relating ϵ_C and e_C as in Example 1.6.

1.5 At $\epsilon = 1.116$, $S = 0.76 \text{ kN/mm}^2$, so $Y = 0.66 \text{ kN/mm}^2$ after correction for friction in the test.

1.6 This graph is useful for many metalworking calculations. It is plotted using information from §1.1. Some typical values are:

r	20%	30%	40%	50%	60%	63.2%	80%
ϵ	0.223	0.357	0.511	0.693	0.916	1.00	1.61

The most convenient form of this graph is in two parts, 0–65% and 65–100%. These can be plotted on A4 paper.

1.7 (a) Using the graph corrected for spread, and assuming $\mu = 0.05$, a suitable linear approximation at high reductions is from $S = 0.80$ at $\epsilon = 2.0$ to $S = 0.74$ at $\epsilon = 0.8$, which extrapolates to $S = 0.7$ at $\epsilon = 0$. This involves no error for strains beyond $\epsilon = 0.8$, 55% reduction of area. For light reductions, large errors would be introduced. Thus for the pass 0–42%, $\epsilon_{01} = 0.545$, the value of $\bar{S}$ deduced would be 0.715 compared with the value derived from the area of the true curve, $\bar{S} = 0.52$.

Straight lines can be used to approximate to selected portions of the curve. Thus from 0–18% a line from $S = 0.22$ at $\epsilon = 0$ to $S = 0.50$ at $\epsilon = 0.198$ gives $\bar{S} = 0.36$ compared with $\bar{S} = 0.37$ from the areas.

The accuracy over any selected range depends only on drawing the appropriate line, and can usually be within about 2%, but a single line approximation to the whole curve is reliable only for very heavy reductions.

(b) To make the exponential approximation, $\log 10S$ is plotted against $\log 10\epsilon$. The best straight line over the larger reductions is found to be one from $\log 10S = 0.9$ at $\log 10\epsilon = 1.20$ to $\log 10S = 0.72$ at $\log 10\epsilon = 0.20$. Over the whole range a straight line can be drawn from $(-0.6, 0.45)$ to $(1.2, 0.93)$.

If this is replotted as S against ϵ, there is a satisfactory agreement up to $\epsilon = 1.2$. From 0–18% /a, the error is negligible. From 18%–42% this exponential underestimates $\bar{S}$ by about 5%. From 42%–64% there is a comparable underestimate.

The equation is sometimes useful in the form $S = 0.753\epsilon^{0.267}$.

1.8 From equation 1.21, $Y \approx 193/0.3 = 643 \text{ N/mm}^2$.

1.9 Maximum load 500 kN. For most purposes the compression test is not required to extend beyond about 80% reduction, because reannealing would be necessary before further deformation. Thus the greatest value of ϵ is about 1.6 and the corresponding yield stress about 1.0 kN/mm², found by extrapolating the graph, from Example 1.3, to 0.92 kN/mm² at $\epsilon = 1.6$ and adding 10%.

The plane-strain compression test platens should have a breadth b between 2 and 4 times the specimen thickness (Chapter 1, §1.3). This suggests a platen breadth $b = 12 \text{ mm}$ at the start. To ensure plane strain, the strip width w should then be $5b$, namely 60 mm. These platens can be used until the yield stress reaches $500/720 = 0.694 \text{ kN/mm}^2$, which permits a strain of only $\epsilon \approx 0.26$. Either (a) the width requirement could be relaxed to say $4b$, permitting a yield stress up to 868 kN/mm² and a strain up to 0.63; or (b) the stock material could be reduced in thickness and reannealed before starting the test.

(a) Suppose that 50 mm wide strip was chosen. At $\epsilon = 0.63$ the thickness would be given y $\ln 6/h_1 = 0.63$, $h_1 = 3.19 \text{ mm}$. The platens could then be replaced by a second set with 7 mm readth. These would then be suitable until the thickness was reduced to $7/4 = 1.7 \text{ mm}$, a strain of 1·26. The load would thus be $50 \times 7 \times 990\,N = 346\,kN$, within the capacity of the machine. The platens could then be changed again, or allowance could be made for friction in the remainder of the test, using equation 3.34.

(b) Preferably the strip should be thinner, e.g. $h = 5\,mm$, with $b = 10\,mm$, $w = 50\,mm$, used from $h = 5$ to $h = 2\cdot5$; and $b = 5$, $w = 50\,mm$ used thereafter. (At $\epsilon = 1\cdot6$, $S = 1\cdot0\,kN/mm^2$, the final load would be 250 kN.)

Chapter 2

2.1 The magnitudes of the principal stresses are found from equation 2.5, which can itself be derived easily from a Mohr circle. This gives

$$\sigma_1 = \frac{900}{2} + \tfrac{1}{2}\sqrt{36 \times 10^4 + 9 \times 10^4} = 450 + 335$$

$$\sigma_1 = 785\,N/mm^2, \qquad \sigma_2 = 115\,N/mm^2. \ (\sigma_3 = 0)$$

The angle between the principal plane and the plane on which σ_x acts is found from Figure 2.1, giving

$$\tan 2\theta^* = 300/600; \qquad \theta^* = 13\cdot3°$$

The results are also obtainable rapidly by locating the points (σ_x, τ_{xy}) and (σ_y, τ_{yx}) on a (σ, τ) diagram. The Mohr circle passing through them is centred on $(450, 0)$ and has a radius given by $R^2 = 150^2 + 300^2; R = 335\,N/mm^2$.

2.2 (a) Following the procedure § 2.1 the stationary value of τ_θ is found by differentiating equation 2.3b w.r.t. θ and equating to zero. Thus $(\sigma_x - \sigma_y) \cos 2\theta = -2\tau \sin 2\theta$. A second

differentiation gives $\dfrac{d^2\tau\theta}{d\theta^2} = -4(\tau\theta)$, showing this value to be a maximum.

Substitution in equation 2.3a gives $\sigma_\theta = \tfrac{1}{2}(\sigma_x + \sigma_y)$ on the plane of maximum shear. This must be valid for any orientations of the axes x and y, including the principal axes. Equation 2.5 also shows that $(\sigma_1 + \sigma_2) = (\sigma_x + \sigma_y)$.

(b) The answer is immediately seen from the symmetry of the Mohr circle.

2.3 If the load is applied along OZ, it is required to find the equal stresses σ_x and σ_y that produce equilibrium at the given strain; $\epsilon_x = \epsilon_y = 0\cdot050/250 = 2 \times 10^{-4}$.

$$\epsilon_x = \frac{\sigma_x}{E} - \frac{\nu\sigma_y}{E} - \frac{\nu\sigma_z}{E}$$

Thus $\sigma_x(1 - 0\cdot3) - 0\cdot3 \times (-150) = 2 \times 10^{-4} \times 207 \times 10^3$

$$0\cdot7\sigma_x = 41\cdot4 - 45\cdot0$$

$$\sigma_x = 5\cdot14\,N/mm^2; \quad F = 320\,kN$$

2.4 The results may be obtained directly from the Mohr circle. The plane on which the maximum shear stress acts is inclined at an angle θ^{**} to the plane on which σ_x acts:

$$\tan 2\theta^{**} = (750 - 150)/300; \qquad \theta^{**} = 31\cdot7°$$

This is also given by $2\theta^{**} = 90 - 2\theta^*$.
The maximum shear stress is equal to the radius of the circle:

$$R^2 = (300)^2 + (150)^2; \qquad \tau_m = 335\,N/mm^2$$

2.5 The Mohr circle passing through $\sigma_x = 450$ and $\sigma_y = 450$ must be centred on $\sigma = 450$. Thus σ_x and σ_y are the direct stresses acting on the planes of maximum shear, and $\tau_m = \tau_{xy}$ $= 150\,N/mm^2$.

The principal stresses are 600 and 300 N/mm².

It should however be noted that in a real system the third principal stress, $\sigma_3 = 0$, ought to be included, so the maximum shear stress in a three-dimensional body would be $\frac{1}{2}(\sigma_1 - \sigma_3) = 300$ N/mm².

2.6 The principal stresses are found from equations 2.5

$$\sigma_1 = \frac{\sigma_x + \sigma_y}{2} + \frac{1}{2}\sqrt{(\sigma_x - \sigma_y)^2 + 4\tau_{xy}^2}$$

$$= \frac{750 + 150}{2} + \frac{1}{2}\sqrt{(750 - 150)^2 + 4(150)^2} = 450 + 335$$

$$= 785 \text{ N/mm}^2$$

$$\sigma_2 = 450 - 335 = 115 \text{ N/mm}^2$$

(They can also be found from the Mohr circle as in Example 2.1.)

In the hypothetical plane-stress system, there are no stresses acting out of this plane so

$$\tau_m = \frac{\sigma_1 - \sigma_2}{2} = 335 \text{ N/mm}^2$$

Thus according to Tresca, $Y = 2k = 2\tau_m = 670 \text{ N/mm}^2$

It is more realistic to recognise that although no stress is applied on the planes xz and yz, a shear stress will arise within the material on a plane normal to the xy plane, because $\sigma_3 = 0$.

Then, according to Tresca $Y = 2k = 2\tau_m = \sigma_1 - \sigma_3 = 785 - 0 = 785 \text{ N/mm}^2$ and, according to von Mises

$$(785 - 115)^2 + (115 - 0)^2 + (785 - 0)^2 = 2Y^2$$

$$Y = 734 \text{ N/mm}^2$$

2.7 The maximum shear stress in Example 2.5 (equal to the radius of the circle) is 300 N/mm², which is not sufficient to cause yielding at $k = 785/2 = 393$ N/mm² (Tresca), but using von Mises criterion, $(600 - 300)^2 + (300 - 0)^2 + (0 - 600)^2 = 735$ N/mm², which would just cause yielding, by shear in the plane containing x and z.

The addition of the stress $\sigma_z = 450$ would prevent yielding because the maximum shear stress would then be 150 N/mm² with a superimposed hydrostatic tension.

2.8 The relative dimensions show that deformation occurs under plane-strain conditions. Since $Y = 340$, $S = 2k = 391$ N/mm². (Equations 2.18 and 2.13.)

The applied tensile stress is $+100$ N/mm². If there is no friction, this is a principal stress. The Mohr stress circle for plane-strain (Figure 2.3) extends from $\sigma_3 = +100$ to $\sigma_1 = -291$, since the diameter is $2k$. This can also be seen from equation 2.18, with due regard to sign

$$\sigma_1 - \sigma_3 = S; \qquad \sigma_1 - 100 = -391.$$

The roll pressure is thus decreased by the applied tension to 291 N/mm². (A more detailed method of evaluating roll pressures for various values of friction and applied tension will be described in Chapter 4, again using the condition of yielding in plane strain.)

Chapter 3

3.1 (a) The strain imparted is $\epsilon_{01} = \ln A_0/A_1$ from equation 1.3. For this pass $\epsilon_{01} = \ln (2\cdot50)^2/(2\cdot15)^2 = \ln 1\cdot35 = 0\cdot301$. $\bar{S} = \frac{1}{2}(0\cdot58 + 0\cdot20) = 0\cdot39$ kN/mm². The minimum drawing load is that required to impart the deformation homogeneously. From equation 3.5 the drawing force

$$F = A_1 \bar{Y} \ln A_0/A_1 = A_1 \bar{Y} \epsilon_{01} = 370 \text{ N}$$

(b) If the prior strain were $\epsilon_{01} = \ln (3\cdot20)^2/(2\cdot50)^2 = 0\cdot493$, the final strain would be $\epsilon_{02} = (3\cdot20)^2/(2\cdot15)^2 = 0\cdot795$ (= $0\cdot493 + 0\cdot301$). Then $\bar{S} = 0\cdot73$ kN/mm² and $F = 693$ N.

3.2 7500 watts = 7500 Nm/s. Speed 0·1 m/s. Drawbench pull F = 75 kN. Equation 3.5 gives $F = A_1 Y \ln A_0/A_1$.

The maximum size of bar that could be drawn would be expected to be the one for which 1·60 mm represented a light pass. Suppose that a reasonable value to choose for the yield stress is S = 450 N/mm², say Y = 400.

From equation 3.5

$$75 \cdot 10^3 = \frac{\pi}{4} d_1^2 . 400 \ln (d_1 + 1 \cdot 60)^2/d_1^2$$

But $d_1 \gg 1 \cdot 6$ so $\ln (d_1 + 1 \cdot 6)^2/d_1^2 \approx \ln (1 + 3 \cdot 2/d_1) \approx 3 \cdot 2/d_1$

$$75 \cdot 10^3 \approx (\pi/4) d_1^2 . 400 . 3 \cdot 2/d_1; \quad d_1 \approx 74 \cdot 6 \text{ mm}$$

This would involve a strain ϵ_{01} = ln 76·2/74·6 = 0·02.

A better value for $\overline{Y}$ would thus be about 240 N, so d_1 would be correspondingly increased:

$$d_1 \approx 74 \cdot 6 \times 400/240 = 120 \text{ mm}; \quad \epsilon_{01} \approx 0 \cdot 01$$

The exact value chosen depends upon the effective mean yield stress for very light deformations, which cannot be found accurately from the data of Example 1.3. The lower yield point of mild steel in the tensile test is however 0·23 kN/mm² (Example 1.1), so $Y \approx 240$ is reasonable, even for a very light pass.

The largest round steel bar that could be drawn under the specified conditions would thus be over 100 mm diameter, but in fact the deformation would be far from homogeneous (see Chapter 6, §6.4).

Such 'sizing' passes are commonly used in the production of bright-drawn standard bars, and the reduction is often specified as 1·5 mm (formerly 1/16 inch) off the diameter, or for larger bars 3 mm.

3.3 The maximum reduction possible under ideal conditions is given by equation 3.6, with the condition $\sigma_1 = Y_1 = Y$, as in equation 3.8

(a) $\sigma_1 = \overline{Y} \ln A_0/A_1$; A_0/A_1 = 2·7, d_0/d_1 = 1·65   so d_1 = 1·28 mm.

(b) The strain ϵ_{01} = ln A_0/A_1 = 1·0 can be applied in each of the three passes, so the maximum possible in three passes is ϵ_{03} = 3·0 ln A_0/A_3; A_0/A_3 = 20, d_0/d_3 = 4·48, d_3 = 0·47 mm.

3.4 (a) h_0 = 0·50 mm, h_1 = 0·30 mm, A_1 = 0·0707 mm², B = 0·8 cot 10° = 4·54. The drawing stress is found as in §3.3.1.

$$\frac{\sigma_x}{S} = \frac{1 \cdot 45}{0 \cdot 45} [1 - (0 \cdot 6)^{0 \cdot 45}] = 3 \cdot 22(1 - 0 \cdot 795) = 0 \cdot 66$$

The yield stress is found from the hardness, equation 1.21. 165 Vickers is approximately the same as 165 Brinell, both being expressed in kgf/mm². Thus $Y_1 \approx 165/0 \cdot 3 = 550$ N/mm², $\overline{S} \approx S_1 \approx 630$. The drawing stress is then 420 N/mm². A better value would be obtained if the hardness were measured before and after the pass, but high accuracy cannot be expected without determining yield stresses directly.

(b) The work done in drawing a length L metres of wire, equation 3.4, is

$$W = FL = 10 . 0 \cdot 30 . 420L \text{ Nm} = 1260 L \text{ joules}$$

The volume of this length is 10 × 0·30 × L × 10^{-6} m³. Since the density of nickel silver is 8·8 × 10^3 kg/m³, the weight of the strip is 26·4 × $10^{-3}L$ kg.

In the absence of accurate data, assume the specific heat to be 400 J/kg (Cu = 380, Ni = 44). Then

$$1260 L = 400 . 26 . 4 . 10^{-3}L (T_1 - T_0)$$

$$T_1 - T_0 \approx 120°C$$

3.5 Equation 3.14b gives the drawing stress. With

$$\epsilon = \ln 0\cdot 40/0\cdot 30 = 0\cdot 288, \quad B = 0\cdot 1 \cot 12° = 0\cdot 470$$

$$\frac{\sigma_1}{S} = \frac{1\cdot 47}{0\cdot 47}[1 - (0\cdot 75)^{0\cdot 47}] = 3\cdot 13 \times (1 - 0\cdot 873) = 0\cdot 40$$

Using a straight-line approximation, $\bar{S} = \frac{1}{2}(660 + 350) = 500$ N/mm², $\sigma_1 = 200$ N/mm²; $A_1 = 3\cdot 0$ mm², $F_1 = 600$ N.

Assuming the density of copper to be $7\cdot 8 \times 10^3$ kg/m³, the length L_1 of the coil is given by

$$3\cdot 0 \times 10^{-6} \times L_1 \times 7\cdot 8 \times 10^3 = 50; \quad L_1 = 2\cdot 14 \times 10^3 \text{ m}$$

The work expended in drawing the full length of the coil is $F_1 L_1 = 1280$ kNm. Speed 2 m/s. Time to draw the coil $1\cdot 07 \times 10^3$ s. Power required, 1200 Nm/s $= 1\cdot 2$ kW. With 85% efficiency, input power $= 1\cdot 41$ kW. Input current for a single-phase motor at 230 V $= 6\cdot 13$ A. Total power consumed in drawing the coil

$$1\cdot 41 \times 107 \cdot 10^3/3600 = 0\cdot 42 \text{ kWh}$$

The cost is thus 0·92p.

3.6 For strip, equation 3.14b gives

$$\frac{\sigma_{xa}}{S} = \frac{1 + B}{B}\left[1 - \left(\frac{h_a}{h_b}\right)^B\right]; \quad \begin{array}{l} B = 0\cdot 07 \cot 6° \text{ or } 0\cdot 07 \cot 15° \\ = 0\cdot 666 \quad \text{ or } 0\cdot 261 \end{array}$$

$$\alpha = 6°: \frac{\sigma_{xa}}{S} = 2\cdot 50(1 - 0\cdot 67) = 0\cdot 825$$

$$\alpha = 15°: \frac{\sigma_{xa}}{S} = 4\cdot 83(1 - 0\cdot 855) = 0\cdot 703$$

For round bar, equation 3.14b gives

$$\frac{\sigma_{xa}}{Y} = \frac{1 + B}{B}\left[1 - \left(\frac{D_a}{D_b}\right)^{2B}\right] = \frac{1 + B}{B}\left[1 - (1 - r)^B\right]$$

Thus the r.h.s. is the same as in equation 3.14c, but the yield stress used is Y, so the force required to draw the round bar is 15% less than that required for the strip.

From the data of Example 1.3, $\bar{S} \approx 0\cdot 30$ kN/mm² so with $\alpha = 6°$

$$F_{strip} = 0\cdot 825 \times 150 \times 0\cdot 45 \times 0\cdot 30 = 16\cdot 7 \text{ kN}$$

$$F_{bar} = 0\cdot 825 \times 150 \times 0\cdot 45 \times 0\cdot 26 = 14\cdot 5 \text{ kN}$$

3.7 The schedule is most easily prepared in an approximate way using equation 3.5, $F_n = A_n Y$ $\ln A_{n-1}/A_n$, and allowing about 20% for friction, e.g. $(1 + 0\cdot 04 \cot 10°)$

The reductions of area after each annealing are $\epsilon' = \ln (6\cdot 0/3\cdot 0)^2 = 1\cdot 39$ and $\epsilon'' = \ln (3\cdot 0/1\cdot 5)^2 = 1\cdot 39$; $r' = r'' = 0\cdot 75$.

(a) From Example 1.2, at $\epsilon = 1\cdot 39$, $S_n = 0\cdot 77$, $Y_n = 0\cdot 67$ kN/mm².

The drawing force that would fracture the final wire is given by $F = A_n Y_n \approx 1\cdot 77 \times 0\cdot 67$ $= 1\cdot 19$ kN. The limit is thus set by fracture rather than by capacity of the machine.

The maximum possible reduction, allowing 20% friction, is given by

$$1 = \sigma_x/Y = 1\cdot 2 \ln A_{n-1}/A_n; \quad A_{n-1}/A_n = 2\cdot 30, r_m = 0\cdot 56$$

Two equal passes of $\epsilon = 0\cdot 69$ ($r = 50\%$) would complete the second stage. The intermediate area would be given by $\ln A_{n-1}/A_n = 0\cdot 69$; $A_{n-1}/A_n = 1\cdot 99$, $A_{n-1} = 3\cdot 53$ mm²; $\bar{Y}_n \approx 0\cdot 65$, $\bar{Y}_{n-1} \approx 0\cdot 52$. Thus

$$F_n = 1\cdot 2 \times 1\cdot 77 \times 0\cdot 65 \times 0\cdot 69 = 0\cdot 95 \text{ kN}$$

$$F_{n-1} = 1\cdot 2 \times 3\cdot 53 \times 0\cdot 52 \times 0\cdot 69 = 1\cdot 52 \text{ kN}$$

(b) The drawing force that would fracture the wire after drawing to $\epsilon' = 1\cdot39$ would be

$F = A_{n-2} Y_{n-2} \approx 7\cdot07 \times 0\cdot67 = 4\cdot74$ kN, so the limit is set by the drawbench capacity, $4\cdot5$ kN.

The maximum permissible pass before the interanneal is thus given, making a rough prior estimate of $\overline{Y}$ for the pass, by

$$F_{n-2} = 4\cdot5 \approx 1\cdot2 \times 7\cdot07 \times 0\cdot65 \times \epsilon; \quad \epsilon = 0\cdot81, r = 0\cdot55$$

The wire would be taken from $\epsilon = 0\cdot58$ to $\epsilon = 1\cdot39$ in this pass. The preceding pass would be similarly limited:

$$\epsilon = \ln A_{n-3}/A_{n-2} = 0\cdot81, \text{ so } A_{n-3} = 15\cdot8 \text{ mm}^2$$

Suppose $\overline{Y} = 0\cdot55$

$$F_{n-3} = 4\cdot5 \approx 1\cdot2 \times 15\cdot8 \times 0\cdot55 \times \epsilon; \quad \epsilon_{n-3} = 0\cdot43, r = 0\cdot35$$

This pass takes the wire from $\epsilon = 0\cdot15$ to $\epsilon = 0\cdot58$. The next preceding pass is calculated in the same way:

$$\epsilon = \ln A_{n-4}/A_{n-3} = 0\cdot15 \quad \text{so} \quad A_{n-4} = 18\cdot4 \text{ mm}^2$$

Suppose $\overline{Y} = 0\cdot35$

$$F_{n-4} = 4\cdot5 \approx 1\cdot2 \times 18\cdot4 \times 0\cdot35 \times \epsilon; \quad \epsilon_{n-4} = 0\cdot58, r = 0\cdot44$$

This would in fact take wire of a greater diameter than that given, so these three passes would be adequate, totalling $1\cdot82$. A suitable schedule could be slightly easier, say

Pass 1 $\epsilon = 0$ to $\epsilon = 0\cdot38$
     2     $\epsilon = 0\cdot38$ to $\epsilon = 0\cdot76$
     3     $\epsilon = 0\cdot76$ to $\epsilon = 1\cdot39$

The corresponding diameters given by $\epsilon = \ln (d_n/d_{n-1})^2$ are

$d_1 = 4\cdot96$
$d_2 = 4\cdot10$
$d_3 = 3\cdot00$ mm

These passes are close to the maximum, and a better schedule for practical purposes would allow a greater margin of safety, so that four passes before annealing at $d = 3$ mm would be preferable. Greater accuracy in load calculation could be obtained by using equation 6.11 and allowing for redundant work if necessary.

3.8 The total nominal strain imparted to the wire is $\epsilon = \ln \dfrac{3\cdot0}{0\cdot075} = 3\cdot68$ ($r = 0\cdot98$). The theoretical maximum in each pass is $\epsilon = 1$. With $20°$ included angle the redundant work at this reduction of area is negligible (Equation 6.11). Even in the fourth pass ($\epsilon = 0\cdot68, r = 0\cdot50$), $\phi = 1\cdot04$, so the total strain is equal to the nominal strain.

With 19% passes, $\epsilon = 0\cdot21$, $\phi = 1\cdot61$; $\epsilon' = 0\cdot338$, ($r' = 0\cdot29$). There will be 17 such passes ($\epsilon = 3\cdot57$) and one pass $\epsilon = 0\cdot11$, ($r = 0\cdot104$). For the latter, $\phi = 2\cdot37$ and the equivalent strain is $0\cdot259$. The total equivalent strain would be $\epsilon_T = 17 \times 0\cdot338 + 0\cdot259 = 6\cdot01$, ($r_T = 0\cdot997$).

3.9 Area $A_0 = \pi \overline{D}_0 h_0 \approx \pi D_0 h_0 = 392$ mm^2, $A_1 = 277, r = 0\cdot293$. Using the stress equation 3.23

$$\frac{\sigma_{xa}}{S} = \frac{1 + B^*}{B^*}\left[1 - \left(\frac{A_1}{A_0}\right)^{B^*}\right]$$

(a) $B^*_{\text{plug}} = (\mu_1 + \mu_2)/(\tan \alpha - \tan \beta) = 0\cdot2 \cot 15° = 0\cdot746$

$$\frac{\sigma_{xa}}{S} = \frac{1\cdot746}{0\cdot746}\left[1 - \left(\frac{277}{392}\right)^{0\cdot746}\right] = 2\cdot34\,(1 - 0\cdot772)$$

$$= 0\cdot534$$

(If the ratio h_1/h_0 were used, the value would be $2\cdot34\,(1 - 0\cdot782) = 0\cdot51$)

(b) $B^*_{\text{mandrel}} = (\mu_1 - \mu_2)/(\tan \alpha - \tan \beta) = 0$

$$\frac{\sigma_{xa}}{S} = \ln \frac{A_0}{A_1} = 0 \cdot 35$$

The load for plug-drawing is thus about 50% greater than for mandrel-drawing.

3.10 $r_{02} = 0 \cdot 65$, $\epsilon_{02} = \ln \dfrac{1}{1-r} = 1 \cdot 05$. Two passes $\epsilon_{01} = 0 \cdot 55$ and $\epsilon_{12} = 0 \cdot 50$ ($r_{01} = 0 \cdot 42$,

$r_{12} = 0 \cdot 39$) could be used. For most drawing operations it is preferable to take a heavier reduction in the first pass, e.g. $\epsilon_{01} = 0 \cdot 60$ and $\epsilon_{12} = 0 \cdot 45$, ($r_{01} = 0 \cdot 45$ and $r_{12} = 0 \cdot 36$), because of work-hardening, but for tandem-drawing this would involve a greater separation of the dies, and the order should be reversed, i.e. 36% in the first die and 45% in the second.

3.11 Initial cross-sectional area $= \pi \times 44 \times 6 = 829$ mm². Final cross-sectional area $= \pi \times 11 \cdot 1 \times 0 \cdot 9 = 31 \cdot 4$ mm². Total strain $\epsilon = \ln 26 \cdot 4 = 3 \cdot 27$.
   Suppose $\mu = 0 \cdot 05$, $\alpha = 15°$, $B^* = 0 \cdot 373$. From equation 3.23, the maximum reduction in a close pass is given by

$$\frac{\sigma_{xa}}{S} \approx \frac{Y}{S} = 0 \cdot 866 = \frac{1 \cdot 373}{0 \cdot 373} \left[1 - \left(\frac{A_a}{A_b} \right)^{0 \cdot 373} \right]$$

$$\left(\frac{A_a}{A_b} \right)^{0 \cdot 373} = 0 \cdot 765; \quad \frac{A_a}{A_b} = 0 \cdot 488$$

$$r_{\text{max}} \approx 0 \cdot 51 \, \epsilon_{\text{max}} = \ln \frac{A_b}{A_a} = 0 \cdot 718$$

The maximum strain permitted before annealing is given by $r = 0 \cdot 8$, $\epsilon_A = 1 \cdot 61$, so the total strain is just too great to allow only one inter-anneal, according to the rough criterion of 80% per anneal. However, the cost of an additional annealing would be considerable, so an attempt might be made to use say $\epsilon_A^* = 1 \cdot 7$ before the first annealing and $\epsilon_A^{**} = 1 \cdot 6$ for the second stage. Each stage would then have three passes of about $\epsilon = 0 \cdot 56$ ($r = 0 \cdot 43$).
   In detail the total thickness strain is $\epsilon'_{06} = \ln \dfrac{6}{0 \cdot 9} = 1 \cdot 90$, and the diametral strain is $\epsilon''_{06} = \ln \dfrac{50}{12}$
$= 1 \cdot 43$, $(\epsilon'_{06} + \epsilon''_{06} = 3 \cdot 33)$. Equally divided, this implies that in each pass $\epsilon' = 0 \cdot 316$, $\epsilon'' = 0 \cdot 238$, $\epsilon = 0 \cdot 554$, $r = 0 \cdot 42$.
   Thus $h_0 = 6 \cdot 0$ mm, $\epsilon'_{01} = 0 \cdot 316$, $h_0/h_1 = 1 \cdot 372$; $h_1 = 4 \cdot 37$ mm and similarly $h_2 = 3 \cdot 18$, $h_3 = 2 \cdot 32$. The diameters are given by $D_0 = 50$, $\epsilon''_{01} = 0 \cdot 238$ $D_0/D_1 = 1 \cdot 268$;

$$D_1 = 39 \cdot 4, \quad D_2 = 31 \cdot 1, \quad D_3 = 24 \cdot 5$$

After the interanneal, $h_4 = 1 \cdot 69$, $h_5 = 1 \cdot 23$, $h_6 = 0 \cdot 90$

$$D_4 = 19 \cdot 3, \quad D_5 = 15 \cdot 2, \quad D_6 = 12 \cdot 0$$

The die diameters would usually be adjusted to standard values, e.g.

50, 40, 30, 25; 20, 15, 12 mm

The drawing stress for $\epsilon = 0 \cdot 554$, corresponding to $A_a/A_b = 0 \cdot 575$, is given approximately by assuming the whole reduction to be close pass, as in equation 3.23:

$$\frac{\sigma_{xa}}{S} = 3 \cdot 68[1 - (0 \cdot 575)^{0 \cdot 373}] = 0 \cdot 686$$

This will overestimate, because the diameter reductions involve a contribution from sinking, as in equation 3.29.
   The area A_1, after the first pass, is $\pi \times 35 \times 4 \cdot 4 = 484$ mm² and $\bar{S}$ for this pass is $0 \cdot 59$ kN/mm²,

so the drawing force is F_1 = 195 kN. The force F_6 for the final pass is $\approx 0.686 \times 0.90 \times 31.4 =$ 19 kN.

3.12 Use equation 3.23 for plug-drawing. Assume $B^* = 0.373$

$$\frac{\sigma_{xa}}{S} = 3.68 \left[1 - \left(\frac{A_a}{A_b}\right)^{0.373} \right]$$

Now $\overline{S} = 0.75$ kN/mm² and $\sigma_{xa} = 200/A_a$ kN/mm²

$$1 - \left(\frac{A_a}{A_b}\right)^{0.373} = \frac{200}{3.68 \times 0.75 A_a} = \frac{72.5}{A_a}$$

But $\dfrac{A_a}{A_b} = 1 - r = 0.75$

$$1 - 0.898 = 72.5/A_a; \quad A_a = 647 \text{ mm}^2.$$

If $B = 0$, as with a mandrel,

$$\frac{\sigma_{xa}}{S} = \epsilon = 0.287; \quad \sigma_{xa} = 0.215 \text{ kN/mm}^2$$

$$A_a = 200/0.215 = 930 \text{ mm}^2$$

Thus $\pi D h = 930$, $Dh = 296$, e.g. $D = 50$, $h = 6$ mm.

3.13 With a floating plug the condition of stability is seen from Figure 3.2 to be:

$$p \pi D \tan \beta \, dx = \mu_2 p \pi D \, dx; \quad \tan \beta = \mu_2$$

If $\mu = 0.04$, $\beta = 2° 18'$; $2\alpha = 24°$

$$A_b = \pi \times 37 \times 3 = 349 \text{ mm}^2, \quad A_a = \pi \times 27.6 \times 2.4 = 208 \text{ mm}^2$$

$$\epsilon = \ln 349/208 = 0.52, \quad \overline{S} \approx 0.28 \text{ kN/mm}^2$$

$$B^* = \frac{0.08}{\tan \alpha - \tan \beta} = 0.47$$

Using equation 3.23

$$\frac{\sigma_{xa}}{S} = \frac{1 + B^*}{B^*} \left[1 - \left(\frac{A_a}{A_b}\right)^{B^*} \right]$$

$$= \frac{1.47}{0.47} \left[1 - (0.595)^{0.47} \right]$$

$$= 0.675$$

$$F = 0.675 \times 0.28 \times 208 = 39.3 \text{ kN}$$

Work done per second = 39.3×1.6 kN m/sec

$$= 62.9 \text{ k J/s} = 63 \text{ kW}$$

$$(= 84 \text{ hp})$$

Allowing 85% efficiency ≈ 75 kW

(Homogeneous work would involve $\sigma_{xa}/S = 0.45$)

In practice, floating plugs are preferably of curved profile and are used with curved dies.

3.14 Using equation 3.29

$$B = 0.05 \cot 15° = 0.187$$

$$\frac{\sigma_{xa}}{1.1\bar{Y}} = \frac{1.187}{0.187}\left[1 - \left(\frac{90}{100}\right)^{0.187}\right] = 6.35(1 - 0.980) = 0.124$$

$$\epsilon = \ln \bar{D}_b/\bar{D}_a = 0.112; \quad \bar{S} = 0.40 \, \text{kN/mm}^2$$

$$1.1\bar{Y} = 0.38 \, \text{kN/mm}^2$$

$$\sigma_{xa} = 0.047 \, \text{kN/mm}^2,$$

$A_a = \pi \times 78 \times 12 = 2940 \, \text{mm}^2$, ignoring any thickening or thinning that may occur. Drawing force $\approx 140 \, \text{kN}$.

3.15 Assuming the volume to remain constant, the width and thickness each increase by $\sqrt{1.05}$ during the compression. The force required is $(60 \times 700 \times 1.05) \approx 31 \times 10^6$ N.

At room temperature $S_1 = 432 \, \text{N/mm}^2$ at $\epsilon_1 = 0.052$ (for mild steel, Example 1.3a). Thus $Y \approx 380$ and the load would be about 200 MN. Note that S_1, not $\bar{S}$, is used.

It will be seen in Chapter 6 that there would be an appreciable increase in the hot-working load due to the high friction in an actual working operation.

3.16 A reasonable approximation is to assume that the load is equal to that necessary to cause yielding in a rectangular billet with $b = 300$ mm and $h = 2b \sin 60°$, under plane-strain conditions. Then, from equation 3.33, at the end of forging

$$\left(\frac{p}{2k}\right)_{\text{max}} = \exp(0.3/1.73) = 1.19$$

The mean pressure is thus about $1.1 \times 2k = 130 \, \text{N/mm}^2$. The contact area at the platen is 3×10^5 mm² so the force is 39000 kN.
With sticking friction, equation 3.35

$$\bar{p} = 2k\left(1 + \frac{0.58}{4}\right) \approx 140 \, \text{N/mm}^2; \quad F = 41000 \, \text{kN}$$

$$p_{\text{max}} = 2k\left(1 + \frac{0.58}{2}\right) \approx 155 \, \text{N/mm}^2$$

3.17 (a) Equation 3.37 shows that at the initial yielding

$$\left(\frac{p}{Y}\right)_{\text{max}} = \exp\left(\frac{\mu D}{h}\right) = \exp 0.10 = 1.105$$

When the cylinder has been reduced by 20% in height, to 240 mm, the area will have increased by 20% to maintain constant volume, so $D = 1.1 \times 600 = 660$ mm

$$\left(\frac{p}{Y}\right)_{\text{max}} = \exp\left(\frac{0.05 \times 660}{240}\right) = 1.147$$

From Example 1.3, the yield stress for $\epsilon = 0.223$ at room temperature is $S = 0.61$, $Y \approx 0.53$ kN/mm². So $p = 1.074 \times 0.53 = 0.57$ kN/mm². The contact area for $D = 660$ is 34.2×10^4 mm² so the steady forging load necessary would be 19.5×10^4 kN.

(b) With sticking friction at the high temperature, from equation 3.36, with $\tau = k$

$$\left(\frac{p}{Y}\right)_{\text{max}} = 1 + \frac{1.15}{240}\cdot\frac{660}{2} = 2.58; \quad \begin{aligned}\bar{p} &= 60 \times 1.79 = 107 \, \text{N/mm}^2\\ F &= 0.107 \times 34.2 \times 10^4 = 37 \times 10^3 \, \text{kN}\end{aligned}$$

3.18 The cross-sectional area of the billet is 78.5×10^4 mm² so the square would have sides equal to 886 mm. Assuming plane-strain and sticking friction, equation 3.35 gives

$$\left(\frac{p}{2k}\right)_{max} = 1 + \frac{b}{4h} = 1.25; \quad \bar{p} = 1.12 \times 1.15 \times 60 = 77 \text{ N/mm}^2$$

The area of platen contact is $88.6 \times 10^4 \text{ mm}^2$, so the forging load is 68×10^3 kN.

Chapter 4

4.1 The strain imparted is $\epsilon_1 = \ln 2.50/2.00 = 0.223$. Approximating to the stress–strain curve of Example 1.3b by a straight line over this region, $S = \frac{1}{2}(108 + 70) \approx 89 \text{ N/mm}^2$.

(It could be somewhat more accurately deduced from $\dfrac{1}{\epsilon_1}\displaystyle\int_0^{\epsilon_1} S\, d\epsilon$, but the difference is very

small.) The length of contact of the roll with the strip is given by equation 4.18, $L = \sqrt{R\Delta h} = 9.35$ mm. The load per unit width (equation 4.19), is $P/w = \bar{S}L \approx 830 \text{ N/mm}$.
    Thus $P = 1660$ kN. Allowing 20% for friction, $P \approx 2.0$ MN.

4.2 The strain imparted is $\epsilon_1 = \ln 2.50/1.75 = 0.357$. A straight-line approximation to the stress–strain curve of Example 1.3b gives $\bar{S} = 90 \text{ N/mm}^2$. (Note that this simple method becomes more accurate as ϵ_1 increases). From equation 4.18, $L = \sqrt{R\Delta h} = 11.5$ mm. From equation 4.19, $P/w = \bar{S}L = 1035$, $P = 2.1$ MN. Allowing 20% for friction $P \approx 2.0$ MN.

4.3 (a) The load permitted is about half that required to complete the operation in one pass. If the mean yield stress were unchanged, the final pass would, according to the relationship in equation 4.19 be about $\Delta h = (0.5)^2 \times 0.50 \approx 0.13$ mm. The stress–strain curve suggests a mean yield stress of about 106 N/mm² for such a pass. The load would then be $P = 1.2\, w\, \bar{S}\sqrt{R\Delta h}$. For $P = 10^6$ N, $w = 2000$ mm, and $\bar{S} = 106 \text{ N/mm}^2$; $\sqrt{R\Delta h} = 3.93$, $\Delta h = 0.09$ mm.
    Choose the final pass to be 0.08 mm and calculate the load:

Pass no.	$\dfrac{\Delta h}{\text{mm}}$	$\dfrac{h_{N-1}}{\text{mm}}$	$\epsilon_N - \epsilon_{N-1}$	$\dfrac{\bar{S}}{\text{kN/mm}^2}$	$\dfrac{P}{\text{kN}}$	$\sqrt{R\Delta h}$
N	0.08	2.08	0.223 − 0.183	0.106	951	3.74
$N-1$	0.09	2.17	0.183 − 0.160	0.104	990	3.97
$N-2$	0.09	2.26	0.160 − 0.101	0.101	960	3.97
$N-3$	0.10	2.36	0.101 − 0.057	0.091	913	4.18
$N-4$	0.14	2.50	0.057 − 0	0.065	772	4.95

The draft for each pass is estimated on the basis of the preceding calculation.
    Thus a suitable schedule for this operation would be five passes, respectively reducing the strip to 2.36, 2.26, 2.17, 2.08 and 2.00 mm. This would actually imply unwarranted confidence in the formula, to allow 1% safety factor! The first pass could in principle be heavier, but $\bar{S}$ is not well defined for the first pass after annealing.
    (b) With mild steel the final pass would involve a mean yield stress $\bar{S} \approx 0.6 \text{ kN/mm}^2$. Equation 4.19 gives the final draft (assuming that the rolls do not deform — see §4.2).

$$1000 = 1.2 \cdot 2000 \cdot 0.6\sqrt{175\Delta h}; \quad \Delta h \approx 0.0028 \text{ mm}$$

This mill is thus quite unsuitable for rolling steel with these dimensions.

4.4 (a) The strain imparted by the first pass is $\epsilon_{01} = \ln\dfrac{2.50}{2.00} = 0.223$; the total of first and second is $\epsilon_{02} = \ln\dfrac{2.50}{1.50} = 0.511$. From the stress–strain curve (Example 1.3) $S_2 = 0.75$, $S_1 = 0.61$. Thus the mean yield stress is 0.68 kN/mm² and the error in assuming the yield stress to be constant at S_2 would be about 10%.

(b) $\epsilon_{03} = \ln 2.50/1.25 = 0.693$. $S_3 = 0.80 \text{ kN/mm}^2$,

$\bar{S}_{23} = \frac{1}{2}(0.75 + 0.80) = 0.78$ and the error in assuming $\bar{S}_{23} = S_3$ is 0.2 kN/mm², about 3%.

4.5 The prior reduction by 30% corresponds to $\epsilon_{01} = \ln 1\cdot0/0\cdot7 = 0\cdot357$. In the first pass $\epsilon_{12} = \ln 6/4\cdot8 = 0\cdot223$; $\epsilon_{02} = 0\cdot580$. The mean yield stress for this pass $\bar{S}_{12} = (0\cdot35 + 0\cdot43)/2 = 0\cdot39$ kN/mm^2. Using the simple roll-load formula, equation 4.19,

$$P/w = 1\cdot2 \times 0\cdot39 \times \sqrt{175 \times 1\cdot2} = 6\cdot8\,\text{kN/mm}, \quad P = 1020\ \text{kN}$$

In the next pass $\epsilon_{23} = 0\cdot233$, $\epsilon_{03} = 0\cdot813$, $\bar{S}_{23} = 0\cdot46$ kN/mm^2

$$P/w = 1\cdot2 \times 0\cdot46 \times \sqrt{175 \times 0\cdot96} = 7\cdot1\,\text{kN/mm}, \quad P = 1060\ \text{kN}$$

The roll flattening is given by equation 4.17.

$$R' = R(1 + 0\cdot022 \times 7\cdot1 \div 0\cdot96) = R(1\cdot16)$$

If Δh is to be maintained, $R(1 - \cos \alpha_b) = R'(1 - \cos \alpha_b') = \Delta h/2$

$$1 - \cos \alpha_b' = 0\cdot48/175 = 0\cdot00274 \qquad \alpha_b' = 4\cdot3°$$

The maximum deflection is $R \sin \alpha \tan \alpha/2 = 0\cdot49$ mm.

4.6 The prior reduction by 30% corresponds to $\epsilon_{01} = 0\cdot358$. In the reduction from $h_1 = 2\cdot50$ to $h_2 = 2\cdot40$, $\epsilon_{12} = \ln 2\cdot5/2\cdot4 = 0\cdot041$, so $\epsilon_{02} = 0\cdot399$. From the σ/ϵ curve $\bar{S} = (0\cdot69 + 0\cdot71)/2 = 0\cdot70$ kN/mm^2.

(a) Using the simple formula, equation 4.19,

$$P/w = 1\cdot2 \times 0\cdot70 \times \sqrt{175 \times 0\cdot10} = 3\cdot5\ \text{kN/mm}, \quad P = 1760\ \text{kN}$$

The roll flattening is given by equation 4.17

$$R' = R(1 + 0\cdot022 \times 3\cdot5 \div 0\cdot1) = 1\cdot77R$$

(b) If tensions are applied, the equivalent yield stress is reduced at entry and exit as in §4.1.3

$$S_b^* = 0\cdot69 - 0\cdot075 = 0\cdot615\ \text{kN/mm}^2$$
$$S_a^* = 0\cdot71 - 0\cdot150 = 0\cdot56\ \text{kN/mm}^2$$

The mean yield stress is thus reduced to $0\cdot59$ and the roll load becomes $1480\,\text{kN}$ and $R' \approx 1\cdot65R$. For more accurate calculation, the method of §4.1 could be used.

(c) The limiting thickness that can be rolled without tensions on this mill is found from equation 4.20, assuming $\bar{S} \approx 0\cdot80$ kN/mm^2

$$h_\text{min} = 0\cdot035\mu\,R\bar{S} = 0\cdot035 \times 0\cdot07 \times 175 \times 0\cdot8 = 0\cdot34\ \text{mm}$$

4.7 The elastic extension is found from the stress and the Young's modulus

$$\epsilon = \frac{\sigma}{E} = \frac{12}{20 \times 10^4} = 0\cdot6 \times 10^{-4}\ \text{mm/mm}$$

The total stretch of the side members is consequently

$$3000 \times 0\cdot6 \times 10^{-4} = 0\cdot18\ \text{mm}$$

This may be compared with the elastic deformation of the rolls calculated in Example 4.5 for a similar mill.

4.8 The total strain $\epsilon_{02} = \ln 0\cdot8/0\cdot4 = 0\cdot693$. Two suitable passes might be $\epsilon_{01} = 0\cdot4$, $\epsilon_{12} = 0\cdot3$. Then, taking appropriate straight-line approximations to the stress–strain curve, $\bar{S}_{01} = (0\cdot74 + 0\cdot39)/2 = 0\cdot56$ kN/mm^2 $\bar{S}_{12} = (0\cdot81 + 0\cdot71)/2 = 0\cdot76$ kN/mm^2. For the first pass $\ln h_0/h_1 = 0\cdot4$; $h_0 = 0\cdot80$, $h_1 = 0\cdot54$, $\Delta h_{01} = 0\cdot26$ mm. Thus $\Delta h_2 = 0\cdot14$ mm. Using equation 4.19 to find the approximate roll load,

$$P_1/w = 1\cdot2 \times 0\cdot56 \times \sqrt{R \times 0\cdot26}$$
$$P_2/w = 1\cdot2 \times 0\cdot76 \times \sqrt{R \times 0\cdot14}$$

Common L/D ratios for the rolls in such a 2-high mill lie between 1·5 and 2. Supposing $D = 450$ mm

$$P_1/w = 5·14 \text{ kN/mm}$$

$$P_2/w = 5·12 \text{ kN/mm}$$

These values are comparable with common practice. The maximum roll load is thus $P_1 = 3860$ kN.

The limiting load for such short rolls is usually set by shear at the roll-neck shoulder. The roll-neck diameter d is often equal to $\frac{1}{2}D$. The cross-sectional area of the roll neck is thus 4×10^4 mm². A reasonable value for the shear strength would be 150 N/mm², so the load to fracture one neck would be 6000 kN, giving a safety factor of about 3 to allow for stress concentration effects and fatigue.

The power input is derived from the torque (equations 4.24 and 4.26)

$$T_1 \approx 0·45\sqrt{R\Delta h}\,P_1 = 0·45 \times 7·65 \times 3860 = 13·3 \times 10^3 \text{ kNmm}$$

(or recalculate using R').

$$2W_R = 2T\dot\theta = 26·6\dot\theta \text{ kNm/sec} = 26·6\dot\theta \text{ kW}$$

Add about 20% for power loss in the bearings (or calculate for an assumed μ) and allow 80% overall transmission efficiency. The motor input is thus $\approx 40\dot\theta$ kW. A reasonable size of motor for such a mill might be 450 kW. This would roll at $\dot\theta = 11·2$, giving a strip exit speed of 2520 mm/sec, $\approx 2·5$ m/sec.

4.9 (a) Use the simple roll-load equation 4.19. If the operation is to be completed in one pass, the strain is $\epsilon_{01} = \ln 3·0/2·4 = 0·223$. For copper $\bar{S}_{01} = 0·18$ kN/mm² and for steel $\bar{S}_{01} = 0·47$ kN/mm²

So for copper: $P = 400 \times 1·2 \times 0·18 \times \sqrt{75 \times 0·60} = 580$ kN

for steel: $P = 1510$ kN

Copper can thus be rolled easily in one pass, but steel requires more than one pass, since P may not exceed 1000 kN.

In two equal passes for steel, $\epsilon_{01} = 0·112$, $\epsilon_{12} = 0·111$.

Then $\bar{S}_{01} = 0·42$, $\bar{S}_{12} = 0·56$ kN/mm²

$$h_0 = 3·00. \ h_1 = 2·68, \ h_2 = 2·40, \ \Delta h_1 = 0·32, \ \Delta h_2 = 0·28 \text{ mm}$$

$$P_1 = 990 \text{ kN}, P_2 = 1300 \text{ kN}$$

Thus steel strip cannot be rolled to this size even in two passes. Three passes might be:

$\epsilon_{01} = 0·10$ $h_1 = 2·71$ $\bar{S}_{01} = 0·39$ $P_1 = 873$ kN

$\epsilon_{12} = 0·07$ $h_2 = 2·53$ $\bar{S}_{12} = 0·54$ $P_2 = 952$

$\epsilon_{23} = 0·053$ $h_3 = 2·40$ $\bar{S}_{23} = 0·59$ $P_3 = 884$

The operation can just be completed in three passes with the mild steel strip.

(b) The power required is found from equation 4.26b,

$$W_M = \frac{1}{\eta_1\eta_2} (2W_R + 4W_N) = \frac{1}{\eta_1\eta_2} (2T_R\dot\theta + 4T_N\dot\theta)$$

which, for constant speed and friction conditions can be written

$$\eta_1\eta_2 W_M = 2\lambda'L'P.\dot\theta + 4\mu_N\frac{P}{2}R\,\dot\theta\,(\approx 0·8\ W_M)$$

$$= (2 \times 0·5\sqrt{R\Delta h} \times 1·2 \times \bar{S}\sqrt{R\Delta h}\,w + 2\mu_N \times 1·2 \times \bar{S}\sqrt{R\Delta h} \times wR)\dot\theta$$

$$= 1·2\bar{S}(R\Delta h + 2\mu R\sqrt{R\Delta h})\,\dot\theta w$$

The following values can be calculated:

	$R\Delta h$	$2\mu R\sqrt{R\Delta h}$	$\bar{S}$	$\dfrac{\eta W}{w\theta}$
Copper	45	5·0	0·18	9·0
Steel				
pass 1	21·8	3·5	0·39	9·8
pass 2	13·5	2·8	0·54	8·8
pass 3	9·8	2·3	0·59	7·1

The power required is comparable for each pass, but the steel requires 3 passes.

Chapter 5

5.1 Sketch an elementary cube δx, δy, δz at the origin of the $Oxyz$ axes. Resolve the forces along Ox and equate to zero for equilibrium:

$$\left(\sigma_x + \frac{\partial \sigma_x}{\partial x} \cdot \delta x\right) \delta y \delta z - \sigma_x \delta y \delta z + \left(\tau_{yx} + \frac{\partial \tau_{yx}}{\partial y} \cdot \delta y\right) \delta x \delta z - \tau_{yx} \cdot \delta x \delta z = 0$$

$$\left(\frac{\partial \sigma_x}{\partial x} + \frac{\partial \tau_{yx}}{\partial y}\right) \cdot \delta x \delta y \delta z = 0$$

Similarly, $\quad \dfrac{\partial \sigma_y}{\partial y} + \dfrac{\partial \tau_{xy}}{\partial x} = 0$

At the point Q (Figure 5.3) where the tangents to the slip-lines coincide with Ox and Oy axes, $\dfrac{\partial \tau_{xy}}{\partial x} = 0$, because $\tau_{xy} = k$ which is a constant. Thus at Q, $\dfrac{\partial \sigma_y}{\partial y} = \dfrac{\partial \sigma_x}{\partial x} = 0$ and since Q is any point at which the axes coincide with the slip-lines, this may be written generally

$$\frac{\partial \sigma_\alpha}{\partial \alpha} = 0 = \frac{\partial \sigma_\beta}{\partial \beta}$$

5.2 $S = 2k = 600$ N/mm². Draw the Mohr circle with centre $(-450, 0)$ and radius 300. The principal stresses are given by the ends of the diameter along the σ axis, namely $\sigma_1 = -750$ N/mm² and $\sigma_3 = -150$ N/mm². The shear stress $\tau_\theta = \pm 300 \sin 40° = \pm 192$ N/mm².

5.3 Consider two pairs of slip-lines. In Figure 5.9, the α-lines AP and BQ are cut orthogonally by two β-lines. The Hencky equation 5.7 shows that along the α-line QB, $p_Q + 2k\phi_Q = p_B + 2k\phi_B$; and along the β-line BA, $p_B - 2k\phi_B = p_A - 2k\phi_A$. Thus

$$p_Q - p_A = (p_Q - p_B) + (p_B - p_A) = 2k(\phi_B - \phi_Q) + 2k(\phi_B - \phi_A)$$

Similarly $p_Q - p_A = 2k(\phi_Q - \phi_P) + 2k(\phi_A - \phi_P)$ since the general rotation by $\pi/2$ does not influence the relationship. These must be the same since the pressure can have only one value at

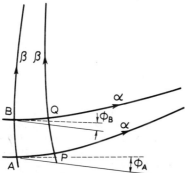

Figure 5.9 Orthogonal slip-lines

a given point, so

$$2\phi_B - \phi_Q - \phi_A = \phi_Q + \phi_A - 2\phi_P$$

$$\phi_Q - \phi_P = \phi_A - \phi_B$$

This is known as Hencky's first theorem.

5.4 Equation 5.10 gives the angle of inclination of the slip-lines to an interface with Coulomb friction

$$2\theta = \cos^{-1} \mu q'/k$$

This cannot however be evaluated unless q' is known. A first approximation is made by supposing that $q' \approx q$, which is found by drawing the slip-line field for a frictionless interface. An example is given in Chapter 6, Example 6.7. In a simple instance such as plane-strain compression of a thin strip, $q = 2k$.

Thus for $\mu = 0.04$ $2\theta = \cos^{-1} 0.08$ $\theta = 43°$ (and 47)

       $\mu = 0.11$ $2\theta = \cos^{-1} 0.22$ $\theta = 39°$ (and 51)

5.5 Two solutions are possible, according to the choice of slip-line field suggested by Prandtl (Figure 5.7a) or by Hill (Figure 5.7b). The hydrostatic pressure distribution is found by drawing the chosen field to scale and ruling a horizontal line 10 mm below the surface.

From Figure 5.7a p/k is constant at the value 1·0 throughout the triangular region BDE, because $\sigma_3 = 0$ and $p = k$ over BD, and the slip-lines are straight. In the fan from BE to BF the pressure rises by increments $2k \times 0.262$ as the horizontal line intercepts successive radii drawn at 15° intervals. The pressure reaches $p/k = 1 + \pi$ at the intersection with BF, and thereafter remains constant over the central region until AF is reached. It then decreases in a symmetrical manner.

From Figure 5.7b the pattern is similar, but the deformation zone does not extend so far outwards from the indenter. In the central region between F and F' it is reasonable to expect that the pressure would remain constant, and Hill's full solution in fact postulates a continuation of the straight slip-lines over this region, as in the Prandtl solution.

Both solutions give a pressure $p = 2.57k$ immediately beneath the edges of the indenter, and the pressure varies almost linearly with distance inwards and outwards from these points.

5.6 Equation 6.13 gives the extrusion pressure for 50% inverted extrusion $P = k \times (1 + \pi/2) = \frac{1}{2} \times 25 \times 2.57 = 32.1$ N/mm². $A_0 = 900$ mm². Load required = 28·9 kN.

5.7 The main features are:

(a) s.l.f. theory allows for redundant work in load evaluation.

(b) Particularly useful for forging and extrusion.

(c) Can be used to predict metal flow pattern.

(d) Can be used to estimate stress and temperature distribution.

(e) s.l.f. theory is limited to plane-strain and in its usual form assumes no strain-hardening. Stress evaluation allows for strain-hardening and can be used for conditions of axial symmetry.

(f) Plane-strain analogies, for which s.l.f. solutions are known, may be useful, for example in wire-drawing and more complex processes.

Chapter 6

6.1 The slip-line field for zero friction divides directly into six equal units, as in Figure 5.5b. The compression stress would therefore be exactly equal to $2k$. (b) With sticking friction the field resembles Figure 6.1. 15° intervals may be chosen at first. Using the same lettering as in Figure 6.1, the field can be drawn as far as $E_3F_2G_1H$, corresponding to a distance 475 mm from the platen edge. To complete the field a boundary α-line $E_3'F_2'G_1'H'$ is drawn at an angular spacing of about 4° further, across the β-lines constructed from F, G and H.

6.2 The stress solution is begun on AC, where $\sigma_3 = 0$ and $p = k$. Anticlockwise rotation along the β-line shows that the pressure along AC_3 is $p_{C_3} = k + 2k\dfrac{\pi}{4} = 2\cdot57k$. Between C_3 and D_2 the α-line rotates clockwise by $15° = \pi/12$, so $p_{D_2} = k\left(1 + \dfrac{\pi}{2} + \dfrac{\pi}{6}\right) = 3\cdot1k$. Following the β-line $D_2 D_3$ a further $15°$ gives $p_{D_3} = k\left(1 + \dfrac{\pi}{2} + \dfrac{2\pi}{6}\right) = 3\cdot62k$. Similarly $p_{E_3} = 4\cdot67k$, $p_{F_2} = 5\cdot2k$, $p_{G_1} = 5\cdot71k$, $p_H = 6\cdot24k$. The pressure at F_2' exceeds that at F_2 by $2k \times \left(4 \times \dfrac{\pi}{180}\right) = 0\cdot14k$, so $p_{F_2}' = 5\cdot34k$, $p_{G_1}' = 5\cdot85k$, $p_H' = 6\cdot38k$ and $p_{E_3}' = p_{E_3} + 0\cdot28k = 4\cdot95k$. To find the mean pressure over the dead zone, the vertical force components are summed. The vertical force F^* acting over the dead zone is

$$F^* = \int k \sin\psi \, ds + \int p \cos\psi \, ds$$

(since the stress acting normal to a plane of maximum shear is p, as seen in the Mohr circle). Since k is constant, the first term is simply $k\dfrac{h}{2}$. The second is evaluated approximately as $\Sigma \bar{p} \, \Delta x$. Along the lines $E_3' F_2'$, $F_2' G_1'$, $G_1' H'$, the mean pressures are $5\cdot15k$, $5\cdot6k$ and $6\cdot12k$ respectively and the horizontal components of the lengths of these lines are $64\cdot5$, 67 and 55 mm, assuming a width of 250 mm for the drawing, representing the 1 m workpiece width. The sum of these products is $332k + 375k + 367k = 1074k$ to which must be added the contribution from the short length of line between H and the centre, $68k$. Thus

$$F^* = 68k + 1142k$$

The horizontal width of this half of the dead zone is 193 mm, so the mean vertical pressure over the dead zone is $6\cdot26k$. The total vertical force is

$$F = 2\left(p_{C_3} AC_3 + \frac{p_{C_3} + p_{E_3}'}{2} \cdot C_3 E_3' + F^*\right)$$

$$= 2(2\cdot57 \times 106 + 3\cdot76 \times 146 \times 1210)k$$

$$= 2k \times 2031$$

The mean pressure $\dfrac{P}{2k} = \dfrac{2031}{900} = 2\cdot25$.

6.3 The area of contact is $8 \times 6 \times 300 = 1\cdot44 \times 10^4$ mm^2. Assume that the plastic zones are initially separate, beneath each ridge, as implied by the Hill solution for indentation (Chapter 5, §5.6.5). Then the pressure is given by equation 5.15:

$$\frac{p}{2k} = 2\cdot57$$

The force W necessary to initiate yielding is

$$W = 2\cdot57 \times 0\cdot15 \times 1\cdot44 \times 10^4 = 5\cdot55 \times 10^3 \text{ kN}$$

After deep penetration, if the plastic zones remained separate, the pressure would increase to $4\cdot14 \times 2k$, according to equation 6.8, requiring a force $W = 8\cdot9 \times 10^3$ kN. It will be seen from Figure 6.2b, however, that the plastic zones would overlap slightly.

6.4 For separate grooves, equation 6.9 may be used: $p = 2k(1 + \theta)$. The value of θ is found geometrically. In Figure 6.2c, $AC = AD$, and for volume constancy the areas of triangles $O'AD$ and $O'AC$ must be equal. The perpendiculars from O' on to these sides must therefore be equal. A circle is drawn with centre O', touching AC, and tangents are drawn to it until one is found such that the intercept AD is equal to AC. This shows that $(\alpha - \theta)$ lies between $12°$ and $13°$, so $\theta \approx 17\cdot5° = 0\cdot1\pi$ radians. If the grooves are 6 mm deep, $OA \approx 6 \tan 30 = 3\cdot4$ mm and the force required is $W = (1 + 0\cdot3) \times 0\cdot15 \times 2 \times 3\cdot46 \times 300 = 408$ kN for each groove, about $3\cdot3 \times 10^3$ kN in all, but the plastic zones will again interact.

6.5 This is a purely computational exercise. It provides graphical results of use in drawing calculations. ϕ is found from equation 6.11, and f from equation 6.10.

6.6 For both strip-drawing and wire-drawing the ratio of drawing stress to mean yield stress (S and Y respectively) is given by

$$\frac{1+B}{B}\,[1-(1-r)^B]$$

The values obtained must be multiplied by the redundant work factors f and ϕ.

$$\phi = 0.87 + \frac{1-r}{r}\,\sin\alpha$$

$$\frac{c}{d} = \frac{2-r}{r}\,.\,\alpha;\quad f(c/d) \text{ is found from equation 6.10.}$$

Thus:

	$\alpha = 2°$	$5°$	$14°$
σ_{xa}/S or $\sigma_{xa}/Y = 0.64$		0.46	0.40
$(1-r)\sin\alpha/r = 0.081$		0.204	0.561
$\phi = (0.95)$		1.07	1.43
$(2-r)\alpha/r = -$		$-$	1.38
$f = 1.0$		1.0	1.06
$\phi\,.\,\sigma_{xa}/Y = 0.64$		0.50	0.57
$f\,.\,\sigma_{xa}/S = 0.64$		0.46	0.43

The optimum angles giving least drawing force for the specified reduction of area and co-efficient of friction are respectively about $5°$ for wire and $14°$ for sheet. The drawing stress is little affected by a small increase in angle, but rises more steeply with decreasing angle.

6.7 The field is constructed as in §6.4, starting with an isosceles $45°$ triangle on AB, and the radial fans centred on A and B. It will be found that the field almost matches the required reduction if there are three $10°$ segments centred on A and five on B. Using the straight-line approximation, without drawing the smooth curves for the true field, the contributions of the sections on the entry slip-line can be summed. Thus, for the segment starting on the centre line, $\phi = 50°$, $\cos\phi = 0.643$, $\sin\phi = 0.766$ and the length $s = 0.78$ (measured in mm, taking $\frac{1}{2}h_b = 125$ mm and $\frac{1}{2}h_a = 100$ mm as suitable diagram dimensions). The pressure increment to the first intersection is $2k\Delta\phi = 2k(0.175)$ so the mean pressure on this section is $p_x + 0.175k$, if p_x is the pressure on the centre line. Thus $\bar{p}s \sin\phi = 0.596p_x + 0.104k$, and $ks \cos\phi = 0.501k$.

The total rearward horizontal force component (equation 6.7) is $\Sigma\bar{p}s \sin\phi + ks \cos\phi$. Equating this to zero (no backpull) gives $-(5.09p_x + 6.25k) + 1.37k = 0$, $p_x = -0.96k$. The pressure at the apex C of the $45°$ triangle is $p_c = p_x + 2.80k = -1.84k$, which is also the hydrostatic pressure at the die face. The major principal stress at the die face is thus $\sigma_1 = q = -(p+k)$ $2.84k$. Thus $q/2k = 1.42$.

The same procedure is followed when $\mu = 0.10$, except that the initial triangle is set at an angle given by $\cos 2\theta = \mu q/k$, taking $q = 2.84k$ as found above. To meet the condition for $45°$ intersection at the centre-line, suitable values for ψ and ζ are $25°$ and $55°$ respectively. Equating the rearward horizontal force component to zero gives $p_x = -0.75k$ and thence $q = 2.88k$. It will be seen that this differs little from the value for frictionless drawing.

6.8 For this pass $r_{01} = 0.20$, $\epsilon_{01} = \ln\dfrac{3.0}{2.4} = 0.223$, but account must be taken of the redundant deformation. From §6.41, $\dfrac{c}{d} = \dfrac{2-r}{r}$. $\alpha = 3.14$, so using Figure 5.6, $f\left(\dfrac{c}{d}\right) = 1.53$ and the effective strain is $\epsilon' = f\epsilon_{01} = 0.341$ ($r = 0.29$). Substituting this in the given ductility equation, $(e\,1\%) - 42 \exp(-2.56) = 42/12.9 = 3.3\%$. Under ideal conditions $(el\%) = 42 \exp(-1.67) = 7.9\%$

(Actually the exponential equation given ceases to represent the ductility beyond about $r = 0.3$, $\epsilon = 0.36$, and the percentage elongation then remains almost independent of prior strain over an appreciable range.)

6.9 (a) The work done per unit volume of strip, if deformed with zero redundant work, is given by

$$\frac{W}{V} = \int_0^{\epsilon_1} 2k\, d\epsilon \approx \overline{2k}\epsilon_1$$

From the data of Example 1.2 the mean flow stress in a pass $\epsilon = 0$ to $\epsilon = 0.223$ is $2k \approx 0.38$ kN/mm²

$$\frac{W}{V} = 0.085\, V \text{ kN/mm}^2$$

The density of brass is 8.38×10^{-3} g/mm³, so for a mass m

$$W = \frac{0.085}{8.38 \times 10^{-3}}\, m \text{ kN/g} = 10.1\, m \text{ J/g}$$

The specific heat of brass is 0.376 J/g so

$$10.1\, m = m \times 0.376 \times (T_1 - T_0); \quad T_1 - T_0 = 26°\text{C}.$$

(b) Allowing for redundant work $W/V = \overline{Y}\, \epsilon'$. The temperature rise is thus increased in ratio ϵ_1'/ϵ_1 to 39°C.

6.10 (a) The field resembles that for strip-drawing, shown in Figure 6.3. A 45° triangle is first drawn against the die face AB. Fan regions are constructed round the two singularities A and B, using 15° intervals. The field is then extended by drawing chords at $7\frac{1}{2}°$ to the radii. Chords inclined at 15° are then drawn from each intersection in turn, as explained in Chapter 6. The field is built up until an intersection near the centre-line is reached. The angles ψ and ζ included in the fans A and B are selected so that the chords meeting near the centre-line are inclined at $52\frac{1}{2}°$ to it, since the real slip-lines should intersect it at 45°. The best values for ψ and ζ for a 15° mesh are thus found to be 15° and 90° respectively, but the nodal point then lies a little below the centre-line. To obtain a more accurate solution, the smooth slip-lines are drawn in, and further slip-lines are then constructed, using the same technique, with closer angular separation near the edges of the field. Thus $\psi = 10°$ gives an intersection above the centre-line. $\psi = 13°$ and $\zeta = 88°$ give a more accurate result.

It should be noticed that the angle of intersection of the exit β-line with the centre-line is $180 - (\theta + 45 + \psi - \zeta)$, θ being the inclination of the die face to the transverse direction (= 15°). For a valid field the slip-lines must meet the centre-line at 45°, so $\theta + \zeta - \psi = 90$ or, in this instance $\zeta - \psi = 75°$.

(b) The field with sticking friction resembles Figure 6.6d. The exit slip-line is straight from the die B to the centre-line, intersecting the latter at 45° in D. A fan centred on B with this radius is constructed with 15° sectors. The second line is extended to the centre-line at D_1 by a chord at $7\frac{1}{2}°$ and so on, adding a ring-shaped area to the field. This still fails to reach the container at normal incidence, and a further ring zone must be added from D_2. This almost satisfies the boundary conditions of 0 and 90° at the container and 45° at the centre-line. The dead zone is thus found to contain an angle 25° at the die and to extend about $3.2a$ along the billet ($2a$ = final strip thickness). To improve the solution, the intersections are joined by smooth curves and lines of closer spacing are drawn. A satisfactory solution is obtained with a field bounded by the α-line from D_3', the latter point being found from the β-line inclined at 26° to the exit β-line. The dead zone then starts with an angle 29°.

6.11 (a) It is simplest to draw the hodograph for the 15° mesh first, though this implies a slightly larger extrusion ratio. The more accurate solution for the real boundary slip-lines can then easily be drawn in. (This procedure reduces the risk of numerical errors in the angles.) The hodograph starts with the line Of = 1·0. In the vicinity of the centre-line there is a shear at 45° represented by a line fF. Similarly on leaving this zone there is shear at 45° in the other direction and the final velocity is along the extrusion direction, Of produced to O'. The exit velocity is determined by the extrusion ratio. The magnitude of the tangential velocity discontinuity is unchanged along the entry slip-line and is represented by radii of a fan centred on f in the hodograph. The radii are each parallel to the appropriate portion of the slip-line, so the fan includes an angle ζ = 90°. The discontinuity on the exit line is also constant, so a second fan can be drawn about O', but this has only one sector ψ = 15°. The fans are then extended one intersection at a time as described in Chapter 6, §6.1.1. It will be found that the final absolute velocity along the die face is not accurately parallel to the die with the 15° mesh, but when the hodograph is smoothed out and the corrected fan angles 88° and 13° are used this is rectified.

(b) For sticking friction the hodograph may be started in the vicinity of the container wall. Again it is simplest to use first the 15° mesh, which approximately fills the actual plastic zone. Near the wall the chords meet at $7\frac{1}{2}°$ and $97\frac{1}{2}°$. The starting line Oa = 1 is followed by a line from a at $7\frac{1}{2}°$ to the normal, representing shear on the entry slip-line, which intersects a line at $7\frac{1}{2}°$ to Oa, representing absolute velocity parallel to the dead zone boundary. The magnitude of the discontinuity along the entry line is constant, so a fan of three radii is centred on a, giving the velocities in the three entry zones. An element leaving the entry zone near the centre-line will cross into the triangular zone where its velocity is parallel to Oa. The diagram is continued by considering the first element, adjacent to the dead zone boundary, crossing to the next zone along that boundary where its velocity is again parallel to the dead zone boundary. This gives the first extension of the fan centred on a, and so the hodograph is built up, mesh by mesh. When the exit-line is reached and the diagram is completed it will be found to correspond to a reduction of area 2·2:1. The hodograph is then filled in by smooth lines joining the intersection and the corrected angles of the bounding slip-lines are used to draw further lines for the accurate solution.

6.12 Draw the approximate field by the chord method using $\Delta\phi$ = 15° intervals. Since the die is frictionless and the semi-angle is 60°, the fan centred on the exit corner B contains an angle 60° or 1·05 radians. The die pressure between B and A is thus q = $(1 + \alpha)$ $2k$ because p on BD is equal to k and on BC is $k + 2k\alpha$. Between A and the next intersection E_1 on the die face, p increases by $2k . 2 \Delta\phi$, and so on.

The contribution of each zone to the extrusion force is

$$q_{AB} \text{ AB } \sin \alpha + q_{AE_1} \text{ AE}_1 \sin \alpha + q_{E_1E_2} \text{ E}_1E_2 \sin \alpha, \text{ etc.}$$

$$= 2k (1 + 1·05)(44·5) + 2k(2·05 + 0·52) (43·8) + 2k (2·05 + 1·04)(68·8) + . . .$$

the lengths being measured on the diagram ($\frac{1}{2}h_2$ = 25 mm).

Thus for a ratio 2·78:1, $P/2k = [(2·05)(43·8)] /68·8 = 1·31$

4·5 :1, $P/2k = (91 + 112)/112 = 1·81$

7·75:1, $P/2k = (204 + 212)/194 = 2·14$

11·5 :1, $P/2k = (416 + 382)/287 = 2·78$

The maximum extrusion pressure available is $2500/(150 \times 25) = 0·67$ kN/mm², corresponding to $P/2k = 0·67/0·25 = 2·66$. The largest possible extrusion ratio is thus about 10:1.

(If the deformation were homogeneous the maximum ratio would be given by $\ln A_1/A_2$ = 2·66, namely 14·2:1. With square dies, using equation 6.14,

$$2·66 = 0·8 + 1·5 \ln A_1/A_2, \text{ giving } 3·4:1)$$

6.13 (a) The field resembles that shown in Figure 6.6b. A 15° mesh is drawn first starting with the exit slip-line at 45° to the centre-line. The fan centred on the exit edge B of the die is then drawn, extending to the 45° triangle on the frictionless die face. The field is then built up from this. This would fit accurately if the extrusion ratio were 9·4:1. A more accurate solution can be obtained by drawing the slip-lines smoothly between the intersections and then extending the field by about 1°, starting with the β-line inclined at 31° to the exit slip-line, following this to its intersection with the centre-line, and then drawing the appropriate α-line.

(b) The field resembles that shown in Figure 6.6d. Again the construction with a 15° mesh starts at the exit slip-line BD. The fan centred on B is first continued round to the die face, since if the slip-lines meet the die face they must do so at 90° and 0°. The radius at 15° to the exit line is extended by a chord at $7\frac{1}{2}$° to meet the centre-line at D_1 and the field is increased by one annular zone of 15° meshes at a time. The fourth such zone, cutting the centre-line at D_4 and D_5 would meet the dead zone boundary at the correct angles ($7\frac{1}{2}$° to the normal and tangential) on the container wall if the extrusion ratio were 8·7:1. The dead zone would then include an angle 15° at the die edge.

To complete the solution the field is drawn with smooth lines between the intersections, and lines of closer spacing are drawn at the entry and dead zone boundaries to fulfil the conditions of sticking friction on the container for the required extrusion ratio. The dead zone is then found to include about 10° at the die edge.

6.14 The slip-line field resembles that shown in Figure 6.6b. It is constructed in the same way as in Example 6.13. A 15° mesh fits accurately. It is convenient to start the hodograph, following the procedure described in Example 6.11 using the approximate chord method. Finally the intersections are joined by smooth curves.

To draw the flow-lines, the smoothed hodograph is used. The mean velocity in any mesh is then represented by the vector from the origin to the mid-point of the appropriate hodograph section, as described in §6.6. Lines parallel to these are superimposed on the slip-line field traversing the meshes to which they refer, starting each one at one of the intersections on the entry slip-line, and following each through successive meshes, as in Figure 6.7. The intersections with the slip-lines are finally joined by smooth curves, which represent the flow of metal elements through the whole plastic zone.

6.15 The slip-line field is of the same type as that shown in Figure 6.6a. The hodograph is started in the corner of the container where an element of approaching metal shears at 45° and then proceeds parallel to the die face. This determines the magnitude of the tangential velocity discontinuity along the inlet slip-line, which remains constant but changes direction with the slip-line until the centre-line is reached. The hodograph is completed by further shear at 45° on the exit line, giving a final longitudinal velocity 3·0.

Mean values of the absolute velocity in each 10° sector are found by joining the mid-point of each in the hodograph to the origin. Lines parallel to these velocity vectors are transferred to the slip-line diagram systematically for each sector, starting at each intersection on the inlet slip-line. These lines are finally smoothed out to represent the actual flow of metal.

6.16 The extrusion can be considered as simultaneous extrusion of three flat bars, two being 6 mm wide and 1·6 mm thick and one 8·8 x 1·6 mm. However, as stated in §6.5.3, if the extrusion ratio is large the extrusion pressure is sensibly that for extrusion of round bar of the same cross-sectional area. Thus, using equation 6.14,

$$\frac{P}{Y} = 0.8 + 1.5 \ln A_1/A_2$$

in this example A_1 = 491 mm². The final area is 2 x 6 x 1·6 + 8·8 x 1·6 = 33·3 mm². A_1/A_2 = 14·7

$$\frac{P}{Y} = 4.83$$

The mean yield stress for aluminium (Example 1.3) is about 0·15 kN/mm² for heavy deformation at room temperature, so $P \approx 0.7$ kN/mm² and the force is about 350 kN.

6.17 Assume $\overline{S} \approx 0.65$ kN/mm², $\overline{Y} \approx 0.56$ kN/mm². If the tube is 25 mm O.D., the final area is 207 mm². From the approximate equation 6.14,

$$\frac{P}{Y} = 0\cdot8 + 1\cdot5 \ln\frac{A_1}{A_2}; \quad \frac{10\,000}{0\cdot56A_1} = 0\cdot8 + 1\cdot5 \ln\frac{A_1}{207}$$

whence $\frac{A_1}{207} = \exp\left(\frac{11905}{A_1} - 0\cdot53\right)$

A first attempt at solution can be made using the expansion $\exp(x) = 1 + x + \frac{x^2}{2!} + \text{etc.}$

$$\frac{A_1}{207} \approx 1 + \frac{11905}{A_1} - 0\cdot53; \quad A_1{}^2 - 37A_1 - 2\cdot46 \times 10^6 = 0$$

$A_1 = 1588$, implying an extrusion ratio 7·6, but this is very inaccurate since x has a large value (6·9). The equation is however quite quickly solved by numerical approximation :

$$A_1 = 1588, \quad \frac{A_1}{207} = 7\cdot67; \quad \left(\frac{11905}{A_1} - 0\cdot53\right) = 6\cdot97; \quad \exp 6\cdot97 = 1\,060$$

= 3 000	= 14·5;	= 3·43	= 31
= 3 500	= 16·9;	= 2·87	= 17·6
= 3 600	= 17·4;	= 2·78	= 16·1
= 3 530	= 17·05;	= 2·84	= 17·15

This implies an extrusion ratio of about 17:1. A standard size may be selected and the pressure checked. Assuming the initial bore diameter of the billet to be 25 mm, to allow clearance for th mandrel, the O.D. would be given by

$$\frac{\pi}{4}D_1{}^2 - 491 = 17 \times 207; \quad D_1 = 71 \text{ mm}$$

If $D_1 = 70$ mm, $A_1 = 3\,357$, $A_1/A_2 = 16\cdot2$

$$\frac{P}{Y} = 0\cdot8 + 1\cdot5 \ln 16\cdot2 = 4\cdot98; \quad P = 2\cdot78 \text{ kN/mm}^2, \quad PA_1 = 9\,357 \text{ kN}$$

(If $D_1 = 65$ mm, $A_1 = 2\,827$, $A_1/A_2 = 13\cdot7$

$$\frac{P}{Y} = 0\cdot8 + 1\cdot5 \ln 13\cdot7 = 4\cdot73; \quad P = 2\cdot64 \text{ kN/mm}^2, PA_1 = 7500 \text{ kN})$$

It should be noted that the calculation does not allow for the initial peak pressure. On the othe: hand, a somewhat lower pressure would be required with a conical die.

Chapter 7

7.1 The slip-line field and hodograph are drawn as in Figure 7.2. A suitable scale represents h_0 by 160 mm and unit velocity by 80 mm. Then

$$\Sigma kus = k(1\cdot41 \times 1\cdot0 + 1\cdot08 \times 0\cdot77 + 1\cdot41 \times 0\cdot59 + 1\cdot08 \times 0\cdot77 + 1\cdot41 \times 1\cdot0)$$

$$P \times 2 \times 1 = k(5\cdot32); \quad P = 2\cdot66; \quad P/2k = 1\cdot33$$

This may be compared with the slip-line field solution, 1·285, and that found from the simpler upper-bound, 1·50.

7.2 With the further sub-division, the upper-bound solution approaches more closely the slip-line field value:

$$\Sigma kus = k(1\cdot41 \times 0\cdot85 + 0\cdot55 \times 0\cdot71 + 1\cdot41 \times 0\cdot28 + 0\cdot55 \times 0\cdot71 + 1\cdot41 \times 0\cdot30$$

$$+ 0\cdot55 \times 0\cdot71 + 1\cdot41 \times 0\cdot28 + 0\cdot55 \times 0\cdot71 + 1\cdot41 \times 0\cdot85)$$

$$P \times 2 \times 1 = k(5\cdot17); \quad P/2k = 1\cdot29$$

7.3 A simple upper-bound solution can be drawn by assuming that the dead zone is bounded by a straight line at 45° to the container wall, passing through the die corner. This gives

$$\Sigma kus = k(1\cdot0 \times 1\cdot0 + 1\cdot27 \times 1\cdot41 + 0\cdot9 \times 9\cdot1)$$

$$P \times 1 \times 1 = k(11\cdot0); \quad P/2k = 5\cdot5$$

More elaborate upper-bound fields can be drawn, and it is instructive to compare the results with the slip-line field. For sticking friction, the latter resembles Figure 6.6d and gives the value $P/2k = 3\cdot3$. An upper-bound field divided into three triangles gives $P/2k = 5\cdot8$. The dominant contribution comes from the work done on the exit shear-line.

It may be noted that the equation 6.14 for axially-symmetric extrusion gives $P/Y = 4\cdot25$, $P/2k = 3\cdot7$, at 10:1.

7.4 An upper-bound solution with five equilateral triangles gives $P/2k = 2\cdot88$; with 45° isosceles triangles, $2\cdot99$. Subdivision of the two triangles related to the fans in the slip-line field gives $2\cdot64$, compared with $2\cdot57$ for the slip-line field solution.

7.5 For zero friction, a simplified version of Figure 7.5 can be used, dividing the left- and right-hand halves respectively by their two diagonals, at 29° to the platens. This gives $P/2k = 1\cdot17$, which can be compared with the s.l.f. solution in Figure 5.6.

If sticking friction is allowed along the platen, this adds a large component, increasing $P/2k$ to $2\cdot1k$.

An alternative solution, introducing a dead zone over both platens, can be represented by a single diagonal cross, extending over the whole platen, at 15°. This gives $P/2k = 1\cdot95$. The slip-line field for sticking friction, shown in Figure 6.1, predicts an average pressure $P/2k = 1\cdot65$.

7.6 The slip-line field construction for wedge indentation has been described in Example 6.4. For a 60° wedge the angle θ is 19° $\approx 0\cdot1\pi$ rad, and equation 6.9 gives $P/2k = 1\cdot33$.

An upper-bound solution, resembling this field but comprising only two equilateral triangles and ignoring the pile-up, gives $P/2k = 1\cdot73$, or $2\cdot88$ for sticking friction. A single triangle, from the apex of the indenter to the edge of the pile-up (20° to the surface) gives $P/2k = 1\cdot22$ and $2\cdot7$.

7.7 A simple approximation to the half slip-line field of Figure 6.3 is a single triangle extending from the entry and exit points A and B to the centre-line. Using an isosceles triangle and assuming zero friction, this upper-bound solution gives $\sigma/2k = 0\cdot24$. The equation for homogeneous deformation (3.6) gives $\sigma/Y = \ln 1\cdot25 = 0\cdot22$. If sticking friction is assumed on the dies, the upper-bound has a dominant additional term giving $\sigma/2k = 1\cdot18$, which is too great to allow drawing without fracture. If a shear stress $\tau = 0\cdot1k$ is assumed on the dies, the result is $\sigma/2k = 0\cdot34$.

7.8 A single-triangle upper-bound field can be drawn, with lines at −5° and +35° to the axial direction, from the die exit. The hodograph shows a sharp discontinuity on the exit boundary.

Taking four elements, each approaching the mid-point of a 10° sector in the 40° triangle, the calculation may be set out as follows, assuming a starting line unit distance from the boundary for element 1 and calculating $\Delta t = \Delta x/V_x$. Element 5 is on the centre-line.

		Element 1		Element 2		Element 3		Element 4		Element 5	
	V_x	Δx	Δt	Δx	Δt	Δx	Δt	Δx	Δt	Δx	Δt
zone 1	1·0	1·0	1·0	1·45	1·45	1·80	1·80	2·15	2·15	2·3	2·3
2	1·35	10·8	8·0	7·0	5·2	4·0	3·0	1·35	1·0	0	0
Total to exit line		11·8	9·0	8·5	6·65	5·8	4·80	4·5	3·15	2·3	2·3

Assume some time allowing all elements to leave the plastic zone e.g. $t = 9\cdot1$. Then Δx in exit zone (3) is $10\Delta t$

zone 3	10	1·0	0·1	24·5	2·45	43	4·3	59·5	5·95	68	6·8
Total x		12·8		33		49		69		70	

These distances from the starting line may be plotted on the respective flow-lines. The result resembles that deduced from a slip-line field, but is clearly less accurate. Try other configurations.

7.9 A slip-line field for this unsymmetrical extrusion shows that the fields based on the two dies intersect away from the billet centre-line (dividing the billet width in ratio about 3·2:1), and the product velocity is inclined to the axis. This suggests an upper-bound field comprising a 45° isosceles triangle based on the smaller die, and a triangle joining the apex of this to the entry and exit points of the other die.

For frictionless extrusion this gives $P/2k = 0.92$ compared with 0·86 from the slip-line field. If sticking friction is assumed on both dies, this upper-bound solution gives 1·85.

7.10 Figure 7.4 may be taken as a basis for this solution. A 45° isosceles triangle is drawn under the punch. The field can then be completed by drawing a line from the apex of the dead zone, parallel to the punch face, until it meets the container wall. This point is finally joined to the punch corner by an exit shear-line.

This solution gives $P/2k = 3.4$, but it ignores friction on the container wall. To include friction a third triangle is completed by a line from the punch corner, meeting the wall at 90°. No work is done along this line, because the velocity is parallel to the wall on both sides of it, but sticking friction (or some value mk) can be assumed against the wall. This gives $P/2k = 5.0$.

7.11 On Figure 7.7, draw a vertical line from 2 to cut 01 in d. Then $12 \sin \phi = 2d = 0d \cot \alpha = (1 - 12 \cos \phi) \cot \alpha$. Hence $12 = \cot \alpha / (\sin \phi + \cos \phi \cot \alpha)$

$$= \frac{\cos \alpha}{\sin \phi \sin \alpha + \cos \phi \cos \alpha} = \frac{\cos \alpha}{\cos (\phi - \alpha)}$$

Selected Bibliography

General texts on metalworking theory

Avitzur, B., *Metal forming: processes and analysis*, McGraw-Hill, New York, 1968.

Baque, P., Felder, E., Hyafil, J. and Descatha, Y., *Mise en forme des métaux*, Dunod, Paris, 1973.

Blazynski, T. Z., *Metal forming: tool profiles and flow*, Macmillan, London, 1976.

Ford, H. and Alexander, J. M., *Advanced mechanics of materials*, Longmans Green, London, 1963.

Johnson, W. and Mellor, P. B., *Engineering plasticity*, van Nostrand Reinhold, London, 1973.

Johnson, W., Sowerby, R. and Haddow, J. B., *Plane strain slip-line fields*, Edward Arnold, London, 1970.

Lange, K. (Ed.), *Lehrbuch der Umformtechnik. Band 2 – Massivumformung*, Springer-Verlag, Berlin, 1974.

Rowe, G. W., *Principles of industrial metalworking processes*, Edward Arnold, London, 1977.

Slater, R. A. C., *Engineering plasticity*, Macmillan, London, 1977.

Thomsen, E. G., Yang, C. T. and Kobayashi, S., *Mechanics of plastic deformation in metal processing*, MacMillan, New York, 1965.

General texts on metalworking processes

Alexander, J. M. and Brewer, R. C., *Manufacturing properties of materials*, van Nostrand, London, 1963.

Datsko, J., *Material properties and manufacturing processes*, Wiley, New York, 1966.

Radford, J. D. and Richardson, D. B., *Production engineering technology*, MacMillan, London, 1974.

Schey, J. A., *Introduction to manufacturing processes*, McGraw-Hill, New York, 1977.

Specific metalworking processes

Anon. Wire Handbook (Steel – Vols 1–3, 1972 Non-ferrous – Vol 1, 1977) Wire Assoc. Inc., Guildford, Conn., U.S.A.

Davies, R. and Austin, E. R., *Developments in high speed metal forming*, Industrial Press, New York, 1970.

Feldmann, H. D. *Cold forging of steel*, Hutchinson, London, 1961.

Hoffmanner, A. L. (Ed.), *Metal forming – interrelation between theory and practice*, Plenum Press, New York, 1971.

Jevons, J. D., *The metallurgy of deep drawing and pressing*, Chapman and Hall, London, 1945.

Johnson, W. and Kudo, H., *The mechanics of metal extrusion*, Manchester University Press, 1962.

Jones, W. D., *Fundamental principles of powder metallurgy*, Edward Arnold, London, 1960.

Larke, E. C., *The rolling of strip, sheet and plate*, Chapman and Hall, London, 1963.

Pearson, C. E. and Parkins, R. N., *The extrusion of metals*, Chapman and Hall, London, 1960.

Pugh, H. Ll. D. (Ed.), *Mechanical behaviour of materials under pressure*, Elsevier, Amsterdam, 1970.

Schey, J. A., *Metal deformation processes: friction and lubrication*, Marcel Dekker, New York, 1970.

Shaw, M. C., *Metal cutting principles*, Massachusetts Inst. Tech. Press, 1960.

Index

Kings of Steam

A collection of trains and weapons produced at the
famous Beyer Peacock works in Manchester, England

P & D Riley

Portions of this book were first published in a different format in 1945 by
Beyer Peacock

This edition first published 2004 by

P & D Riley
12 Bridgeway East
Cheshire
WA7 6LD
England.

This edition and format © P & D Riley
Introduction © 2004 by Peter Riley

ISBN:1 874712 69 7

British Library Cataloguing in Publication Data
A catalogue record for this book is available from the British Library

Printed in England.

Introduction

Charles Frederick Beyer (1818-1876), was the son of a poor weaver from Saxony, but managed to work his way through Dresden Polytechnic, frugally spending only just above £20 a year during his three years there.

In 1834 he obtained a travel grant that allowed him to travel to England to study textile machinery., and he even turned down job offers in Germany to stay in England where he entered the drawing office of Sharp Roberts & Company in Manchester. This company began to build railway locomotives in 1837, and Charles was moved to that department where he worked until 1843 when he became Chief Engineer at the tender age of 25.

Despite his position, however, he was disappointed at not being offered a partnership, (and there were rumours that he had also been refused in marriage by one of Sharp's daughters), and this made him leave in 1853. The following year he became a partnership with Richard Peacock and the pair started a firm of mechanical engineers whose business was mainly the manufacture of steam locomotive engines.

Richard Peacock (1820-1889), who had been locomotive superintendent of the Manchester & Sheffield Railway, knew Beyer through trading with Sharp Bros, for engines and because the two of them had been founder members in 1847 of the Institution of Mechanical Engineers. Richard had left Leeds Grammar School when he was 14 years old to take up an apprenticeship with the Leeds firm of Fenton Murray & Jackson. When he was only 18 years old his unique ability had made him the locomotive superintendent of the Leeds & Selby Railway. In 1840 this railway was taken over by the York & North Midland Railway and Richard Peacock went to work under Daniel Gooch on the Great Western. Obviously a restless and very ambitious soul, Richard's connection with Manchester began in 1841 when he was only 21 years of age and he became the locomotive superintendent of the Manchester & Sheffield Railway and laid out their running sheds at Gorton where later the railway workshops, nicknamed "Gorton Tank, were established. It was mainly thanks to Peacock's huge influence that rural Gorton was transformed into one of Britain's major engineering centres.

The firm also had a third partner, Henry Robertson (1816-1888), who was born at Banff. He had graduated from Aberdeen University and spent some time in the mining industry in Lanarkshire before joining Robert Stephenson & Locke who were building railways in southern Scotland and parts of England. Among his other work for the company was the levelling of part of the West Coast route over Shap Fell. After a varied career in Scotland, he helped build the Chester to Shrewsbury, Shrewsbury to Birmingham, and the Shrewsbury to Hereford lines as well as others on the Welsh borders. He was also responsible for designing a 19 arches viaduct over the River Dee at Ruabon and a second over the River Ceiriog at Chirk. A very ambitious man, Henry had originally joined the firm of Beyer, Peacock to provide capital to the fledgling company but he was also responsible for bringing in many orders for engines.

It has been recorded that between 1856 and 1966, Beyer Peacock took photographs of almost every type of engine which they built, leaving a unique collection of archive material for the nation and posterity.

The reputation of both Beyer and Peacock was already remarkable and their first order for engines was from the East Indian Railway before any part of the works had even been built! However, their first completed engine at Gorton, which left the works on 21 July 1855, was one of eight 2-2-2 tender engines for the Great Western Railway, and cost £2, 660.

The new works at Gorton were built by Beyer himself, and he also built many of the firm's machine tools. It was something that became a tradition at Beyer Peacock who built machine tools for most of their 110 year history.

Richard Peacock died on March 3, 1889, and his son Ralph, who had been in the works since 1862, became Managing Director. In 1902, he felt that the firm should become a public company and he retired from active management though he remained on the Board of Directors until 1905.

For the next 60 years Beyer Peacock manufactured an enormous range of locomotives that were shipped all across the globe. During the Second World War the company had to produce an amazing array of items, both in locomotive orders and in the production of tanks and other weapons that was demanded by the British Government. It should have been the start of a completely new and prosperous era but changes in the travel superstructure of Britain and other countries soon made steam locomotives obsolete and after 1958 no further orders for steam engines were received. The firm continued to trade for the next eight years, but as more and more business slipped to overseas markets, Beyer Peacock closed its doors for the last time in 1966.

Peter Riley

<u>Acknowledgements</u>

The publishers would like to thank the following for their valuable help during the preparation of this book

Derek Duckworth, Alex Shiel, Brian and Rosemary Halpin
Fenton Tennant, Sid Riley, and Ken Bryan for the loan of illustrations
Peter Sharples of the *Manchester Evening News*

Original Foreword

THIS Foreword to the story of the war effort of a British Engineering Group of Companies is written in the victory month of May, 1945. It is written within a stone's throw of Westminster Abbey, within sight of Big Ben and the bomb-shattered House of Commons. We are proud to record that in spite of the worst the enemy could do to blast, burn and terrorise this great and noble Capital City – in spite of buildings blitzed the ground next door and all around us – in spite of repeated but fortunately minor damage to our own offices, we never closed our doors. Not for a single day did the Luftwaffe sever our contacts with the nerve centres of Government demand.

At the outbreak of war in 1939 this company and its main subsidiary were listed by His Majesty's Government as essential undertakings. The control thus imposed meant briefly two things – firstly, we were given instructions as to what our activities were to be, and secondly, we were compelled to discontinue many peacetime contracts going through our factories and to postpone any not then commenced.

For nearly six long years considerations of national security precluded us from explaining in detail to our many friends all over the world the reasons why we were not able to give them the service they rightly expect in times of peace.

With the end of the war in Europe and the lifting of many censorship restrictions we are now able to tell our friends what we have been doing. It is hoped that this volume will be of interest in that sense. Certain of our activities are still on the Secret List, but the following pages indicate the wide variety of our problems and achievements on the Production Front during these momentous years.

Abbey House, London, S.W.1
May, 1945

Reproduction of map taken from an enemy pilot in Holland in 1945
This particular pilot was over Manchester on January 9th 1941

Call to Service

WAR BETWEEN BRITAIN and Germany started on the 3rd September, 1939. The impact of that event on our works at Gorton, Manchester, had immediate repercussions of the most far-reaching character. Since 1854 we have manufactured railway locomotives of the widest variety of design and type for service in almost every country in the world.

It is clear that rail transportation is one of the main sinews of war. The deployment of large armies necessarily involves the use of railways for the multifarious needs of movement and supply. We were not at all surprised, therefore, when we were immediately ordered to produce with all speed locomotives to serve the British overseas armies. We were told to sacrifice anything which might in any way impede the promptest execution of these instructions.

The immediate situation in our factory may well be imagined. Materials purchased for other purposes were commandeered wherever it was found possible to utilise them for the requirements of the new war production. Thousands of tons of interrupted work-in-progress were sorted and either modified for war service or stored for future consideration. Out of the seeming chaos our new production schedule gradually emerged. The pulse quickened slightly. Our first war job was under way.

While this early work was being planned and put into execution other matters claimed our urgent attention. One of the most important was the provision of air-raid shelters for our employees. Of equal urgency was the organisation of the many-sided activities covered by the term Civil Defence. Fire-fighting equipment on a scale unknown in times of peace had to be secured and fire parties trained. First-aid classes were organised. Anti-gas methods and equipment were devised and procured. Emergency telephone lines had to be laid from shelters and action posts to a newly constructed underground control room. Black-out materials were ordered and fitted to all buildings, completely masking all top and side lights.

The dangers to workpeople of suddenly throwing out the main electric switches were visualised. Dim battery lighting was therefore provided for passage to the many shelters. Every individual was allocated a place in a specific shelter, and practice 'alerts' were organised to ensure smooth and swift operation of raid plans. A multitude of other necessary war measures had to be taken as required by the host of departmental instructions and orders which were showered on industrial war establishments.

It became necessary immediately to organise security measures against sabotage in the works or the entry therein of any unauthorised person. Patrols were set to work day and night and passes were provided for the use of staff, workpeople and authorised visitors. The efficacy of our provisions had to be tested from time to time. This was done by plans laid by our own security officer, and also by attempts at unauthorised entry by agents of the central authority. Our patrols could not be drawn from production personnel, and had to be specially engaged.

The problem of identification was therefore somewhat difficult in the early stages. It was not unusual for senior executives to be challenged when a patrol thought they were taking a suspiciously keen interest in some aspect of the lay-out or production processes. The humour of such situations was appreciated by both parties. The patrol was usually complimented on his keenness. The incident ended with a laugh and possibly a joke, thus drawing together in common plight and for a common cause some of those who do not normally fraternise quite so easily or so freely.

At a later stage, in the middle of 1940, when France was over-run by the German armies and capitulated, it became necessary to take into consideration the possibility of the invasion of Britain by the continental forces of the enemy. We organised our own works Home Guard Company. Reinforced concrete fire points were sighted and constructed. The volunteers were trained in all the intricacies of hand-to-hand fighting in built-up areas, and the vitally necessary technique of maintaining contact with one another and with adjacent forces outside the factory area.

All this planning, all this organising, all the necessary lectures, training, equipping, testing, exercising and inspecting were added to the urgent and primary demands for production. Continuous blackout in the shops affected ventilation. Hours of work were increased to, and often beyond, the limit. Transport was difficult, the shopping of essential food and other supplies, the shortage of beer and tobacco and the multiplicity of regulations, controls, forms and cards all added to common burden of war strain. The average worker stood up to it all magnificently.

It is true that tempers were sometimes a little hotter and patience occasionally gave way to the strain. Above all, however, both John and Jane Citizen proved beyond doubt the sturdy qualities of our

Beyer Peacock Home Guard Company

national character. They exhibited a strong sense of duty, a sane and calmly balanced outlook. They toiled and sweated. They groused and swore. And to every situation they brought that typically British sense of humour which makes them capable of an everlasting hope, and denies any possibility of their ever admitting defeat.

On the 13th May, 1941, there came into force what was known as the ' Essential Works Order.' One of the main features of this Order was that it imposed two vital restrictions. Under its provisions no workman was allowed the freedom to leave his job and seek employment elsewhere, and no management was permitted to discharge or employ personnel except through the Ministry of Labour. Judged by national standards this war-lime legislation was the obvious answer to a number of malpractices growing up here and there. It was inevitable, however, that the restrictions thus imposed resulted in initial friction and irritation. With a stroke of the pen the whole practice of management in Great Britain was revolutionised.

Speaking very broadly, management prior to the 13th May, 1941, was 10% leadership and 90% discipline. On and after that date the position was reversed, and management willy-nilly had to be 90% leadership and 10% discipline. There was undoubtedly much resentment on both sides of this very necessary Order, but we in this Company feel that the lessons we have learnt under it are of the most vital importance in our future relationships between management and labour. We believe those lessons will exert a powerful and ineradicable influence on our production policy in the future.

LOCOMOTIVES

'WE MUST REGARD the locomotive as just as much a munition of war as the gun, tank, or shell.' Such is an extract from a letter written by the Controller-General of Munitions Production, stress-

ing the imperative necessity of locomotive production for war purposes. Transportation of every sort is necessary to all organised communities in times of peace. In times of war our conception of what is required has to be drastically revised. Methods of living must be altered, ways of life must be changed, but the importance of transportation suffers in no way under this metamorphosis. Indeed, the needs of a modern fighting machine depend to a much greater extent on efficient transportation than at any time in history. Gone are the days when a lightly equipped and lightly armed band of warriors could move by skirmish and encounter to battle and victory, living the while (for a large part) on the land. The modern Moloch in its most mechanised form demands a lavish, constant and uninterrupted supply of all those myriad requisites which sustain a 20th-century force in the field.

In addition, the speed with which attack is mounted, and at which the advance or retreat moves, necessitates not only the requisite number of everything for a planned operation, but requires a large surplus to minimise the factor of strategic danger which might otherwise result from tactical surprise. The flowing tide of events cannot be predicted with certainty in times of peace.

During the struggles of a world conflict it is evident that the future is even less predictable. In spite of this, it is clear that victory depends not a little on the right quantities of the right things being at the right place at the right time. Transportation services of every kind bear that responsibility and must shoulder that burden.

In planning for military victory it is also essential to foresee some of the problems which will immediately become paramount on the conquest or liberation of any given territory. In this sense it is, therefore, necessary to envisage transport requirements not only for the armed forces of fighting units and their base organisation and their supplying industries, but also for the civil populations which may in the processes of victory find themselves deprived of the essentials of life, unless supplied through an organisation closely keyed to the military operational plan.

The calls on transportation are, therefore, mainly divided into three composite headings. Firstly, the movement of men and supplies to the points of battle. Secondly, the movement of manufacturing equipment, raw materials and food to the factory front and supporting civil population. Thirdly, the conveyance of such things as are essential to organised community life in freed or occupied territories. How difficult it is to assign priority as between these three main requirements can easily be imagined by the briefest contemplation of the enormous problems involved during the progress of a world conflict. The movement of metallic ores and other minerals from Africa, of food from Australasia and Canada, of jute and other important items from India, of machine tools and specialised equipment from the U.S.A., and of a multifarious list of diverse necessities from other parts of the world - all these are of vital importance to those who have the duty and responsibility of planning the nation's war effort.

The unexpected always happens even in times of peace. In times of war, when the success of a campaign depends on guarding against unpleasant surprises, transportation planning inevitably imposes a burden which may become at times almost intolerable. There may be a sudden increase in U-boat activity, with consequent loss of convoys, or some country producing an essential item of supply may be overrun, or some group of factories in a specialised industry may be obliterated by bombing. These considerations and the concomitant problems of rail and shipping availability demand the provision and planning of alternative sources of supply, the accumulation of ample reserves, and the decentralisation of specialised manufacturing. Such plans inevitably throw additional loads upon transportation services.

For these reasons unparalleled traffic demands arose in many parts of the world. Frequently it happened that the total traffics were far beyond anything envisaged when the railways were built. In a number of cases single lines had to be doubled or new lines constructed. These factors had of necessity to be related to a balanced but changing strategic plan.

It is well to visualise something of this background of over-all planning when endeavouring to appreciate the necessity for vital mechanical equipment being sent to certain countries. His Majesty's Government set up machinery which dealt rigorously with

Part of Frame Shop looking south

Above: Boiler Shop No 1 Bay looking North

Multi-head Frame Slotting Machine

problems of this nature. Nothing was permitted to pass through the fine mesh of Government control unless it was considered to be of paramount necessity to the nation's war needs.

How all this affected the question of the supply of locomotives is too complicated to relate in this small book, but it can be stated that to certain manufacturing companies there were allocated large quantities of standard engines, and to our Company fell the difficult but important task of meeting varied demands from many different operational or supply countries. It was thus our lot to be responsible for more new designs of locomotive than all other British locomotive companies put together. The value, therefore, of this Company's locomotive contribution in war-time is a combination of total output in physical units, and the technical work connected with a large number of designs.

By reference to the illustrations, the variety of locomotive designs dispatched from our Works during the war will be appreciated. Nineteen different designs have been delivered, and these cover

the following gauges - 2' 6", metre, 3' 6", 4' 8½", 5' 3", and 5' 6". With the European war in retrospect it is interesting to note the geographical distribution of these locomotives. They were produced for India, Iran, France, the Near East, Kenya, Brazil, Sierra Leone, Nigeria, Gold Coast, French Equatorial Africa, South Africa, the Burma Front, Northern Ireland, and Ceylon. Of these engines a number were of conventional design, these being locomotives for the 5' 3", 4' 8½", 3' 6" and metre gauge respectively, and were dispatched to Northern Ireland, the Middle East, Brazil and South Africa.

The 4' 8½" gauge locomotives for France and the Near East were standard Ministry of Supply War Locomotives based on the London, Midland & Scottish 8F class design, and a large number of these were provided for the War Department. After the fall of France, engines of this class were dispatched to

Dismantling for shipment

Egypt and Iran, and the initial supplies to Russia by way of the Trans-Iranian Railway were hauled by these engines as an addition to those already operating on that railway.

The claims of Northern Ireland for motive power are not difficult to understand when one remembers that at the outset of the American entry into the European War, Northern Ireland became a forward base for forces of the United States of America. The huge general-purpose 3' 6" gauge South African conventional locomotives of a type designated '15F' were required by reason of the tremendous traffic increases occasioned by this world-wide conflict.

A brand new steam engine in the yard at Beyer Peacock Gorton works

Above: A Beyer Garratt 2-8-0 + 0-8-2 (Burma) manufactured during the Second World War

Above: A Beyer Garratt 2-8-2 + 2-8-8– produced for Burma Railways during the Second World War

Above: A Standard Heavy Freight Beyer-Garratt locomotive, (SHEG) once the most powerful steam locomotive in Great Britain

It is fresh in the memory that as a main route the Mediterranean was for a considerable period denied to British Merchant shipping, and that a constant stream of convoys passed from the West to the East by way of the Cape. The industrial resources of South Africa were also of considerable importance. In this connection it may be mentioned that the mining of South African coal, and the moving of this to the ports for bunkering and for export, increased in a fantastic manner.

Total coal transported by the S.A. R. in 1939 was 13 million tons - this had risen in 1944 to nearly 18½ million tons. The delivery of '15F' locomotives - a total of more than 1¼ million lb. of tractive effort - was, therefore, a very welcome addition to South African engine-power.

Apart from engines of a conventional type it will be noted with interest that there has been a large official demand for articulated locomotives of the 'Beyer-Garratt' type for war purposes. We are particularly proud that this should be so, as for many years we have advocated the advantages of the large train-load. In peacetime our argument is the economic one. The necessity of moving abnormal tonnages in war-time makes the need for big power units obvious. 'Beyer-Garratt' engines of high tractive effort have enabled greatly increased loads to be hauled on already highly congested lines, thus enlarging their capacity and achieving this without the necessity of additional engine crews, a very important point with staffs depleted by the calls of war. The demands of the War Department for articulated locomotives of our special type

were both numerous and varied. They include engines of varying wheel arrangements for the 2' 6", metre, 3' 6" and 5' 6" gauges, with axleloads varying from 5 tons to 17 tons. In a number of cases the designs supplied were the most powerful operating on the railways concerned.

Conditions of service in the matters of grade and curvature of line were exceptionally severe in certain instances. We may quote as an example, 1-in-25 grade combined with curves of 300-feet radius.

It was evident at an early stage that it would not be convenient or indeed possible in every case to provide locomotives specifically designed for individual territories. After consultations with us on the subject of special designs, the War Department finally decided that the over-riding motto, as it were, must be 'the best for the most.' Translated into practical language this meant that we had to design ' Beyer-Garratt locomotives suitable for employment under widely varying conditions of climatic and territorial service. For the first time in the history of the Company we embarked on projects for 'Standard Beyer-Garratts.' The two outstanding examples of this war standardisation were the 3' 6 " - gauge 'Sheg" - essentially an African engine for 60-lb. rail use, and the metre-gauge 'Stalig' - essentially an Indian engine for 50-lb. service.

The so-called 'Sheg' was designed under the limiting conditions of a number of 3' 6"-gauge railways and has in fact operated with complete satisfaction in the Gold Coast, French Equatorial Africa and Rhodesia. The wheel arrangement of this engine was 2-8-2 + 2-8-2 and the tractive effort at 75% B.P. was 51,400 Ib. It had a total running weight of 150 tons, on an axleload of 13 tons.

Company bosses in 1945

The metre-gauge 'Stalig' was designed to conform to all loading gauges of metre railways east of Suez. The wheel arrangement was 4-8-2 + 2-8-4, with a 4' 0" coupled wheel. The axleload was kept to 10 tons, this giving it the widest possible field of application as a general-purpose engine. It had a tractive effort of 38,400 Ib. at 75% B.P., and a total service weight of 137 tons. This engine is the most powerful metre-gauge locomotive operating in the Far East.

War standardisation has brought to light a number of interesting side issues. It is our confident expectation that the lessons which we have learnt in the hard school of war may in years to come be applied with advantage to the requirements of our customers all over the world.

In addition to the Standard 'Beyer-Garratt' locomotives of the two main types mentioned above, we produced 'Beyer-Garratt' engines for specific war requirements in the following territories : Sierra Leone, Nigeria, Kenya, Ceylon, India (including Burma), South Africa and Brazil.

Many interesting stories could be told of the production problems arising from unexpected Government demands. One will suffice to illustrate the point. In 1943 we were informed that the highest priority was attached to a new requirement for locomotives for the Burma Front. These locomotives were required specifically for the Ghats section (1 in 25) of the Burma Railway between Mandalay and Lashio. The direction thus given to us was notified as of such overriding importance that it was necessary that we should, as far as was practicable, relegate other production to a secondary place and 'leap-frog' this priority job over work already in production so as to produce the required locomotives at a given date.

The work of designing was a problem of some intensity. The difficulties of procuring materials at short notice and in such quantities severely tried our suppliers as well as our own organisation.

Our workpeople were naturally somewhat bewildered at the temporary confusion in the factory, but so far as security considerations would allow we explained the position to them. Their response was immediate. How effective it was can be gauged from the fact that from the date of receiving the official instruction, the designing, material procuring, and manufacturing processes were completed, and the first engine was in steam within 118 days - 4 days ahead of programme. These engines were delivered temporarily to Assam to participate in the vital preliminary phase of the 14th Army's attack on Burma.

We cannot pretend that our organisation, flexible though it is, likes this kind of specialised direction, but we are proud to know that the resources of the Company, placed whole-heartedly at the disposal of the demanding authority, produced results so exceptional as to merit special letters of appreciation from the War Office and the Ministry of Supply. Reproductions of these are to be found above.

Many of our engines have put up remarkable performances under the stress of war-time conditions. For instance, mileages to general repairs, both on the metre and 3' 6" gauges, have exceeded 200,000 and some ' Beyer-Garratt' engines have averaged over 6,000 miles per month for three consecutive years. In one case mileages of over 200,000 have been obtained with 4-8-4 + 4-8-4 'Beyer-Garratt' engines without the necessity for any tyre turning. This occurred on a metre-gauge line having many grades and much sharp curvature.

In 1941 we received a somewhat novel instruction from the War Office through the Ministry of Supply. Six 2-10-2 Tender engines built by Fried Krupp of Essen were intercepted in Eastern waters and diverted to Iran. We were asked to convert these locomotives so that they would be suitable for service on the Trans-Iranian Railway. Very few drawings were available. We had to re-design the outer structure to conform with the loading gauge, alter the buffing and draw-gear arrangements, provide oil-firing equipment and a number of other incidentals. This job was carried out at high speed and the parts shipped to Iran, where the engines were modified on the spot without difficulty and put into service. They have done good work and were a welcome addition to the severely strained resources in engine-power of the Iranian State Railways.

After the invasion of North Africa, we received instructions to supply spare parts for many classes of locomotives on the Algerian State Railways. These locomotives included a number of fast and powerful 'Beyer-Garratt' locomotives constructed under our licence in the factory of the Société Franco-Beige de Matériel de Chemins de Fer. We also carried during the war period an enormous Order Book for spare parts.

War locomotives were shipped with 'Combat' spares and these were quantitatively of an order greatly exceeding those which are normally required in peace-time service. In addition to this there were many cases where large numbers of spare parts were required to keep in service locomotives which were really ready for retiring, but owing to shortage of locomotive capacity, wherever possible it was decided as a policy to put old engines back into service rather than wait long periods for the delivery of new power. Our own commercial customers in many cases suffered serious inconvenience because the excessive load thrown upon our manufacturing resources in the way of priority locomotives and spares did not leave capacity for the usual flow of spare parts. We regret

4' 8½" War Standard 2-8-0 type

that in some cases severe hardship has thus been sustained.

At all times since the outbreak of war we have suffered an acute shortage of skilled labour, and have been glad to take advantage of the services of both male and female trainees. It cannot, of course, be pretended that the quantity of work performed per worker-hour has been quite up to what it would have been with our normal proportion of skilled labour. Our system of inspection has enabled us, however, to maintain the high standard of workmanship for which our products have been renowned all over the world for the best part of a century.

Our collaboration with the authorities has had a number of other railway aspects. We have been gratified at being in a position to supply detailed information on railway matters connected with systems all over the world, and we believe that the information thus put at the disposal of the Government from our archives, and as a result of the world travels of our engineers, has been of great value. We have also been able to supply technical information as to the manner in which locomotives could be sabotaged, and the type of first-aid services required to remedy various kinds of sabotage.

Our relationships with the War Department and the Ministry of Supply in the matter of railways and locomotives have throughout been cordial, and, although we have been subject from time to time to demands of a most peremptory nature, we record with gratitude the courtesy and assistance received at all levels of authority.

A FEW SENTENCES EXTRACTED FROM LETTERS OF APPRECIATION RECEIVED FROM OVERSEAS

A war casualty

. . . ' *Thank God, we got all these new locomotives from you before this show started. Where we would have been without them I do not like to think. We have been going all out now since Italy entered the war, and there seems to be no let up. The big engines saved our lives . . .*

'*. . . I have never known such a record, or anything approaching it, in my experience."*

'*. . . They have been doing excellent work and hauling trains ... 50 per cent, heavier than we have previously shifted:*

'*. . . Thanking you for a good design, well made*

From a foreign railway, with no previous experience of 'Beyer-Garratt' locomotives or, indeed, British-built locomotives of any type :

'*... In conclusion we may say that the ——— Railway is especially satisfied with the performance of the 'Beyer-Garratt' locomotives . . .*

Top Pic: Hilton 'George' Duckworth, a Ganger Slinger, (right) with a boiler in Beyer-Peacock's works. He is also pictured in the bottom pic (second from right) with some of his work mates. 'George', a one time social club steward at the works almost lost an eye when a slinging wire snapped.

Train for Belfast & County Down Railway, built 1859. Gorton 'Tank' railway works in background

Right: Mock up of a steam locomotive that stood outside the office at Beyer Peacock's Gorton works

Left: Locomotive No 18 in Australia where it still runs (pic by Rosemary Halpin)

C.F.B. loco in yard at Gorton

Train no 2395, LNER Railway, in the countryside

TANKS

ONE OF THE MOST interesting tasks entrusted to us during the war was the production of heavy tanks. At a very early stage we had been invited by the appropriate authority to consider the possibility of tank manufacture, but at that time the overall weight and general type of British tanks under construction or in prospect was, in our view, too small for the general shop facilities of a factory tooled for the production of the largest size of main-line locomotives.

It had been agreed that our factory could be more usefully employed on work of a heavier nature. At the time of the fall of France, however, the position came under urgent review once more. The Government was aware that there was a serious possibility that the Germans would attempt to invade the shores of Great Britain, and a type of tank was, therefore, conceived for defensive purposes quite different from preceding models. It was larger and heavier and it was proposed to carry armour in excess of anything previously visualised. This design was known as A.22.

Tanks at Overloon that were built in Gorton

Responsibility for the engineering of this new fighting vehicle was accepted by Vauxhall Motors Ltd., who also undertook to act as 'parent' for high-speed co-ordinated production. We were invited to collaborate in this matter and to undertake the manufacture of a number of hulls and other components and to be responsible for assembling, testing and final trials.

A number of other distinguished engineering firms joined in this collaboration and the over-all demand for these vehicles was divided by agreement between them. Some idea of the nature and extent of the difficulties of this problem may be gathered from a realisation that the whole project was of such extreme urgency that there was no time to make a few prototypes for trial purposes. It is probable that the A.22, now known as the Churchill tank, is the only heavy fighting vehicle which was ever produced under such pressure and without previous experimental work. It normally takes several years from the conception of a new design to the first production model.

Of the origin and purpose of this tank the following official information may be of interest. In the House of Commons (*Hansard, Volume 385, column 1773/4*), the Prime Minister said : ' . . . On the 20th July (1940), we met again, Major-General Pope also being present. The Tank Board had approved the specifications subject to certain modifications, and it was agreed to go forward with the utmost rapidity with the production of what became known as the A.22 Tank. The General staff expressed themselves entirely in favour of the project.

'Work proceeded with the utmost enthusiasm. We could not afford the time to wait to carry out exhaustive trials with pilot models. This would have set us back at least six months; our paramount aim was to get the maximum number we could into the hands of the troops in 1941. The pilot model was running on 12th December 1940. Production began to flow in May 1941, and by the autumn 400 were available for battle.

'Meanwhile, the German armies had been launched against Russia and the danger of invasion had lessened. The possibility of using the A.22 tank in an overseas offensive role was therefore considered, and modifications were introduced to make the tank more suitable for extended operations abroad. That winter we began reworking these tanks, and large numbers are now in a fit condition for use in the assault of strong positions for which their armour fits them.

'Reports have been received from the brigades in this country now armed with these tanks which are on the whole strongly favourable. There are between one and two thousand in the hands of troops. They are said to be the best weapons yet received by the units concerned.

'It will be seen that this tank was never intended for the fast-moving long-range warfare of the desert. However, a certain number were sent to the Middle East in the autumn of 1941 for trial. It will interest the House to hear that a small number took part in the attack on Rommel's lines at Alamein, and reports show that they gave a good account of themselves, and stood up to very heavy fire.

'I am glad to have had this opportunity of informing the House of the history of this tank and of publishing the names of those who took the bold decision to introduce it. No one would go back on that decision now. The A.22 is naturally surpassed by the latest types, but the production in large numbers in less than a year of an entirely new tank of much heavier pattern than anything we had before and thoroughly capable of going into action in Home Defence is highly creditable to the British engineering industry and to all concerned.'

General Oliver Leese, referring to the fighting in Italy, wrote : 'It may interest you to know of the fine performance of the Churchill tanks, which supported the Canadian Corps when they attacked and broke through the Adolf Hitler line last month. They stood up to a lot of punishment from heavy anti-tank guns. Several tanks were hard hit without the crews being injured. They got across some amazingly rough ground. Their 6-pounder guns made good penetration and were quick to load and aim.'

The decision to produce Churchill tanks involved us in a number of major problems in our factory. The first and most obvious one was switching over a portion of our Works from locomotive production. This switch necessarily involved the fairly wholesale movement and

Top: Suspension Unit shop

Above: Water testing a tank

Bottom: View of Machine Shop

rearrangement of machinery, the clearance of floor space for the various sub-stores, and the arrangement of a number of special-ised small departments for the economical production of components and their sub-assembly.

The tank chassis, or hull as it is called, was a fairly straightfor-ward locomotive boiler-shop job, and our skilled boilermakers found little serious difficulty in coping with their new type of pro-duction. The same, however, cannot be said of either the armour-plate or the revolving turret, and although the problems were of an engineering nature, and as such were capable of resolution by our technical staff, the nature of the material imposed an unusual strain upon our equipment.

Any engineer will appreciate the nature of the tool difficulties of manipulating armour-plate on equipment designed for normal work in mild steel. Standards of speed and feed, types of tooling equipment, the technique of welding, etc., etc., all had to be re-vised. We believe that our organisation showed up very favourably in these matters, and we have documentary evidence that our welding of armour-plate was second to none in the country.

The amount of electrical wiring in a tank is considerable, and in addition to power and light wiring a certain amount of inter-communication telephone work and also radio installation is in-volved. Our own maintenance electricians were assigned to this work and put up an excellent performance.

The final erection of sub-assemblies and components was a mat-ter of the greatest intricacy and required an unusual amount of thoroughness and precise method. Anyone who has inspected this assembly will appreciate how important it is that each part shall go in in exact sequence. The amount of clearance between parts and sub-assemblies is so small that in many cases there is no room for a hand to be inserted, and each small crevice had, there-fore, to be plugged temporarily as assembly proceeded to avoid

The Machine Shop at Beyer-Peacock

Testing ground for tanks

Delivering tanks by railway from the Gorton works

any possibility of small parts or tools disappearing into the interior if dropped by accident. Otherwise part of the work would have had to be undone to recover the missing item.

The Churchill had to be made water-tight, and water tests had to be carried out during the process of construction. This involved the provision of a large water test basin in our boiler shop, and there was a further basin constructed on the proving grounds.

For proving the tanks by final trials, we leased an old brick-field. This was ideal terrain for such work, as, in the 20 acres or so of ground, surface irregularities were most severe and included a number of small ponds with mounds rising almost vertically and of the roughest possible nature. On these proving grounds we erected a tank garage with underground fuel-storage and power-washing facilities. It would have been out of the question to have run the tanks over the road after they had been through their trials. As it was, we were in trouble more than once with the Local Authority for the amount of debris unavoidably carried out on to the main road. We trained our own test drivers, who collaborated in a spirit of friendly camaraderie with personnel from the Tank Corps and officials and drivers of the Ministry of Supply.

The photographs cannot do justice to the variety of production activity entailed by the manufacture of these tanks. The photograph

Somewhere in Holland

of the suspension unit details does, however, indicate the large number of small parts which had to be manufactured for a single sub-assembly, and it should, of course, be remembered that of this item there are twenty-two sets required for each tank.

Another point which cannot be adequately illustrated in such a small volume is the number of different types of Churchill tank manufactured. The photograph showing tanks outside our tank garage at the proving ground illustrates two different types of turret, both revolving, one cast steel and the other welded armour-plate, and the photograph of tanks on railway trucks awaiting dispatch from our factory shows a third class of turret, the fixed armour-plate turret with a 3-in. gun in position. Incidentally, on the latter photograph the entrance to No. 20 Air Raid Shelter can be seen in the left-hand bottom corner, and the entrance to two other shelters can be seen on the extreme right of the photograph, although the numbering cannot be seen. The variety of operational duties envisaged called for a differentiation in turret and other features, and it will be appreciated that in the factory there was, therefore, an additional problem which must inevitably be encountered when such variations have to be incorporated at short notice.

We are very pleased to be able to record that, despite the enormous difficulties of producing a major weapon of this type without an experimental period, our relations with Vauxhall Motors Ltd., during the whole period of our co-operation with them were in the highest degree friendly and co-operative.

Whatever difficulties we had, they also experienced, but in addition to our difficulties, they had the added complexities of handling detail matters with the Government authorities concerned. Their type of organisation was essentially different from our own, owing to the fundamental differences in the nature of our normal peace-time production. Their system was, however, fitted into ours without serious inconvenience to either party, and the contacts we had from Managing Director through the various grades of executive control were at all times pleasant, and were the means of establishing personal friendships which may be mutually advantageous in the years to come.

We are very proud to have been associated with the production of Churchill tanks, and although space is inadequate to tell the story fully, perhaps the most suitable words with which to close this section are those of the Secretary of State for War in the House of Commons (*Hansard, Volume 388, column 1042*). The Minister, in referring to the Churchill tank, said 'The latest and best test of all, in battle, shows that the tank is giving very good service.'

In action at Caen

GUNS

Gun Mountings

The wartime demand for guns of every type has been enormous and apart from Royal Ordnance Factories and regular armament manufacturers it is clear that locomotive-manufacturing plants have the equipment and can rapidly acquire the technique for the manufacture of carriages and mountings. It is not surprising, therefore, that our factory at Gorton has been for a number of years engaged on work of this kind.

Our first order was for mountings for the new 4.5-in. anti-aircraft gun and we, in company with a number of other manufacturers, received instructions to manufacture a number of these mountings. Almost immediately it was realised by the authorities that the system of giving small numbers of mountings to several manufacturers involved jig and tool manufacture at each factory. The urgency of the job was such that conversations were opened with a view to eliminating this if possible by arrangement.

4.4-in A.A. Gun Cradles

Finally our company and two other leading Manchester engineering firms agreed to pool resources, each firm doing its share of the work by an agreed division, thus providing the possibility for larger batches and more expeditious construction. Our section of the work involved the manufacture of the steel castings and the construction of the carriage. The steel castings consisted of upper and lower racer plates, forming the base of the mounting, the large gun-cradle, gear boxes, and a number of other details.

We finish-machined racer plates and ground the roller paths, and we rough-machined the cradles. The carriage was of a construction necessitating the employment of highly skilled boilermakers, whom we were fortunate in being able to make available, and also required machining and fitting of a precision quite beyond anything normally called for in locomotive construction. This in turn demanded a number of accurate jigs and a considerable amount of measuring equipment for use by our inspection department.

One of the problems which arose in connection with the heavy 4.5-in. anti-aircraft gun and its mounting was that of providing a firing base and fastening devices of such a nature that the whole could, if required, be rapidly moved from place to place. We were asked to provide a large number of these structures in the form of holdfasts, holdfast pedestals and sub-bases. We also supplied a number for the 9.2-in. howitzer.

Another interesting gun-mounting job which we tackled in the early stages of the war concerned 18-in. howitzer railway truck mountings. A number of these enormous railway vehicles had to be stripped, overhauled and re-assembled. When it is realised that this mounting was carried on fifteen axles and the gun alone weighed nearly 100 tons (the total equipment weighing approximately 250 tons), it will be appreciated that the work involved could only be undertaken by factories having cranage facilities of an exceptional character.

In addition to the general overhaul we gave to these vehicles, we were also responsible for a number of important modifications. It can readily be appreciated that the amount of floor space occupied by equipment of this size and nature created a number of engineering problems.

After the fall of France in the summer of 1940 it was increasingly evident that the shores of Great Britain might be subject to enemy invasion. At our subsidiary company's works at Leiston in Suffolk we were at that time, amongst other things, manufacturing 12-pdr. naval gun mountings for the Admiralty. After some conversations on the subject of dispersal, the Admiralty instructed us to set up a duplicate line of 12-pdr. mounting manufacture at Gorton. As similar work was being done at Leiston the preliminaries were fairly straightforward and we quickly got into production.

Suffice it to say here that the working at Gorton of a product al-

18-in
Railway
Mounting

ready being manufactured at Leiston eliminated much of the preliminary detail investigation into methods of operation, estimates of man-hour requirements, and the like. Very fortunately the threatened invasion did not mature, but the advantages of dispersal were none the less very real and will be immediately appreciated by our engineering friends.

We illustrate one of these mountings with a gun fitted and the front splash shield in position. In the foreground a number of cast-bronze cradles and gear pillars are to be seen on the floor of the shop. These castings were made in our own non-ferrous foundry. We should like to mention the achievement of our foundry in successfully overcoming the great difficulties associated with the cradle casting. The internal chambers of this casting have to be tested to extremely high pressures without any sign of 'weeping'

12-pdr Naval Gun and Mounting

The intricacy of the internal design and the severe differences in contiguous wall thicknesses called for advanced casting technique. Some thousands of these cradles were successfully cast in our works at Gorton for the works' use and for supply to our Leiston factory. The advantages of our modern metallurgical research department in a matter of this nature are obvious.

The new 4-in. twin naval mounting afforded us a further opportunity of collaborating with our Leiston subsidiary company. When our subsidiary company was invited by the Director of Naval Ordnance to manufacture these complicated modern mountings, the utmost emphasis was placed on the necessity for speed. We, therefore, decided that we would manufacture the steel castings at Gorton and would also build a number of the carriages to enable a quicker getaway with delivery. Among the steel castings required were the twin cradle and the racer plates.

At that time the demand for steel castings of every kind for war purposes was enormous and it was, therefore, a great advantage to be able to produce these difficult castings within our own organisation. The general precision of this work is extreme for riveted structures, overall limits being within one or two thousandths of an inch. This necessitated the manufacture of precision jigs and special measuring tackle, and we are proud to relate that all the jigs and measuring equipment were produced in our own toolroom and the first carriage had passed its inspection successfully within sixteen weeks of the original Instructions To Proceed. We also produced in Manchester a number of canopies and shields and other details for this important cruiser mounting.

One of the interesting developments in firearms during the war was the virtual supersession of the .303 machine gun by 20-mm. cannon. Of the types produced probably the most popular was the Oerlikon. The Oerlikon gun was used by all three fighting forces. Many different types of mounting were devised and manufactured for the special use of this weapon in H.M. ships of all types. We

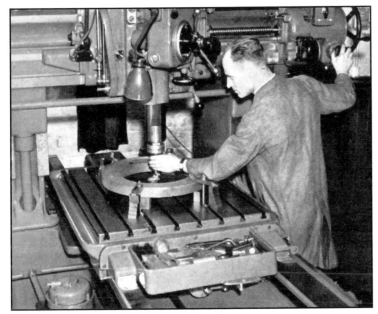

Top Left: Twin 4-in Gun Cradle

Top Right: Twin 4-in Gun Carriage

Middle Left: Twin 4-in Racer Plate

Middle Right: In the Test Room

Bottom: Jig Boring

had a number of contracts from the Admiralty for these mountings and produced many hundreds of them.

The supply of all kinds of guns and their mountings was of such urgent importance for our fighting forces that it was not always possible to give recruits their complete training with fighting equipment. Practice loading devices were one of the methods used by the authorities to provide recruits with opportunities for drill on structures which dimensionally were representative of the arms they were to use. Gun crews could thus receive their preliminary training, especially in loading drill, by means of these simple structures. Throughout the greater part of the war period we have continuously provided the authorities with these practice loading devices.

Top: Vital work is carried out in the Beyer-Peacock Laboratory

Right: The 20mm Oerlikon gun, used by all three fighting services, pictured in action

Gun Bodies

There was a time when the total production of 12-pdr. naval mountings in our factories at Leiston and Gorton rose to such a figure that a shortage of gun barrels was envisaged. The problem, therefore, was whether to slow down the production of mountings or, on the other hand, to increase the production of guns. The latter procedure was not easy, for gun manufacture is a very specialised armament technique and requires single-purpose machinery which is not normally available from stock but has to be ordered considerably in advance of the date it is required.

After consultation with the authorities concerned, and after due consideration of the inevitably extended period which must elapse before new gun-making machinery would become available, we decided to adopt the unusual course of protesting against a reduction of mounting production, but of offering instead of this to design and manufacture the gun-making machinery and undertake the manufacture of guns. These gun machines were designed and manufactured at Leiston.

HMS 'Turquoise' mounting 12 pdrs

It was decided, however, that the dispersal of key manufacture was of sufficient importance to necessitate the installation of duplicate lines. The original line was laid down at Leiston and the duplicate line was installed at Gorton. Gun manufacture of anything like the calibre of 3-in. and above requires large floor areas, and we decided to allocate for the purpose of the 12-pdr. gun our locomotive packing shop. The area was adequate and the cranage facilities were ideal.

Certain non-specialised operations such as planing the gun keyways were taken care of by adapting our own locomotive machine tools, but all the boring, turning, rifling, and breech-clearance machines, etc., were designed and manufactured by Richard Garrett Engineering Works Ltd., and delivered to Gorton from their Leiston factory. The layout and installation of these machines were effected at high speed and no difficulty was experienced in maintaining the rated output of guns. In this connection it is interesting to note that the whole manufacture of the guns and their breech rings was undertaken by female trainees with the minimum staff of skilled male machine-setters and charge hands.

Incidentally, all inspection gauges were made in our own toolroom, and the production officers concerned with this work had great reason to be satisfied with the splendid results they achieved. Hundreds of guns came off this production line, which must be regarded as an outstanding example of the adaptability of our technical organisation.

Breech Mechanisms

It is obvious that the stepping-up of guns to meet the high production of mountings involved an investigation by the authorities of breech-mechanism production. The breech mechanism of a gun is normally regarded as the most intricate piece of precision engineering in the whole unit. On investigation it was disclosed that potential suppliers would not be able to cope under the existing arrangements with the demand which would be made upon them for these largely increased quantities.

The Admiralty, therefore, asked whether we would collaborate in producing the breech mechanisms. The technique of mechanism production is so far removed from the engineering with which our Gorton works is usually associated that we approached this problem with some caution. Our doubts were reinforced when it was realised how many small parts were involved and the degree of precision required on these parts.

Normal practice in mechanism production requires a big proportion of skilled fitters' time after the parts leave their final machining operations, and skilled fitters in Manchester at that time were more difficult to come by than water in a desert. The whole success, however, of the 12-pdr. production depended on an even production balance between the three components mountings, guns and mechanisms. We therefore regarded this problem as a challenge to our ingenuity.

Breech Mechanism Shop

After careful thought we agreed to accept the responsibility for mechanism production, and we eliminated the necessity for a high proportion of fitters' time by carefully re-figuring all production drawings, and drastically cutting down the machining limits. We improved the tooling normally used on machines for this purpose and

12-pdr Breech Mechanism Details

provided specialised fixtures and jigging which ensured that any machining operation could not be undertaken unless the previous operation had been performed within the greatly reduced limits. By these methods we finally succeeded in producing a line which in the hands of female trainees manufactured the component parts to such a high degree of accuracy that fitting was virtually eliminated.

The completed mechanism

The final assembly was mated to a special gun breech in which the limits had been so fixed that if mating was possible then that breech mechanism would fit any standard 12-pdr. breech which had been manufactured within drawing limits. In this way we not only produced mechanisms of com-

'Bore Clear' in the Second World War

plete interchangeability, but we also decreased the time normally required to mate the mechanisms to the guns. Indeed, to such a degree was this successful that finally we made no charge whatever for the mating process.

To accomplish all this meant we must have a special department with its necessary bond stores, inspection benches, and the like. It also meant the provision of a large number of jigs, machine fixtures and gauges to high precision limits. Our technical staff undertook this work in a full realisation of all its difficulties, and produced a unit which met all Admiralty requirements and solved the serious problem of production balance on this important piece of armament. Incidentally, we made mechanisms not only for the guns produced from our Gorton gun line, but also to cover the requirements of our gun production at Leiston, and at the height of production we had sufficient elasticity in the department to be able to make good any casual deficiency which arose elsewhere.

The novel technique thus developed at Gorton was of the utmost assistance in the national effort. Incidentally, it reduced the cost of our mechanisms to something less than one-third of the normal cost, and in this way the nation obtained a double benefit. units.

SHELLS & BOMBS

Shells

At an early date in the re-armament programme, before the outbreak of war, one of the questions occupying the minds of the authorities was the provision of capacity for the production of shell of about 6-in. calibre by mass-production methods. Machine-tool manufacturers in this country had not at that time devoted their attention to the design and manufacture of a rough-turning lathe which would adequately meet the requirements of this type of production. When the problem was mentioned to us we saw possibilities for being of service to the country in a degree which is not usually considered to attach to the work of shell-case manufacture, and with our background of semi-heavy engineering technique we were confident that we could solve some of the more serious problems involved.

There are between 30 and 40 operations in the production of 6-in. shells, taking as raw material the pierced forged steel billet and delivering the shell varnished internally to the filling factory. Of all these operations the chief difficulty centred round that of rough-turning. The weight of the pierced billet was about 180lb., and this, when machined, had to be reduced to just over 80lb. The amount of material removal, therefore, to be done at high speed was phenomenal, and it was found that the use of conventional-type lathes was not possible owing to the continual jamming of cuttings on the slides, etc. We are not normally lathe designers, but naturally have a vast accumulation of experience of lathe work.

The Beyer-Peacock Shell Shop in Gorton

We discovered that the only suitable lathes available were two types of German manufacture of very complicated design and great cost. We considered that it would be unwise to plan production with the use of German equipment, so we immediately set our Leiston subsidiary company the task of designing a powerful automatic multi-tool shell-turning machine totally enclosed, inverting the slides so that all the mechanism was carried overhead, thus allowing the cuttings to drop clear into a large hollow base containing a swarf bin.

Our preliminary designs and calculations appeared to us to be so satisfactory as to be worthy of submission to the Government authorities concerned. The then Director-General of Munitions Production, Sir Harold Brown, took the bold step of entrusting us with the production of a complete line of machinery and equipment for the 6-in. howitzer shell. The whole of the machines for centring, rough turning, boring fuse hole and cones, finish turning, blending interior, etc., were designed and produced by our subsidiary company, Richard Garrett Engineering Works Ltd., of Leiston, Suffolk.

The job was of great urgency and there was, therefore, no time for the design and production of pilot or prototype models for testing. As quickly as the machines were manufactured they were set in position, tooled up, and started operation. The reliability of these machines under continuous heavy production over a number of years was a complete justification of our designing policy and of the courage of the Ministry in backing our project.

The large quantity of turnings to be removed from the rough turners set us an interesting problem in floor cleanliness, which we overcame by designing a turnings skip on wheels which fitted into the lathe base from the back. The catch which retained this skip in position was connected by a hydraulic control valve to a patented flap inside the machine in such a manner that when the catch was lifted to withdraw the skip for swarf removal the flap

Above: Lifting shell from roller conveyor to finish borer
Right: Transferring from bench tray to fuse-hole borer

automatically came to rest in a horizontal position, retaining the turnings coming off the machine while the skip was out of position. After the skip had been emptied and was returned to the base, the retaining catch automatically lowered the flap, dropping the turnings made in the interim into the emptied skip. By this means it was possible to maintain a clean floor and to secure continuous operation during the process of the removal of turnings.

In laying out this mass-production unit, we gave considerable thought to the problems which would arise should war break out, when manpower would be in short supply. We therefore planned the whole lay-out so that without undue fatigue women could handle more than 90 per cent, of the work.

The forgings flowed on roller conveyors from the stock bank (at truck floor level), down the production line, and at each operation the removal from the conveyor to the machine and back again was accomplished by easy lifting or transferring devices of a mechanical nature designed and made in our Gorton works. In order to put down this line we entirely cleared one small shop.

As we had planned this unit for operation by female labour and as

Annealing Furnaces

Corner of the bomb machine shop

we visualised that most of the women we would employ would never have seen the inside of an engineering factory before, we decided to make the plant as attractive in appearance as possible, and all machinery was painted a bluey-green. This is a small, psychological point, but we believe it was helpful in creating an interest in our employees.

It is interesting to note that from the commencement of operations this department maintained its rated output without difficulty. Our lifting and conveying devices have been illustrated in Government publications and our general layout has been the reason for many requests from the Government for us to allow other shell manufacturers or potential manufacturers to inspect this department. The women we have employed have been able to meet the demand upon them without undue fatigue and the flow of shells from this department was continuous for nearly seven years.

Provision was made for form-bars and other tooling for 5.25-in., 5.5-in. and 6-in. shell, and large quantities of these calibres have been delivered without any hitch or break-down.

Bombs

Both the general purpose and the medium casing types of medium weight British bombs are of cast steel. Whilst we have been engaged from time to time on other types of special bombs, the bulk of our production has been of the cast-steel variety.

We are the only British locomotive manufacturing company possessing a steel foundry. Normally we do not compete in the open market for steel-casting contracts as we have regarded it a matter of policy to develop this side of our activities as a service to the locomotive manufacture of our main works. Steel castings for locomotive wheel centres and for other locomotive components must be of very high grade on account of the onerous duty they perform and of the serious possible consequences in the way of damage to life and property should an engine fail at high speed. For this reason we have associated with our steel foundry a modern metallurgical department equipped with the finest appliances known to science for research into and control of steel-manufacturing processes.

The casting of bombs is a process of some intricacy. Relative to the bulk of the casting, the walls of the bomb are thin. The bomb itself must be made in such a fashion as to conform *inter alia* with two major requisites. In the first place, it must be made so as to enable the greatest possible degree of accuracy in dropping. This requires that it shall be carefully balanced. Secondly, it must be made in such a way as to give on explosion the correct degree of fragmentation whilst resisting disintegration on impact the moment before explosion. These over-riding requirements necessitate a high degree of dimensional accuracy in the casting and a very strict control of the metallurgical qualities of the steel.

Machining bombs

After numerous experiments on core forms, angle of pouring, location of risers, and liquid-steel temperatures, both from open-hearth and electric furnaces, we developed a technique which has proved highly successful and has led to the production of bomb castings of a quality second to none in the country. Because of the thinness of the wall, especially in the case of medium-casing bombs (less than ½ in.) and the liability of premature 'freezing' of the metal in the mould, we decided that maximum fluidity of the molten metal was essential. For this reason we finally selected electrically melted steel in preference to steel melted by the open-hearth process.

The annealing of the castings thus made was a matter of critical importance, and annealing temperatures had to be controlled to within twenty degrees Centigrade. This control is a matter of no difficulty with the modern Priest annealing furnaces which can be seen in the illustration. These furnaces are coupled up to Kent automatic control gear, with a revolving drum recording the temperature throughout the process. A continuous control on the analysis of the steel has also been maintained by our metallurgi-

Bombing-up (1,000 lb. Medium Casting

cal laboratory and a percentage of all castings was taken for destruction test, so that we were continuously advised of physical properties including that of the impact the casting would stand without rupture. We have cast and machined large numbers of a variety of sizes and types of bomb.

The machining of this bomb is done on semi-mass-production lines, and the bomb machine-shop was laid down with complete run-ways and small electric hoists for the rapid and orderly movement of the bombs through the various production stages. The whole of this equipment had to be specially laid out. Special arrangements were also made for grinding, pressure testing, degreasing, welding of carrying lugs, varnishing, stoving and painting.

The Ministry of Aircraft Production arranged for single-purpose machinery to be designed and manufactured for the various machining operations. This was done on a somewhat novel basis. The bomb was inserted in a pot-jig which was a component part of each of the various machines. The two tool slides with their driving arrangements, gear-boxes and controls were designed and manufactured by our subsidiary company at Leiston.

The hoists are of push-button control, and the women operatives were quickly trained to manipulate this machinery and equipment at high speed without undue fatigue. The novelty of this layout lies in the fact that once the bomb casting has been located and fixed in the pot-jig-cum-machine-component it is not removed until the whole of the machining operations are complete. Thus the jig is a component part of each machine and travels with the bomb from the beginning to the end of the machining cycle.

The obvious benefits to be obtained from this lie mainly in the entire absence of necessity for re-centring the bomb in the different machines, and the Ministry of Aircraft Production, who have sponsored so many mechanical novelties, have been amply justified by results in the action they took in backing the ingenious inventor of this machinery layout.

In addition to the specialised turning and boring machines, other single-purpose equipment was used for thread-milling at nose and base, drilling and tapping, etc. After the castings were fully machined and carrying lugs welded on, the whole being varnished and stoved inside and painted outside, various components had to be fitted, including exploder containers, nose plug, transit base and transit rings.

Apart from a few cases of male specialists necessarily employed in the department, the whole of the work was carried out by women operatives without any previous engineering experience. They were quickly trained to their duties, and performed them in an efficient and satisfactory manner.

Our major war productions have been briefly described in the foregoing pages. The perusal of those pages will also give the reader some indication of the nature and excellence of our scientific and production facilities. These have been at the disposal of the authorities in many other ways which cannot conveniently be grouped under preceding headings.

We have, for instance, undertaken metallurgical research with a view to the production of war goods previously considered impossible other than by laboratory methods and have worked out techniques for large-scale production which have been brilliantly successful. We have also undertaken from time to time miscellaneous prototype work which has been much appreciated by the authorities.

Elsewhere we describe the Civil Defence and Security measures so necessary in war-time for a protected establishment. In addition to these measures we secured occupation of country quarters well away from vital targets. At a point approximately equidistant from

Manchester, London and Leiston we established our war-time Registered Office at Flore Manor, Northamptonshire, and after converting the stables to splinter and fireproof storage we there collected vital documents, drawings, etc., from the more vulnerable operating addresses.

To Flore there were sent each day photographic copies of current transactions and carbon copies of all important documents. Visualising the possibility that enemy bombing might destroy internal communications in England, we instituted a Dispatch Rider service for daily inter-communication, and this was tried out and time-tables planned, although we never had occasion to put it into full regular operation. Nearer to Manchester, in the peaceful Cheshire countryside, we had other quarters equipped as emergency offices and also for the temporary-residence of any of our staff who should suffer the misfortune of having their homes blitzed.

In 1943 our Company suffered a grievous loss by the death of Mr. Samuel Jackson, who as Technical Director was responsible for the designing and producing functions

'Bombs Away!' the tragic but inevitable end to weapons made in Gorton

Members of the Beyer-Peacock ARP organisation

and whose brilliant contributions to railway engineering over many years have made his name both well known and honoured all over the world. The Company received some hundreds of letters of regret on this sad occasion.

There are many other matters we should have liked to record in this story of our Company's war effort, but space will not permit. We should have liked to make reference in some detail to our Joint Production Committee and its work, to our wall newspapers, which Government authority told us were outstandingly good, and to those domestic matters concerned with labour relations.

Train no. 6003 in Beyer Peacock works

In spite of war difficulties and the problems of dilution and sudden changes in production occasioned by the exigencies of war, these remained on a high level of cordiality. We should have liked to mention by name many of our workers of every grade, both men and women, who with unobtrusive efficiency and true British determination have rendered valuable service on the production front. The honour and the glory are theirs in no less degree, although they are not specifically named.

We should also have liked to mention by name those of our staff who are serving in the Forces, and particularly those who have made the supreme sacrifice. The war with Japan, however, is still not won and it would not be proper to issue an incomplete Roll of Honour.

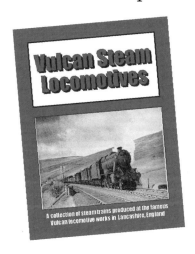